The Politics of Speed

D1809721

Everyone agrees that the world is accelerating. With advances in communication, transportation and information processing technologies, it is clear that the pace of events in global politics is speeding up at an alarming rate. The implications of this new speed, however, continue to be a significant source of debate. Will acceleration lead to a more interconnected, productive, peaceful and humane world; or a nightmarish descent into ecological devastation, economic exploitation and increasingly violent warfare?

The Politics of Speed attempts to map the contours of the new global space of speed, and investigates key issue areas – including democratic governance, warfare, capitalism, globalization and transnational activism – to uncover the ways in which acceleration is shaping the world. The book uses contemporary political theory (especially the works of Deleuze and Guattari) to develop an ontological account of speed, showing how its effects are frequently far more complex and surprising than we might expect. The result is an attempt to craft a way of engaging with global acceleration that might help avoid the dangers of speed, while embracing the possibilities it provides us with to produce a safer, more egalitarian, democratic and pluralistic world.

Simon Glezos is an assistant professor in political science at the University of Regina, and has a PhD in political theory and international relations from the Johns Hopkins University. His research applies contemporary political theory to questions of speed and technology in global politics.

Interventions

Edited by Jenny Edkins, *Aberystwyth University* and
Nick Vaughan-Williams, *University of Warwick*

As Michel Foucault has famously stated, "knowledge is not made for understanding; it is made for cutting." In this spirit The Edkins–Vaughan-Williams Interventions series solicits cutting edge, critical works that challenge mainstream understandings in international relations. It is the best place to contribute post disciplinary works that think rather than merely recognize and affirm the world recycled in IR's traditional geopolitical imaginary.

Michael J. Shapiro, University of Hawai'i at Mānoa, USA

The series aims to advance understanding of the key areas in which scholars working within broad critical post-structural and post-colonial traditions have chosen to make their interventions, and to present innovative analyses of important topics.

Titles in the series engage with critical thinkers in philosophy, sociology, politics and other disciplines and provide situated historical, empirical and textual studies in international politics.

Critical Theorists and International Relations
Edited by Jenny Edkins and Nick Vaughan-Williams

Ethics as Foreign Policy
Britain, the EU and the Other
Dan Bulley

Universality, Ethics and International Relations
A grammatical reading
Véronique Pin-Fat

The Time of the City
Politics, philosophy, and genre
Michael J. Shapiro

Governing Sustainable Development
Partnership, protest and power at the World Summit
Carl Death

Insuring Security
Biopolitics, security and risk
Luis Lobo-Guerrero

Foucault and International Relations
New critical engagements
Edited by Nicholas J. Kiersey and Doug Stokes

International Relations and Non-Western Thought
Imperialism, colonialism and investigations of global modernity
Edited by Robbie Shilliam

Autobiographical International Relations
I, IR
Edited by Naeem Inayatullah

War and Rape
Law, memory and justice
Nicola Henry

Madness in International Relations
Psychology, security and the global governance of mental health
Alison Howell

Spatiality, Sovereignty and Carl Schmitt
Geographies of the nomos
Edited by Stephen Legg

Politics of Urbanism
Seeing like a city
Warren Magnusson

Beyond Biopolitics
Theory, violence and horror in world politics
François Debrix and Alexander D. Barder

The Politics of Speed
Capitalism, the state and war in an accelerating world
Simon Glezos

The Politics of Speed

Capitalism, the state and war
in an accelerating world

Simon Glezos

 Routledge
Taylor & Francis Group

LONDON AND NEW YORK

First published 2012
by Routledge
2 Park Square, Milton Park, Abingdon, Oxon, OX14 4RN

Simultaneously published in the USA and Canada
by Routledge
711 Third Avenue, New York, NY 10017

Routledge is an imprint of the Taylor & Francis Group, an informa business

First issued in paperback 2012

British Library Cataloguing in Publication Data
A catalogue record for this book is available from the British Library

Library of Congress Cataloging-in-Publication Data
Glezos, Simon, 1981-
The politics of speed : capitalism, the state, and war in an
accelerating world / Simon Glezos.
p. cm. -- (Interventions)
Includes bibliographical references and index.
1. International relations. 2. Globalization--Political aspects.
3. Cosmopolitanism. 4. Capitalism--Political aspects. 5. State, The.
6. Speed--Political aspects. I. Title.
JZ1308.G54 2011
327.1--dc22
2011008748

ISBN: 978-0-415-78261-6 (hbk)
ISBN: 978-0-203-80472-8 (ebk)
ISBN: 978-0-415-82054-7 (pbk)

Typeset in Times
by Taylor & Francis Books

Contents

Acknowledgements

This book began its life as my dissertation while studying at the Johns Hopkins University. As such the first, and most important, people I need to acknowledge are my advisors, Bill Connolly and Jane Bennett. They were unfailingly generous with their time, their criticisms and their enthusiasm; this book simply would not be what it is without their involvement. Everyone should be so lucky as to have teachers like them.

Following that, there are an enormous number of people who contributed to the writing of this book in a multitude of ways, from providing commentary on the entire work, to simply listening to me try to work out an argument for the umpteenth time over drinks. Daniel Deudney, Paola Marrati, Joel Andreas, Warren Magnusson and Rob Walker all provided extensive commentary on the work as a whole, and Arthur Kroker, Marilouise Kroker, James Tully, Misao Dean, Jennifer Culbert and Siba Grovogui provided comments on several sections of the text. Renee Marlin-Bennett helped with Chapter 3 and Margaret Keck provided important sources for Chapter 5. Incalculable types and amounts of help were provided by my cohorts at both the Johns Hopkins University, as well as the University of Victoria, including Erin Ackerman, Libby Anker, Jeremy Arnold, Brad Bryan, Elisha Cohn, Adam Culver, Bill Dixon, Cristie Ellis, Stefanie Fishel, Jorge Gonzalez, Sam Gottlieb, Jake Greer, Marion Gutwein, Nina Hagel, Meghan Helsel, Robert Higney, Ryan Holston, Suvi Irvine, Serena Kataoka, Allison Kavey, Alex Lefebvre, Daniel Levine, Jennifer Lin, Noora Lori, Neena Mahadev, Liam Mitchell, Nobutaka Otobe, Johnny O'Doherty, George Oppel, Smita Rahman, Matthew Scherer, Mina Suk, Lars Toender, Chloe Thurston, Rob Watkins, Dylan Weller, Melanie White and Mabel Wong. Jairus Grove's help was invaluable. Not only did he contribute countless ideas and suggestions for the book, he also provided extensive material support, not least by being the instigator of the trip to join the protest discussed in Chapter 5 (which turned out to be a good idea despite early moments when it seemed like it might just be us facing the entire Winston-Salem police force alone). Hadley Leach was enormously supportive throughout much of the writing of the book, and for that I thank her sincerely. The ideas and insights which led to this book came, with alarming frequency, from conversations with Stephanie Doerksen, a fact which inclines me to keep her around. Amanda Kosonen has always been a source of wisdom for me, and, as such, I'm grateful that she's inclined to keep me around. Michael Erickson was a crucial component in keeping me sane during the writing of this book. And Emily Shoichet always provides me with support, insight and a comfortable chair to hide away from the rest of the world in, something for which I'll always be grateful. (I should also probably thank the staff of Habit Coffee in Victoria, BC, who were always kind enough to let me occupy one of their tables for hours at a time, pouring over manuscript pages. Probably the best office I've ever had.)

Many of the final revisions for this book took place while I was a post-doc at the Pacific Center for Technology and Culture at the University of Victoria. I thank them for their support in this project. They also published an article version of Chapter 3 in the centre's journal *CTheory*: 'Creative Destruction versus Restrictive Practices' was first published as part of a special theme issue, 'Code Drift', in the scholarly journal *CTheory* (www.ctheory.net), edited by Arthur and Marilouise Kroker. It is reprinted with the permission of the editors.

Material from Chapter 1 also appeared in an article in *Contemporary Political Theory*, under the title 'The Ticking Bomb: Speed, Liberalism and *Ressentiment* against the Future', and is also reprinted here with their permission.

Finally, I want to thank my family, Peggy, Jim, Matthew, Dawn, James, Ben, Caleb and Silas Glezos. I'm grateful to the accelerative technologies that let me remain in their lives.

Introduction

Fear of a fast planet

This project started in despair and ended in hope; despair over the acceleration of the world and hope for the possibilities that speed can bring.

I would be lying if I said this sense of fear and anxiety wasn't in some way influenced by my move to the United States from Canada in mid-2002. Arriving in a country still reeling from the September 11th attacks, I was overwhelmed by the runaway pace of events (and in this I'm sure I was not alone). The war in Afghanistan not even over, the Bush administration had already started the push to invade Iraq, justifying the rush to action by the imminent threat they claimed Saddam Hussein posed. We were told that action had to be taken immediately, that we could not wait for inspectors to determine if the threat was real, that we could not allow 'the smoking gun to come in the form of a mushroom cloud'. Implicit in these statements was the exposition of the new temporal order of the political world: in this accelerated world, the pace with which new threats can materialize leaves no time for hesitation. Decisions must be made quickly and efficiently by a centralized and authoritative executive. Slow-moving processes of deliberation and debate (not to mention investigation) are no longer viable. Indeed, they potentially threaten our survival.

I, like many in both America and around world, was not convinced by the President's claims of the imminent threat posed by Iraq, and joined the hundreds of thousands in the streets of Washington, DC (and millions in cities all over the world) in protest. However, as these protests were systematically ignored I was oriented to another worrisome aspect of speed. At the same time that the pace of events in the world encouraged the government to act in ways too fast for democratic deliberation, it also allowed them to act so quickly as to escape democratic censure. At this point, almost eight years into the war, it feels as if those in power have gone from one reckless action to another, always moving too fast to be held accountable for their destruction, lies and illegalities. A quote from an article in the *New York Times Magazine* in 2004, profiling the character of the Bush administration, seemed to get to the heart of this new freedom. In it, reporter Ron Suskind interviewed a high-level aide within the Bush administration:

The aide said that guys like me were "in what we call the reality-based community," which he defined as people who "believe that solutions emerge from your judicious study of discernible reality." I nodded and murmured something about enlightenment principles and empiricism. He cut me off. "That's not the way the world really works anymore," he continued. "We're an empire now, and when we act, we create our own reality. And while you're studying that reality – judiciously, as you will – we'll act again, creating other new realities, which you can study too, and that's how things will sort out. We're history's actors ... and you, all of you, will be left to just study what we do."

(Suskind 2004)

In addition to informing us that, apparently, members of the Bush administration had been reading a lot of Baudrillard, this quotation provides insight into the new temporal order of politics. It tells us that the actions of those in positions of political power now move too fast for traditional mechanisms of oversight and accountability. And the news media which is supposed to exercise this accountability must itself move so fast that, in moving from scandal to scandal, those in power need only wait for the news cycle to move on. Thus, when a decision is made, by the time we figure out what has happened, and discuss whether or not it is a good thing, the decision-makers have 'act[ed] again, creating other new realities'. The process of democratic deliberation and popular accountability becomes a never-ending game of catch-up, freeing the powerful of any real responsibility. This is because responsibility and accountability are necessarily backward looking, while, in a fast paced world, we are pressed to focus our eyes on the future (there is no time to play the 'blame game').

This sense of despair about the effect of speed on the political process was mirrored by an equal sense of fear at the effect of speed in the economic realm. There is little need for me to describe the myriad ways in which technological acceleration has set the stage for the further immiseration and exploitation of the world's poor. Countless studies of post-industrialization and post-fordism have recounted the way in which the new speed and flexibility of capital and capitalism free corporations and the wealthy from the fordist compromises that had been forced on them by traditional territorial politics.[1] In the new era of globalization, it seemed as if the accelerating forces of capitalism were free to roam the globe, seeking out cheaper labour and laxer regulations, while national labour pools found themselves trapped behind borders, left to decide whether it was better to be exploited by multinational corporations or ignored by them (neither choice seeming all that attractive).

The more I thought about the facts of acceleration at a global scale, the more I became convinced that there was developing a fundamental disjunction between the time and pace of the progressive politics to which I was attached (a politics which seemed tied to the slow-moving, territorially bounded mechanisms of grassroots organization and large-scale social movements); and the time and pace of the elites, the powerful, who were able to go where they wanted and act when they wanted. Of course, there has always been an asymmetry between the elites and the masses, between the powerful and the powerless. But now it felt as if the two were on completely different playing fields.

At the height of my despair over speed, however, I began to be concerned about some of the implications of this line of analysis. First of all, I became uncomfortable with some of the theoretical bedfellows I was making. My feelings of anxiety over acceleration seemed to be tinged with nostalgia for a slower, more idyllic time (at the very least, my conception that acceleration somehow inaugurated a new era of unaccountability in government was, I realize, particularly naïve). I started to see how easily this anxiety over acceleration could be transformed into a reactionary drive against change. My concern over the speed of globalization could become a kind of nationalistic, xenophobic drive against immigrants in the style of, say, Lou Dobbs or Pat Buchanan. In the same vein, my desire for a period of slower-moving democratic deliberation also shared something with conservative critics who fear the way in which the current fast-paced world unsettles their comfortable assumptions of family, community, culture and society. Indeed, in a more general way, I became aware there is a tendency in any given generation to view itself as undergoing a breathless and overwhelming acceleration of the pace of events.[2]

I had, however, an even greater concern with my original line of thought. If these anti-democratic and anti-egalitarian trends *were* inherently rooted in processes of technological acceleration, then I could think of no way in which real change could be effected short of some nigh-impossible attempt at turning back the clock. In trying to think through acceleration, I had introduced an element of technological determinism (the idea that major social and political formations find their root causes in technological changes) into my thought, which seemed to curtail – if not outright abolish – the possibility of productive political interventions. In this regard there was a tinge of apocalypticism to my thinking. I had begun to see a world spiralling towards a dystopic future with no conceivable remedy. This was the true root of my despair over speed. It is one thing to say that things are bad. Indeed, those of us on the democratic Left have come to accept this as a pretty common state of affairs. But to say that there was no way of making it better – that is another matter entirely. From this perspective, the steady worsening of the world appeared as the result of large-scale changes in the material context of human processes so diffuse and complex that we could never hope to intervene in them successfully – were we to de-invent the wheel, do away with the jet-plane, the computer, the mobile phone?

Of course, neither of these concerns served to disprove the analysis which I had built up. It could very well be true that we were on a path to a dystopian future and that the only possible fix to this state of affairs would be some sort of fundamental reversion of all of our technological advancements. That this was an unpleasant state of affairs was not reason enough to say that it cannot be so.

However, these concerns did open up another avenue of thought, which I realized might lead away from the theoretical and political dead-end at which I had arrived. Specifically, I began to consider the elements of technological acceleration which enhanced my life, both personally and politically. For example, I had seen, in 2000, the protests in Seattle that managed to shut down the World Trade Organization (WTO) meetings, and was aware of the crucial role that advanced communications technologies played in organizing this massive demonstration of resistance and alternative political possibility. I was aware of the role that a new freedom of information served in bolstering movements against oppressive regimes the world over (China's endless attempts to block the internet provide an example of the threat that these new technologies pose to totalitarian structures. If the Chinese government is trying to censor you, you're probably doing something right). The rise of institutions such as Wikileaks hinted at the possibilities of a new era of transparency and accountability in government dealings. And the news media, which I had maligned earlier, was now, at least in principle, capable of gathering information, and provoking outrage, at injustices perpetrated the world over.

Indeed, following my new sense of the seemingly reactionary politics which flowed from a fear of speed, I began to acknowledge some of the liberatory possibilities which new speed technologies might provide. So much of the violence and exploitation of the past had been rooted in a logic of firm borders and strong, slow-moving, static communities. As Bill Connolly puts it, 'A slow, homogeneous world often supports undemocratic hierarchy because it irons out discrepancies of experience through which constituencies can become reflective about self-serving assumptions they habitually use to appraise themselves in relation to others' (Connolly 2002: 144).

I realized that, despite my fears, I also felt attached to the power and possibility of speed. I appreciated the way in which new transportation and communication technologies destabilized the privileging of many fixed, territorial borders (and the reactionary, xenophobic politics and moralities that went along with them). The new scope and pace of information and culture often provide possibilities for breaking up the oppressive, conservative environment which suppressed different forms of identity and existence. Growing up in deepest suburban Canada, I drew much comfort and strength from the ability to partake of arts, culture, politics and ideas from all over the world. I can only imagine what sort of boon this new pace would be to those living in genuinely oppressive environments. In many ways, acceleration was crucial to making the world the kind of place I wanted to live in, a world open to periodic change and becoming, a world of play and multiple connections across difference. A world which warped and deformed the calcifications and reifications of borders, identities and ideologies; that refused the separation of those who might wish to be connected and who might be able to work together to build new possibilities and new opportunities (as well as resist old oppressions and exploitations).

Was the answer, then, that acceleration is an essentially ambiguous phenomenon? That if I wanted the freedom and possibility that accelerative technologies sometimes provide, I would also have to accept the violence, exclusion and exploitation that they seemed to foster?

That there is an ambivalence to acceleration, and that new technological formations invariably bring with them both new possibilities and new dangers is undoubtedly true. However, I became suspicious that there might be more to the question of speed than mere ambiguity. I began to wonder if the bivalence I saw might not in fact be the result of an inherent disjuncture in the phenomenon of acceleration itself. That the problem of speed might be the result not so much of an inherent ambiguity, but of an analytical unification of what was, fundamentally, a multiple phenomenon.

While reading Deleuze and Guattari's *A Thousand Plateaus*, I stumbled across a passage that seemed to offer both a language and an ontology to describe the internal multiplicity of acceleration. In the context of their discussion of the nomad war-machine, and its relation to space and time (as distinct from the space and time of the state-form and its military apparatus), Deleuze and Guattari had this to say:

> It is thus necessary to make a distinction between *speed* and *movement*: a movement may be very fast, but that does not give it speed; a speed may be very slow, or even immobile, yet it is still speed. Movement is extensive; speed is intensive. Movement goes from point to point; *speed, on the contrary, constitutes the absolute character of a body whose irreducible parts (atoms) occupy or fill a smooth space in the manner of a vortex,* with the possibility of springing up at any point.
>
> (Deleuze and Guattari 1987: 381)

This passage, with its seemingly counterintuitive (and yet, as I will argue, ultimately almost commonsensical) distinction between speed and movement, provided the entryway into a different investigation of acceleration; a way of complicating, differentiating and multiplying what had been received as an inherently unitary phenomenon. I will go further into analysing what I take this passage to mean on pp. 19–26, and in Chapter 1. For now, the point is that distinguishing between speed and movement was the first step to developing the tools with which to differentiate between those elements and effects of acceleration which I appreciated and revelled in and those which worried me. What was more, by breaking the unity of acceleration I also broke the monolithic and unilinear narrative of technological determinism. If acceleration is a multiple and multi-valent phenomenon, then that might mean that certain types of acceleration could be deployed against other types, and certain effects of acceleration could be deployed against certain others. The choice therefore was not simply between progression or regression, acceleration or deceleration, the future or the past. The question became: what kind of progression or acceleration? What kind of future? This is not to suggest that, in making a distinction between speed and movement, one of them was entirely 'good' and the other entirely 'bad'. Rather, the point is, introducing multiplicity generates a fundamental tension and instability into what had appeared to be a unitary and inexorable phenomenon. That means that there exists the possibility of emphasizing the desirable aspects of acceleration while suppressing the dangerous ones.

Indeed, this new attentiveness to the duality of acceleration also made me aware of another fact: that speed is not autonomous. In the dystopic, technological determinist narrative of acceleration I had accepted, I was assuming the autonomy (indeed, the primacy) of the technological over the social. However, attention to the multiplicity of acceleration highlighted the way in which specific technological machines entered into assemblage with different social, political, cultural, economic, legal and psychological machines. This produced the possibility of different social outcomes from similar technological infrastructures (not to mention the way in which such assemblages influence the development of these infrastructures). Different kinds of assemblage would emphasize different tendencies of acceleration. In terms of the concerns listed above, it made no sense to discuss the effect of technological acceleration on democratic politics without noting the way in which it entered into assemblage with different social formations; social machines for the formation of political identities, state machines for the organization of military apparatuses, economic machines which affected the functioning of media technologies. To discuss the effect of technology on economic well-being separate from the specificities of the capitalist assemblage is to accept the neoliberal account of capitalism's transparency, autonomy and naturalness.

The goals of this project then began to crystallize. They are twofold. The first is to develop an analysis of speed and acceleration. This analysis investigates the ontological characteristics of speed, and the attendant phenomena of velocity, movement and acceleration, as well as their political characteristics, seeing how they enter into assemblage with diverse social, political, cultural, economic and legal formations. In performing this analysis, the second goal is to explore the ways in which it is possible to constructively engage with the phenomenon of speed, and technological acceleration, in ways that promote democratic governance, pluralistic social formations, egalitarian economic structures, and reduce violence and suffering.

Each chapter seeks to investigate a different aspect of the contemporary landscape of speed and acceleration, tracing out its contours and attempting to identify faultlines which might be open to intervention or productive political action. The goal of this analysis is always to reclaim the possibility of political action from narratives of technological determinism, showing how accelerative technologies are more diverse and potentially pliable than we might initially acknowledge. This does not mean that we need to give up the possibility of material analysis and view technologies as completely value neutral, entirely subordinate to human action. Rather, the goal of this analysis is to expand the bounds of what we consider materiality to be (Bennett 2005), including technical machines, as well as social, cultural, legal, libidinal and economic assemblages.

This book is primarily a work of what could be called global political theory. This is not to say that all of the issues that it deals with are related to what we conceive as 'international relations' or, even more, that it is a work of 'international relations theory'. Rather, it attempts to use the insights of political theory to investigate the space of global flows in which contemporary politics takes place. In this regard, it oscillates between an analysis of theoretical texts and the investigation of crucial sites, events and issues within global politics, in the hope that each will shine light on the other.

In Chapter 1, we look at the question of democratic governance, under the rubric of the so-called 'ticking bomb scenario' in relation to the liberal narrative of speed. The liberal narrative of speed argues that, with the acceleration of the pace of events in the context of global politics, a shift is necessary within the democratic state, away from the slow-moving, deliberative actions of the legislative branch, and towards the energetic and unitary executive. According to this perspective, democracy is becoming anachronistic (indeed, even 'quaint') and increasing executive autonomy is necessary for the survival of the state. I argue, however, that this analysis is not rooted in the material necessities of acceleration. While it is true that technological acceleration produces new challenges to democratic governance, it also provides new tools, in some cases introducing the possibility of greater popular participation in politics. I then argue that this push for increased executive autonomy is not rooted in the functional challenge of acceleration, but is, rather, one kind of response to the existential challenge it poses. This is to say that the 'social acceleration of time', by introducing a fundamental element of uncertainty into the future, challenges the stable narratives of political identity. This produces a sense of what I call *ressentiment* against futurity, a generalized social resentment against time for its refusal to subject itself to our desire for certainty and stability. This *ressentiment* in turn produces the desire for an authoritative rendering of the narrative of a political community, which only a centralized and unitary executive can provide (as opposed to the potentially unsettling compromises and mediations that come with democratic engagements in a time of uncertainty).

In Chapter 2, we investigate the apparently tight relationship between speed, war and the state, primarily through an analysis of the works of Paul Virilio. Virilio's work argues that technological acceleration brings with it the perfection of the practice of warfare, which in turn reinforces the authority of the state-form. This results in the arrival of what he terms the 'globalitarian' state, a global military state which controls and organizes civilian life through a generalized time of violence and fear. I note how similar this account of the perfection of the practice of war through accelerative technologies is to that advanced by proponents of the revolution in military affairs (RMA) within elite military and political circles. However, I argue that both Virilio and the proponents of the RMA are mistaken in believing that acceleration brings with it the omnipotence of the military apparatus because these thinkers fail to differentiate between kinds of speed. In doing so they also fail to notice a fundamental tension between some types of speed and war (and especially between speed and the military apparatus). This analysis shows how, despite the increasing speed and power of what Deleuze and Guattari call the 'worldwide war machine', local 'war-machines', deploying local speed, also tend to spring up. These local war-machines escape some of the attempts at capture and control, and divert others into new directions unplanned by their carriers. The goal of this chapter is to argue not that speed has not made war quicker or deadlier, but rather that it has not made the state military apparatus as omnipotent as many of its proponents (and critics) seem to think. Pointing out this continual vulnerability of even the most advanced state militaries might hopefully encourage a more chastened approach to war-fighting.

Chapter 3 investigates the common assumption about the privileged relationship between speed and capitalism. I begin by analysing that brilliant prophet of capitalist innovation Joseph Schumpeter, describing how, in addition to his theories of the dynamism of capitalism through entrepreneurship and 'creative destruction', he theorizes a collection of 'restrictive practices' which slow down or moderate the rate of technological innovation under capitalism. I argue that this serves to dramatize the inherent tension in capitalism's relationship to speed, based in the dual character of the capitalist 'axiomatic' as a machine for the deterritorialization of flows and as an apparatus of capture. I exemplify this tension through an engagement with the struggle over contemporary information technologies, noting the way in which modern capitalism seeks to accelerate the flow of information to improve profitability and efficiency while at the same time blocking and curtailing it to ensure ownership and control of content.

Chapter 4 continues this investigation of speed and capitalism, now from the perspective of globalization. First I engage the neoliberal argument that capitalism, bolstered by technological acceleration, is engaged in a project of organizing the entire world into one homogenous system ('the earth is flat'). I challenge that account by arguing that, under globalization, we see an increasingly complex stratification and variegation of the earth's surface as a way of policing the various deterritorialized flows of globalizing capitalism. In this chapter I develop the concept of the 'regime of (im)mobility' to describe the proliferation of political, legal, economic, cultural and infrastructural mechanisms to regulate and channel various kinds of global flows (money, knowledge, goods, workers). These regimes of mobility ensure that new accelerative technologies do not, in fact, 'flatten the earth'; they instead work to maintain the control and separation of various flows and groups the world over. This separation is enhanced by the development of a sense of *ressentiment* against exteriority (similar to the *ressentiment* against futurity addressed in Chapter 1), where local populations resent and fear migrant populations because they identify them as the cause of their new instability and see in them the source of their impotence in the system of global production. This is particularly unfortunate, since these groups are frequently in a similar subject position with regards to globalizing capitalism. The national politics of *ressentiment* serves to forestall the possibility of new forms of political connection.

However, in Chapter 5, we see how, in spite of the pressure for this *ressentiment* against exteriority to proliferate, we also see the development of extensive networks of global activism and mutual aid. These networks are frequently described in terms of an emergent cosmopolitan ethos. However, I argue that traditional conceptions of cosmopolitanism, which I term 'arborescent cosmopolitanism', represented by thinkers such as Immanuel Kant and Martha Nussbaum, fail to grasp the true complexity of these new movements. According to the narrative of arborescent cosmopolitanism, global politics introduces a mode of transcendence, abstracting from local identities and affective attachments in favour of universal moral norms and essentialist conceptions of human nature. I argue instead that many of the movements, organizations and campaigns engaged in global progressive politics are organized by a logic of 'rhizomatic cosmopolitanism'; a cosmopolitanism that encourages global-level political action without requiring abstraction from locality, diversity and particularity. Indeed, an analysis of rhizomatic cosmopolitanism can help us see the strange geographies and conjunctions of eccentric flows which accelerative technologies produce, as well as make us more attuned to positive political possibilities which these new technologies present.

Note that, though in each of these chapters I seek to introduce a measure of hope into my political analysis, this should not be understood as an unqualified, uncritical or, indeed, even particularly optimistic hope. When I say that I am hopeful for the future, this does not deny that technological acceleration produces grave challenges to political, economic and social life. Indeed, throughout the text I provide accounts of many such dangers. I am aware that combating these threats requires immense stores of creativity, energy, will, patience, intelligence, openness, strength, forgiveness and love. The struggle to produce a future in which oppression, exploitation and violence become more the exception than the norm is a difficult one, marked by tremendous effort and sacrifice. However, it seems to me that the first step in this struggle is a mode of analysis that shows how such actions are not necessarily in vain. Having done that, the next step is to identify some of the potential levers, constituencies and sites of effective intervention. One of the major contentions of this book will be that speed introduces a fundamental uncertainty into time – an openness to the future. That openness means possibility; possibility means hope; and it is that hope which leads us to act.

1 The ticking bomb

Speed, democracy and the politics of the future

The affair cries haste, and speed must answer it.

(*Othello*, Act 1, Scene 3)

The ticking bomb

It's called 'the ticking bomb scenario': imagine a terrorist has planted a nuclear bomb somewhere in a major metropolitan centre. The terrorist has been captured, and knows where the bomb is, but the bomb is set to go off soon and torture is the only way to find out its location. Do you torture the terrorist?

What's important about this particular thought experiment is not the extreme utilitarian calculus that it seems to call into being (the lives of many versus the pain of one) but rather its very explicit temporal element. It is not just that there is a bomb, but that it's a ticking bomb. The imminence of the threat precludes any action other than torture (or at least so the scenario claims). Implicit in the narrative is the idea that the pace of events makes following traditional moral prohibitions – not to mention legal rights and due process – unfeasible and inefficient.[1]

The scenario is, like most thought experiments, absurd in its premises. It assumes, first of all, that we know for a fact that a nuclear bomb has been planted, but we have absolutely no other information about its location (or, apparently, any other avenues for acquiring that information). It assumes absolutely certainty that we have arrested the culprit responsible for planting the bomb. It assumes that he will be unable to withstand torture for long enough to allow the ticking bomb to go off, or that he will not provide false information, sending the authorities on a wild goose chase. Furthermore, it assumes that by focusing on this potentially false information, the authorities are not being distracted from other, more concrete leads (which, of course, we've assumed don't exist). However, as a philosophical exercise, it does lead to the interesting question of how urgency and speed might trump ethical commitments and legal regimes of rights and protection.[2]

Unfortunately, just because something is absurd doesn't mean it will lack political efficacy (indeed, frequently it seems just the opposite). In recent years, there have been many invocations of the ticking bomb scenario as a way of justifying a legitimate – and most importantly executive-centred – right to torture. It has been brought up during senate subcommittee hearings on torture. It has also been advanced by well-known legal scholars such as Alan Dershowitz, in defence of his plan for 'torture warrants' in cases of pressing concerns (Dershowitz 2004, 2006). These arguments in favour of a right on behalf of either the executive or the judiciary to authorize torture (or, rather, the revocation of the right *not* to be tortured) necessarily take the temporal element as their justification. Torture is not to be used in most criminal cases because there is no urgent threat to disqualify the (apparently) inefficient requirements of due process. However, the 'new era of terrorism' inaugurated with the 9/11 attacks has placed a premium on rapid, flexible responses. In other words, we no longer have the time not to torture.

The ticking bomb scenario and the right to torture are simply the leading edge of a much broader move within politics to use an accelerating pace of events (and threats) as justification for an abandonment of traditional ethical constraints, legal structures of due process and political checks and balances, in the name of a more efficient and unitary capacity for executive action. For example, in a series of memos to the White House, members of the Department of Justice such as Alberto Gonzalez and John Yoo argued for an increased scope in executive powers (such as the ability to wage wars, abrogate foreign treaties and determine the status of foreign combatants) on the basis of, amongst other rationales, the new urgency of the pace of events and threats in the political world. While justifying the executive's right to torture enemy combatants (and more broadly the executive's right to withdraw from treaties which might constrain its ability to torture), Department of Justice lawyer Alberto Gonzalez argues for the mitigating circumstances of the need for speed and flexibility in response to terror threats:

> As you have said, the war against terrorism is a new kind of war. It is not the traditional clash between nations adhering to the laws of war that formed the backdrop for GPW [the Geneva Convention]. The nature of the new war places a high premium on other factors, such as the ability to quickly obtain information from captured terrorists and their sponsors in order to avoid further atrocities against American civilians, and the need to try terrorists for war crimes such as wantonly killing civilians. In my judgment, this new paradigm renders obsolete Geneva's strict limitation on questioning of enemy prisoners.
>
> (Gonzalez 2002)

Though these memos were circulated in secret, the claim to increased executive authority in the face of an accelerating pace of threat has become increasingly common, and public, in the last few years. John Yoo, author of an earlier Department of Justice memo claiming increased presidential powers, published a book arguing that there is constitutional support for expanded executive authority. At least part of his argument relies on the need for an increased 'flexibility' in executive decision-making (Yoo 2005: 8–9). The new, post-9/11 world requires a unitary, autonomous executive, he says, unchecked by standards of divided government or constitutional restrictions:

> The cost of inaction, for example, by allowing the vetoes of multiple decisionmakers to block warmaking, could entail much higher costs than scholars in the 1990s had envisioned. At the time of the Cold War, the costs to American national security of refraining from the use of force in places like Haiti, Somalia, or Kosovo would have appeared negligible. The September 11, 2001, terrorist attacks, however, demonstrate that the costs of inaction can be extremely high – the possibility of a direct attack on the United States and the deaths of thousands of civilians.
>
> (Yoo 2005: x)

In a world of proliferating and accelerating threats, the greatest danger is inaction, says Yoo. Decision-making processes must be streamlined, authority centralized, and the executive freed of legal, political or ethical encumbrances which might limit the flexibility of its response. The novelty of this threat is not just the magnitude of the danger, but the speed with which it materializes. Like the ticking bomb scenario, the problem is not the utilitarian calculus but the fact that we no longer have time to allow for democratic consultation and constitutional limitations. The executive must be able to respond quickly and authoritatively to whatever new threats the world might throw at America.

At this point, however, we might take yet another step backwards. We might notice that the logic of the ticking bomb and its attendant claim about the need for increased executive authority is, in fact, not a new one. Though its application has unquestionably intensified in the post-9/11 era, it has in fact justified a steady transition of authority to the executive for years now. This increase of executive authority has extended beyond issues of national security, although this has certainly been its strongest quarter. In the United States, the executive has lobbied for, and received, increased ability to negotiate trade treaties, conduct diplomacy and even influence domestic legislation. What is more, this is not a uniquely American experience. In democracies all over the world, there has been a steady empowering of the executive on the basis of, amongst other factors, the acceleration of the pace of events (Scheuerman 2004: 92–3, 108–9).

In this chapter, I will examine the threat that speed supposedly poses to democracy. I will begin by investigating William Scheuerman's account of what I call the 'liberal narrative of speed', the tradition within liberal democratic thought which, I argue, accepts the logic of the ticking bomb, and believes that speed is a threat to democratic practice and requires an expansion of the power of the executive. However, I will then go on to argue that the liberal narrative is based on an inherently flawed account of acceleration; that it ignores the way in which technological acceleration can also provide important tools which foster democratic practice. Then, through an ontological analysis of speed, I argue that the move to expand the power of the executive in the face of acceleration is a result not of the *functional* threat which acceleration poses to a political community, but rather of the *existential* threat. I will argue that the push for increased executive authority is the result of a sense of *ressentiment* against speed, against the uncertainty and destabilization which acceleration brings to stable narratives of political community and identity. Finally, I will investigate how this fear of speed is manifested in the democratic thought of Sheldon Wolin. Note that the choice of liberalism, on the one hand, and the work of Sheldon Wolin, on the other, is deliberate, insofar as both are, to a greater or lesser degree, deeply attached to democratic practice and governance. It is useful, then, to investigate how, in even a strongly democratic character, a *ressentiment* against speed can foster anti-democratic sentiments. In (post)modern life, the spectre of the ticking bomb haunts democracy. It claims a kind of necessity for itself, arguing for the increasing impossibility of democracy in periods of acceleration. It will be the goal of this chapter to challenge this necessity, to argue that the anti-democratic impulse should be located not primarily in the ticking bomb, but in ourselves.

Speed and liberal democracy

According to the liberal narrative, the central threat that speed poses to democracy is that it enhances the power of the least democratic branch of government, the executive. Within the liberal tradition, it is argued that the executive is best adapted to deal with an accelerating pace of events, while the legislative branch is ill equipped for an environment of substantial instability and rapid change. The liberal narrative of speed argues that

> the widely endorsed conception of the unitary executive as an 'energetic' entity best capable of acting with dispatch means that social acceleration often promotes executive-centered government and the proliferation of executive discretion while weakening broad-based representative legislatures as well as traditional models of constitutionalism and the rule of law.
>
> (Scheuerman 2004: xiv)

The liberal democratic tradition has always assumed that the processes of democratic debate and decision-making are necessarily cumbersome and slow, making the legislative branch incapable of acting in the face of fast-moving events:

> Legislative politics is typically conceived as resting on a process of free-wheeling deliberation involving a rich sample of public opinion, and liberal thinkers have repeatedly emphasized the necessarily measured and unhurried prerequisites of a legitimate process of reasonable debate in

which participants possess a fair chance to express distinct political views and defend a multiplicity of interests.

(Scheuerman 2004: 38)

This is in contrast to the unitary, 'energetic' executive, which is able to make decisions in a rapid and efficient manner.

Now, within liberal democratic thought there was always an understanding that there would be some events that would be too rapid to be dealt with by the legislative branch, and hence the executive was to be assigned some power to act independently in response to unexpected occurrences.[3] Because there always exists the potential for events which the legislative body cannot deal with in a timely manner, the liberal narrative of speed says that the executive must be legitimately able to act unilaterally. The narrative goes on, however, to argue that there has been a fundamental and general acceleration of the pace of modern life, and that this acceleration has increased the number of situations in which a rapid governmental response is required. This means that the legislative branch is becoming increasingly incapable of managing the political sphere, leading to more and more government action via independent executive order. Says Scheuerman about this shift,

Assumptions about the energetic executive potentially open the door to an executive-dominated system of constitutional adaptation, because appeals to the executive's high-speed character typically justify its impressive power. The dictates of speed cry out for flexible, rapid-fire institutional responses and the classical temporal portrait of the executive will lead many political and legal actors to deem the executive best attuned to tackling the imperative of constitutional adaptation.

(Scheuerman 2004: 100–1)

And, says Scheuerman, this prediction is playing out. Increasingly, liberal democratic polities around the world are seeing a steady transfer of authority, either *de jure* or *de facto*, from legislative to executive bodies. Executives the world over (although this has been most easily seen in the American context) have been using the liberal narrative of speed and the volatility of world events as an argument for the increased transfer of power from legislative oversight to executive directive.[4] This is sometimes lamented for the injury which it does to democratic process, but is frequently accepted as necessary to ensure the government's continual effective responsiveness to crisis and cata-strophe. Democracy – at least robust, 'free-wheeling' democracy – was a luxury of the past, which is impossible in today's fast-paced, unpredictable world.[5]

What is remarkable, however, is that, after laying out this narrative, Scheuerman then goes on to argue that it is, potentially, a deeply flawed argument; saying, 'perhaps the traditional contrast between slow-going *deliberare* and high-speed *agere* no longer makes sense (Scheuerman 2004: 101)?' This is because the liberal narrative of speed assumes that the general acceleration of modern life has affected only the context *in which* the legislative and executive branches function, but has had no significant effect on *the way* in which they function. Scheuerman argues this is not true in the case of either branch.

First, the idea of the unitary executive, energetic and capable of acting quickly and efficiently, is, in many ways, a left-over from the early days of liberal democracy, when the executive was a much smaller administrative organization. In response to this image, Scheuerman argues:

> the contemporary executive is a complicated institution, made up of a rich variety of (oftentimes conflicting) bureaucratic units: the emphasis on traditional reflections on the unitary and even solitary nature of the executive badly obscures the empirical executive decision making. Even when the executive branch acts unilaterally, seemingly straightforward undertakings can prove toilsome and time consuming, as anyone familiar with the less-than-efficient operations of the modern executive can attest.
>
> (Scheuerman 2004: 101)

Ironically, as the executive appropriates more and more spheres of authority to itself on the basis of its perceived efficiency, it becomes more fragmented and inefficient.

The United States was given an unfortunate and chilling example of the potential slowness, ineptness and inefficiency of executive action in the bungled response to Hurricane Katrina and the flooding of New Orleans and surrounding areas. And this was a natural disaster, second only, perhaps, to a surprise military attack in terms of the paradigmatic emergency situation which the executive is supposed to deal with, and not even part of that creeping sphere of influence which the executive has begun to procure for itself under the rubric of the liberal narrative of speed. (Indeed, the failures of the administration were all the more glaring to the extent that, unlike a surprise military attack, the threat of Katrina was known well in advance.) Now, of course, one instance of bureaucratic incompetence does not necessarily disprove the thesis. But it does bring to the fore the various complications which the increased speed and scope of a political community can bring to the supposedly unitary, energetic executive: overlapping jurisdictions, ineffective lines of communication, poor preparation and the lack of situational awareness. There are various efforts that can improve these problems, but it is unlikely, given the character of modern governance, that they will ever be completely eliminated. The image of the executive as custom made for the challenges of modern acceleration is therefore more present in the narrative than in real life.

Conversely, the image of the slow, inefficient legislative branch is also somewhat anachronistic, based as it is on the transportation and communication technologies of centuries past. Says Scheuerman:

> early modern discussions of popular deliberation arguably presuppose underdeveloped forms of transportation and communication: well into

the nineteenth century, elected representatives were forced to engage in time-consuming travel to meet their colleagues, and correspondence or news might require weeks or even months to reach its target. In an age of instantaneous communication and high-speed travel the temporal pre-suppositions of popular deliberation are dramatically different than in the days of Hamilton, or even Mill, as new technologies potentially allow huge numbers of people to exchange views at unparalleled speed. The association of popular deliberation with 'slowness' no longer deserves the self-evident character that it possessed for so many of our historical predecessors.

(Scheuerman 2004: 102)

Here we see how accelerative technologies can aid in the practice of demo-cratic legislative politics in key ways. Scheuerman later invokes the example of the anthrax scare which shut down Congress and several other buildings in Washington, DC. Despite being physically dispersed, Congress continued to communicate and govern through the use of mobile and handheld communication technologies. Additionally, he discusses the way in which high-speed media can provide an opportunity to change the 'sequential' char-acter of deliberation which supposedly slows down democratic legislative decision-making. In principle, the mass media can provide a useful forum for large-scale debates on important social issues, allowing for increased oppor-tunities to disseminate information and to sample public opinion. Indeed, new accelerative technologies can provide opportunities for citizens to bypass representatives in the legislative process altogether, as theorists of deliberative democracy have discussed (209), resulting in accelerative technologies making legislation not just faster, but also potentially more democratic. New accelerative technologies provide the legislative branch with the possibility of being, if not as 'energetic' as the executive, certainly a lot less sluggish than the liberal narrative of speed takes for granted.

This argument does not suggest that the legislative will be able to handle all events that occur. But it does argue that the number and type of events beyond the reach of the legislature are not necessarily expanding, or at least not expanding as quickly as proponents of increased executive power would have us believe. Nor does this argument deny that a general social acceleration of time poses specific challenges for the practice of democracy (Scheuerman spends substantial time noting the obstacles that acceleration places in the way of democracy). The central point, however, is that accelerative technologies and a general social acceleration of time provide at least as many possibilities for democratic activity as they do pitfalls, and that a careful consideration of these possibilities can serve to foster democracy in spite of these changes, as well as because of them. Acceleration, though a challenge to democracy, is not fundamentally opposed to it.

However, if we choose to reject the liberal narrative's technological pessimism, and instead argue that the 'assertion that social acceleration undermines liberal democracy may rest on a historical myth' (189), then why does this narrative still carry so much weight in politics? Why is it that, in spite of all the new opportunities for democratic deliberation, the accelerating pace of events is accepted as justification for the steady transfer of power to the executive branch?

Scheuerman explains this willingness to accept the liberal narrative of speed primarily as the result of a series of misunderstandings. In addition to misunderstanding the various characteristics of the executive and legislative branches (as described on pp. 15–16), there is also, he says, a crucial misunderstanding of the actual pace of threat. This misunderstanding has its roots in the uncritical acceptance of the rhetorical trope of the state-as-body. Scheuerman's claim is that metaphorically identifying the state with the body necessarily raises the perceived stakes of (as well as the necessary speed of response to) acts of violence and terrorism. As he puts it,

> when physically assaulted, individuals lack the luxury of debating with their peers or allies about the best conceivable response. Instead, they must move quickly to ward off immediate threats to their physical well-being, and such moments call for action rather than deliberation, dispatch instead of delay. If physical violence is imminent or already at hand, individual self-preservation can only be achieved by the imperatives of physical self-defense, where agility and swiftness are at a premium. In the political universe, the unitary executive, and not a numerous deliberative assembly, is the most likely source of such agility and swiftness.
>
> (Scheuerman 2002: 496)

Of course this metaphor is crucially faulty, as, though a single violent physical blow can be fatal to the human body, only in the most extreme, nuclear-related circumstances would the same be true for a state. Therefore, the necessary pace of response in political matters might not be as great as we tend to believe.

I certainly agree with Scheuerman that these misunderstandings contribute greatly to the temporal politics of the contemporary world. My concern, however, is that he explains the increasingly anti-democratic reforms of the liberal democratic world in a purely exogenous way. This is to say that, on his account, the error of the liberal narrative of speed is primarily in how it is applied, in the way that it misunderstands the actual pace of events, and the speed of the various actors and institutions involved. This is problematic, because it doesn't so much solve the problem of speed as delay it. Its response to the liberal narrative of speed – and the anti-democratic sentiments it fosters – is to say that things haven't accelerated that much yet. Though this may be true, it leaves open the problem of what happens when things do reach such a terminal velocity.

What is more, by pursuing a purely exogenous critique I feel that Scheuerman misses out on something very important in the relationship between speed and liberalism, something which I believe points to crucial anti-democratic sentiments at the heart of liberal doctrine.[6] Ferreting out these anti-democratic sentiments means tracing in greater detail the relationship between liberalism and speed, and this means developing a much more nuanced understanding of the nature of speed.

In the next three sections I will investigate the ontology of speed, discuss its character and effects, and the way in which it changes the social and political landscape. Only then will we be able to return to this question of speed and politics, and provide an answer to the question of why, if acceleration does not necessitate the decline of democratic governance, it seems to do so all the same.

Vague ontologies

To pursue these questions we need to develop an ontology of speed. To begin, it is pertinent to discuss what is meant by 'ontology' and how it is used in relation to the concept of speed. Here 'ontology' is used in a somewhat complex and ambiguous sense since speed is not properly a 'being' (in the sense that a chair, or a human is), but is rather a particular organization of beings. This is therefore a relational ontology, the ontology of the specific relation of a set of objects and actors. Additionally, this ontology should not be taken as a strong, transcendent or categorical one. Rather, here the nature of speed is better understood in terms of what Deleuze and Guattari refer to as vague or minor essences (Deleuze and Guattari 1987: 367). This is a term Deleuze picks up from Husserl's *The Origins of Geometry*, which he uses to describe a concept which is somewhere between an ideal essence and a concrete thing (Deleuze 1979). Vague essences can be understood as 'morphological essences in opposition to fixed or formal essences ... these are inexact essences, or better, anexact ones' (ibid.) These vague essences, says Deleuze, are defined not by 'thingness', as are concrete objects, or 'essentiality', as pure ideal essences, but rather by a kind of 'corporeality', which is to say a form of becoming that 'is inseparable from processes of deformation of which it is the site [*siège*], that's its first characteristic: ablation, deletion, increase, passage to the limit, events' (ibid.).

There is never speed *tout court*, but rather specific speeds, specific appropriations and assemblages of speed which modify, mediate and moderate its character. A vague essence is 'inseparable from events ... inseparable from affects' (ibid.). In this book I will produce a kind of bestiary of different assemblages of speed; a state-speed, a capitalist-speed, a war-machine-speed, etc. This is a crucial point, for I will argue that many of the criticisms which are levelled at speed are levelled only at these particular modes of speed, and not at speed as it could exist in other assemblages. A proper understanding of speed, and the assemblages into which it can enter, opens up a wider frame of political possibility. This will also require an understanding of the idea of how speed is intertwined with another concept, movement, which has been the focus of many more investigations.[7] As we shall see, the close connection between speed and movement stops either one from being a fully autonomous category. It also produces each as a minor essence which checks and mediates the other. This is thus a lived ontology of speed, tied to the plasticity of vague essences.[8]

This attempt at developing an ontology of speed, of identifying a group of primary characteristics essential to understanding speed, also serves an important analytical purpose. This is to say that in ordinary language we use the word 'speed' to refer to a host of phenomena, some of which, as I will argue, carry contradictory characteristics. When I differentiate 'speed' from concepts such as 'movement' and 'velocity' (as well as introducing distinctions such as 'quantitative speed' and 'relative speed'), I am saying that philosophically and politically useful effects result from classifying the phenomenal world in this way. It seems to me that many wholesale criticisms of speed emerge in part due to a diverse set of processes being lumped together under the same term. The framework I will be using separates out certain elements that are potentially useful for various political, philosophical and ethical projects from other elements which are potentially harmful. I retain common terms like 'speed' and 'velocity' out of a twofold attachment to some form of Wittgensteinian analysis: first, inspired by his idea of an analysis based on family resemblance, an attempt to figure out what connects the various diverse uses of a word; and, second, through an attachment to a more creative process within Wittgenstein, wherein we attempt to 'bring words back' to a more useful meaning (Wittgenstein 1958: 48; Cavell 1989).

On the ontology of speed

I begin, then, with a distinction that is simultaneously obvious and counter-intuitive. This is the distinction, introduced by Deleuze and Guattari in *A Thousand Plateaus,* between speed and movement (1987: 371). This distinction is obvious because, in the first place, while we are always in motion, even by the most conventional understandings, we do not always have speed. Speed is an intermittent phenomenon in the context of ubiquitous movement. All movement cannot be said to possess speed, unless we wish the word speed to be meaningless. This assertion, at least, seems relatively uncontroversial. Deleuze and Guattari go on, however, to make a more jarring claim. They argue that movement and speed are ontologically distinct phenomena: 'It is thus necessary to make a distinction between *speed* and *movement*: a movement may be very fast, but that does not give it speed; a speed may be very slow, or even immobile, yet it is still speed' (1987: 381).

In response to the claim that all movement is not speed, one might say that of course all movement does not possess speed, but rather only certain movement(s), movement that takes place above a certain velocity. (Here velocity indicates the objective measurement of movement as displacement over time.)[9] In this response, speed becomes a subset of movement, attributed once it has passed a certain threshold. At the risk of sounding tautological (though so much of what we think of as common sense is tautological), speed is a quality possessed by movement when it becomes fast. The trouble with this perspective is that it assumes a binary threshold of velocity, which, when passed, transforms a movement into speed. There can, however, be no absolute threshold of speed, since the human capacity for velocity has changed so frequently in history. The runner's velocity was displaced by the horse, only to be overtaken by the train, car, plane, etc. There is no number, no absolute point beyond which movement becomes speed. We must therefore probe the distinction between speed and movement further.

'Well of course there's no absolute threshold of speed,' our imaginary interlocutor might say. 'But that does not mean that there is no objective measure of speed. This is because speed is relative. Speed is a measure of difference, not an absolute characteristic. Something only has speed, is only fast, in comparison to something else, something slower than itself. But of course this difference is objective. Speed is therefore inseparable from movement, insofar as it describes a particular differential of movement. It is a function of movement.'

It is true that velocity is calculable and that it describes a relative differential. But this does not mean that speed is an objectively attributable phenomenon. For, as physics tells us, when describing velocity as the differential of displacement over time between two points, the velocity can just as accurately be ascribed to either point. Though we might wish to say that something has speed when it is moving faster than something else, a shift of perspective can have it be that 'something else' which is moving away in the opposite direction. To put it another way, we can, with a little imagination, see the train as standing still, and the landscape taking off backwards at a high velocity. Velocity as an objective measurement of a differential cannot, therefore, be enough to attribute speed to an object. We might say the two points exist in a 'relationship of speed', but that seems a substantially more ambiguous statement. How, then, do we go about attributing speed?

Well, in the everyday, the attribution of speed comes about as a result of a conscious experience. Something has speed when it 'feels' fast, when we experience it as speed. It produces particular corporeal and perceptual effects (the sense of acceleration, the drop in the pit of the stomach, the tingle of adrenaline). This is not to say that speed is only a psychological phenomenon. Rather, speed is a material phenomenon attested to by subjective insight.

However, this introduction of experience substantially complicates matters. For, given enough time and stability, any velocity can be experienced as stasis. Take, for example, the passenger on a jet-plane who, though she may be travelling at a little under 1,000 km/hr, experiences no sense of movement or speed. The earth orbits the sun at a velocity of 29.77 km/second and yet none of its inhabitants feels any indication of, or would describe themselves to be, travelling at great speeds when standing on the ground. Furthermore, observe how speed is rarely experienced continuously. Imagine merging on to a freeway, accelerating from 50 km/hr to 90 km/hr. At first the new velocity seems incredibly fast. You feel that familiar rush of speed, that exhilaration of acceleration. And yet, after a short period of time, this feeling leaves, and you begin to experience a general sensation of movement, no different from your earlier velocity (a phenomenon known as 'velocitization'). What is more, if you were forced to decelerate, even to say 60 km/hr, it would undoubtedly feel unbearably slow, slower somehow even than the 50 km/hr you were originally driving, an experience which itself seemed fast when you first pulled out of the driveway.

We now begin to get an idea of what it is that defines speed. Speed is identified by change. It is only at the moment of change that one has the experience of speed, at the moment of acceleration that one *feels* speed. We should now have some idea of what Deleuze and Guattari mean when they state, 'It is thus necessary to make a distinction between *speed* and *movement*: a movement may be very fast, but that does not give it speed' (1987: 381). Though the relative velocity of an object may be high, that doesn't mean that it can't functionally be considered stable or immobile. The second half of the quote, however, where they state that 'a speed may be very slow', is still slightly opaque. But if we accept the point made above, that speed is experienced through change, then its objective velocity is not relevant. What is important is the moment of change. The experience of speed *qua* speed in the runner is the same as the experience of speed *qua* speed in the aeroplane. Hence a speed may be objectively 'very slow' and yet still be experienced as speed. This is what it means to say that speed is a 'relational' phenomenon.

It is in the duration of change that speed lives. The acceleration of the aeroplane, the runner shooting out of the starting gate. This is different than the claim made above that speed is identified through the differential between velocities. This is because such an attribution is based on an objective measurement which necessarily persists in time. Thus it makes speed a state, a quality. But as we saw above in the process of velocitization, speed is not a state that endures. Rather, it is in the nature of speed that it is fleeting. Speed *possesses* movement, and then *drains* away. Speed is not a state or a quality. It is an *Event* (Deleuze 1990: 148). To describe it in another register, speed occupies the time of *Kairos* (Negri 2003). It is the moment which is singular, which is not extended through *Chronos*, though it does open up into the future, and is informed by the past (163).

The attribution of speed must be immanent to the subject/object of speed. It is an absolute, rather than a relative property of an object (which is not to say that it's devoid of an element of relationality). Or as Deleuze and Guattari put it, not an extensive property, but an intensive property:

> Movement is extensive; speed is intensive. Movement goes from point to point; *speed, on the contrary, constitutes the absolute character of a body whose irreducible parts (atoms) occupy or fill a smooth space in the manner of a vortex*, with the possibility of springing up at any point.
> (Deleuze and Guattari 1987: 381)

Speed is a function of an intensive experience of alteration. But it is more than acceleration; for acceleration, when expected, also ceases to be felt (the smooth steady acceleration of a car which can also, *almost*, feel like stasis). It is not just the process of change which identifies speed, but also the element of the unexpected, the unpredictable, the surprising. The swerve of the car; the sudden burst of acceleration. This is why in the passage above Deleuze and Guattari speak of the *'possibility* of springing up at any point'. Speed is the transition that introduces the (in principle) unpredictable.

In this regard, speed functions as, or perhaps is the crucial element of, Lucretius' clinamen, the instantaneous deviation from the expected, the swerve from the apparently foreordained path (Lucretius 1995). This is where the element of relationality comes into play, as the intensive nature of speed is only activated in reference to a pre-existing trajectory. Deleuze and Guattari speak to this point when they describe the distinction to be made between speed and movement:

> The opposition is both qualitative and scientific, in that speed is not merely an abstract characteristic of movement in general but is incarnated in a moving body that deviates, however slightly, from this line of descent or gravity.
>
> (Deleuze and Guattari 1987: 371)

I have identified the experience of speed with the experience of change (hence the identification of speed in the quotation above with a 'deviation' from a line of descent). But it cannot just be any change. For the world is constantly changing in ways that are unrelated to speed. It is a particular kind of change which is bound up with speed. The change which marks speed possesses, and is defined by, two characteristics, the first (primarily) temporal and the second (primarily) spatial. I term these characteristics futurity and exteriority.

To say that the change which speed brings must possess the characteristic of futurity is to say that it is that change which brings the New. Note here that we are ill served if we think of futurity solely in terms of 'surprise', for this is to attribute it to a failure or limitation of human foresight, and keep our analysis solely in the realm of the subjective. Instead, we are talking about a future which is unpredictable, *even in principle*. This is an ateleological future, a future which cleaves to no set plan or idea. Here, Henri Bergson's work developing an image of time as duration will be helpful. For Bergson, time is marked by a creative movement of becoming, an 'unforeseeable novelty' (1974: 91). According to Bergson, time functions according to a principle of open futurity. This is to say that

> time is what hinders everything from being given at once. It retards, or rather it is retardation. It must, therefore, be elaboration. Would it not then be a vehicle of creation and of choice? Would not the existence of time prove that there is indetermination in things? Would not time be that indetermination itself?
>
> (Bergson 1974: 93)

According to Bergson, our intellect attempts to impose an orderly, teleological progression on this unruly creativity of becoming. But it is a primordial unpredictability that truly marks the durational unfolding of time:

> Reality is global and undivided growth, progressive invention, duration: it resembles a gradually expanding rubber balloon assuming at each moment unexpected forms. But our intelligence imagines its origin and evolution as an arrangement and rearrangement of parts which supposedly merely shift from one place to another.
>
> (Bergson 1974: 95–6)

The work of the intellect, then, is simply what Bergson terms the 'retrograde movement of the true growth of the truth', our projection after the fact of an orderly, stable progression within the creative flow of becoming. As Bergson puts it,

> [t]o every true affirmation we attribute thus a retroactive effect; or rather we impart to it a retrograde movement. As though judgment could have pre-existed the terms which make it up! As though these terms did not date from the appearance of the objects they represent! As though the thing and the idea of the thing, its reality and its possibility, were not created at one stroke when a truly new form, invented by art or nature, is concerned!
>
> (Bergson 1974: 22)[10]

In the image of time which the intellect seeks to project on to duration (which Bergson calls the scientific or cinematographic image of time) time is viewed spatially, and is modelled by an unbroken line, unfolding into the future, the present acting as a joint between an always already existing past and future. Contrary to this image of time which the intellect presents us with, Bergson points us towards the faculty of intuition (and a form of metaphysics which starts from intuition), a faculty which orients us towards the primordial uncertainty and creativity of time. Time is duration, it has duration, and 'it has duration precisely because it is continuously elaborating what is new and because there is no elaboration without searching, no searching without groping. Time is this very hesitation or it is nothing' (Bergson 1974: 93).

There is a slight problem here, however. We have identified speed as an irruption of the new. But, if we have accepted the view of time which Bergson (amongst others) presents us with, then we must acknowledge that the New is not something which emerges only occasionally, but rather is something with which we are faced at every moment. As Bergson puts it, 'real time ... eludes mathematical treatment. Its essence being to flow, not one of its parts is still there when another part comes along. Superposition of one part on another with measurement in view is therefore impossible, unimaginable, inconceivable' (12). That time seems to be unfolding spatially is a result of a mental operation, the suppression of difference and an imposition of similarity which makes the passing of time a manageable experience within which we can act in the 'future'-oriented ways necessary to our survival. The major works of Bergson are dedicated to mapping the techniques of thinking which have evolved to help us suppress the coming of the new: 'An attention to the rules of efficient causality makes us better capable of navigating the world, and the world takes the form of a *mechanical* causality' (Bergson 1998: 44). This mechanical causality is implicitly teleological, and assumes an unfolding of time.

In the context of this generalized suppression of the future, then, we can think of the coming of the New not as the New which comes with every moment, but rather as the coming of a particular kind of event (Event) which cannot be smoothly subsumed or integrated into a prior teleological projection of the unfolding of time. For Bergson, it is a turn towards intuition and away from the intellect that opens us up to the creative flow of durational time. However, this attentiveness to durational time, this awareness of the inadequacy of the spatialized image of time, is also forced by the speed-event, the unexpected swerve, the surprising occurrence that cannot be comfortably subsumed under our teleological projection of the future;[11] speed as the irruption of intuition into the intellect.[12]

Thus futurity is always a relational phenomenon, relative to an expectation or projection. This does not, however, mean that speed is a purely subjective phenomenon. Teleological projections of time can happen at any number of different registers: at the physical level of embodied, corporeal movements; at the level of conscious, subjective projections of the future; at the level of societal expectations; at the level of narratives of history; even potentially at the evolutionary level of species-life, or the geological or cosmological level of great physical upheavals. We can think of speed in terms of a deviation from a projected path, however that projection is taking place. Speed is thus the 'moment' when the ateleological nature of time is laid bare, when a mechanical narrative of time's unfolding is shown to be inadequate to the creative becoming of this world.[13] This is why there is a qualitatively different experience of speed between driving a car on the freeway and being a passenger in a car, though the velocity in both cases may be the same. In the one, we are better able to project the path of the movement of the car, and hence we do not experience the speed in the same way as if every swerve or acceleration of the car is unexpected.

The second characteristic of speed – exteriority – can be understood as the spatial mapping of futurity (something quite different from the intellect's attempts to spatialize temporality). Speed operates necessarily through the breaking of barriers, through the opening up of space and the decoding of flows. Speed is that which overcomes limitations which we have come to take as given. (Recall how expectation and standardization are the enemies of speed, transforming speed-as-event into velocity-as-state). This idea seems to have a poetic resonance which speaks in its favour, as the experience of speed is often accompanied by a feeling of overcoming, of breaking free. Here Deleuze and

Guattari's classification of spaces into the smooth and striated is useful (1987: 474–500). The striated is the space of interiority, formed and organized on logics of bounding and limitation. This is not to say that striated spaces are smaller, weaker or more 'limited' than smooth spaces; rather, they operate according to a distinctive logic of limitation (475). These are spaces which produce velocities, movements which are measured according to displacement; travel between and within bounded territories. Say Deleuze and Guattari, '[i]n striated space, lines or trajectories tend to be subordinated to points; one goes from one point to another' (478). This is a space of relative distance over time (the measurement of velocity). In contrast, smooth space is the space of speed, a space which is 'infinite, open, and unlimited in every direction; it has neither top nor bottom nor center; it does not assign fixed and mobile elements but rather distributes a continuous variation' (475–6). Contrary to the projected, teleological movements of the striated space, in the smooth space 'the points are subordinated to the trajectory' (478). This is precisely the spatial movement of futurity, which is to say a path which can only be identified with confidence retroactively, as a plotting of the emergent singularity of becoming. And it is this movement which occurs, and is described, through speed. As was said on p. 21, speed *'constitutes the absolute character of a body whose irreducible parts (atoms) occupy or fill a smooth space in the manner of a vortex, with the possibility of springing up at any point'* (381). The special kind of change experienced in speed is one that overcomes a barrier, decentres and unsettles fixed spatial boundaries; that, in short, deterritorializes (381).

This should not be taken to mean that speed is simply more 'expansive' than movement or velocity. Much as speed can be slow, it can also be small. Exteriority is not a logic of scope, but of organization and coding; or rather a reorganization of elements and a decoding of flows. It changes the shape and functioning of a system, shifting it from an arborescent to a rhizomatic model (8). Deleuze and Guattari provide an example of this in the world of music: 'When Glenn Gould speeds up the performance of a piece, he is not just displaying virtuosity, he is transforming the musical points into lines, he is making the whole piece proliferate' (8). Speed must be understood, then, as a line of deterritorialization. Think of the speed of the runner. The element of speed in the runner lies not in the increased velocity she experiences (or not entirely), since this acceleration unfolds along a projected line of control. Rather, the speed of the runner comes from the deterritorialization of her body, the transformation of her body's assemblage with the earth. Speed transforms her from a walking assemblage into a running machine. The spatial characteristic of speed is then not one of scope but, we might say, of direction. Speed comes at movement transversally. Hence the 'instantaneous deviation' mentioned on p. 22.

This allows us to finally fully understand the earlier quote in its entirety, where Deleuze and Guattari state that 'a speed may be very slow, or even immobile, yet it is still speed' (381). Indeed, it is not just *possible* that speed should be immobile; it is, in fact, *necessary*. For speed always constitutes a

break in movement, a caesura, an 'instantaneous deviation' and hence a moment
(an Event) of immobility within the smooth unfolding of mobility, a moment
which reorganizes the spatial logic of a system or makes us pass to a new
system.[14] Speed therefore only ever happens in the *milieu*, in the middle of
a flow.

Speed is a moment of absolute immobility, and yet one that is only ever
present within the context of movement. It is this paradox which returns us to
the discussion of vague essences which began this section. For though I have
described speed and movement as ideal, 'pure' types, it has become clear
from the examples we have used that the one is never present without the other.
The two types are deeply intertwined. We can see this if we think through the
temporal implications of speed's immobility. Since, in principle, speed is an
event, taking place in the singular time of *Kairos*, we can think of it as
instantaneous, and therefore existing as pure possibility. However, in practice,
every *Kairos* is extended within a *Chronos*, and thus every pure speed is seated,
to a greater or lesser extent, within a movement. To the extent to which we
can see speed as present in immobility, it is a virtual presence. Deleuze and
Guattari describe 'the Japanese fighter, interminably still, who then makes a
move too quick to see' (1987: 356). In this fighter, interminably still, there is
the possibility of 'springing up at any point'. He is thus full of a virtual speed,
an immobile speed, waiting, straining, to be instantiated through movement.

Every *Kairos* is extended in a *Chronos*, every speed-event extended in a
velocity-state. The irruption of the new which speed brings to a settled teleological projection is quickly subsumed into a new projection. The line of flight
or of deterritorialization is always reterritorialized. Or, even worse, it isn't,
and to disastrous consequences, for we know that the unreterritorialized line
of flight is 'a line of death' (229–31) (the speeding car crashes into a wall, unable
to return to a controlled, regular movement). And conversely every acceleration
of velocity produces a shifting of forces, a ratcheting up of intensities which
carries with it new possibilities, and new threats, of producing the Event (like
Glenn Gould's acceleration of a piece of music). Futurity and exteriority,
while on the one hand being binary categories, are also analogue, creating a
kind of creeping continuum between the ideal types of 'speed' and 'movement'.
Our political analysis must then, on the one hand, be careful not to confuse
these two phenomena, and must learn to discriminate between them, while at
the same time being aware of how they are intertwined, and thus how they
might implicate one another or call one another into being.

Technology, acceleration and zones of time

In developing this ontology of speed, I have focused primarily on physical
movement. But speed, and the experience of speed as the irruption of the
New, extends beyond the physical movement of bodies, though it always
involves movement of some kind or another – the movement of electrons in a
computer, the movement of electrical impulses in the brain, the movement of

memes through a culture. There is speed in communication technologies, speed in information processing, speed in creative processes and transformations, speed in social movements, speed in the sequence of events. Though these processes don't necessarily carry with them the physical shock of acceleration (that lurch in the pit of the stomach), they do have the potential to provoke the experience of the radically new, the experience of futurity and exteriority which I identified as central to speed (and usually carry with them some sort of experience of shock, either corporeal, mental, social or physical).

In this section, I want to connect our analysis of the ontology of speed and movement to the acceleration of the pace of events in the social and political worlds. I begin with Hartmut Rosa's identification of three types of phenomena in the modern world, where we see the experience of increasing velocity, producing what he terms 'social acceleration': 'technological acceleration', 'social change and transformation' and 'the heightened tempo of everyday life' (Rosa 2003: 6–9).[15] Rosa identifies the first as 'the speeding up of intentional, *goal-directed* processes of transport, communication and production' (6); the ability to travel faster, the ability to transmit more information over longer distances and to process it more quickly. However, in addition to faster engines, processors and fibre-optic cables, there is a second order to technological acceleration, which is the rate of technological innovation itself (Scheuerman 2004: 10). The pace of modern life is determined not just by the quantitative capabilities of various technologies, but also by the rate at which these technologies are replaced by improved versions. The computer is thus the quintessential artefact of (post)modernity not just because of the pace at which it functions, but also because of the pace at which each iteration becomes obsolete.

Additionally, in understanding speed in the social world, we cannot restrict ourselves to physical, or rather punctual technologies, but must look also at a whole universe of infrastructural, social, political, legal and linguistic technologies to which they are connected. For example, the speed of a particular jet engine is meaningless, socially speaking, without a global infrastructure of airports for it to land in, or the systems of customs, immigration and tourism which allow people to use them. The ability of fibre-optic cables to transmit enormous amounts of information is useless without a physical infrastructure of such cables crossing the globe, and an informational infrastructure of shared protocols which allow for the information to be effectively routed and translated through this physical network. Félix Guattari theorizes this idea by noting that all punctual technologies are also physical machines which enter into assemblage with a host of other social, economic, political or even libidinal machines. He takes the example of the Concorde supersonic jet, and notes that for it to 'work', much more than the immediate technological breakthroughs are necessary:

> The ontological consistency of this object is essentially composite; it is at the intersection, at the point of constellation and pathic agglomeration of Universes each of which have their own ontological consistency, traits

of intensity, their ordinates and coordinates, their specific machinisms. Concorde simultaneously involves:

- a diagrammatic Universe with plans of theoretical 'feasibility';
- technological Universes transposing this 'feasibility' into material terms;
- industrial Universes capable of effectively producing it;
- collective imaginary Universes corresponding to a desire sufficient to make it see the light of day;
- political and economic universes leading, amongst other things, to the release of credit for its construction.(Guattari 1995: 47–8)

Guattari notes that the Concorde failed as a regular flight between London and New York. At the time of his writing it was not in regular service, and has since been entirely taken out of use: 'The Concorde object moves effectively between Paris and New York but remains nailed to the economic ground' (48). As a result, understanding the 'pace' of a particular era, or even geographic area, is not solely determined by the capabilities of the most advanced technologies alone, but also by a broader social environment. This also brings into play questions of access, and the development of different strata of velocity – the idea that different agents will be capable of travelling at different velocities, according to their location within a global matrix of access or denial.[16] Velocity does not exist in a vacuum. Though we may have the technological possibility of travelling at the speed of sound, social, organizational, economic and political factors may keep us from doing so (at least as a regularized, integrated part of social movement). This also brings into relief a point that I will raise often, which is that neither acceleration, velocity nor speed can be abstracted from the social, political, economic, etc. forces with which they enter into assemblages.

Rosa's second category of social acceleration, 'social change and transformation', refers to the rate at which we see changes in social, political and economic patterns (2003: 7). This can refer to everything from changes in business models or political movements to small matters of fads and fashion. Indeed, perhaps one of the central characteristics of the (post)modern era is the way social patterns which in the past seemed to change slowly and with great effort increasingly take on the fluidity of popular fashion.

Finally, we have the 'heightened tempo of everyday life'. This category refers to the experience had by many that in (post)modern life there is the ability (and pressure) to perform an increasing number of tasks and activities in a decreasing period of time (8–10). It's important to note that much of the literature which recounts this phenomenon tends to describe this phenomenon in pejorative terms. Rosa states that the 'heightened tempo of everyday life' will 'cause people to consider time as scarce, to feel hurried and under time pressure and stress. Typically, people will feel that time goes by faster than before and they will complain that "everything" goes too fast; they will worry that they might not be able to keep up with the pace of social life' (9). However, I fear that interpreting this category through this lens inhibits its usefulness. One could just as easily find those who described this new tempo as exhilarating, or productive. This is not to discount the ample empirical evidence which social science has produced detailing a sense of exhaustion and lack of time on behalf of many people within western (post)modernity. It is, rather, to again point to the ambiguity of acceleration, and its ability to produce myriad affective encounters. This speaks to the danger of thinking of technological change abstracted from particular social and political assemblages. Here the apparently harried sense of the modern American can be attributed to the pace of modern life, but that sense of exhaustion and overwork must also be understood in the context of declining real wages and an increase in work hours. This question of leisure and time is also based on certain patterns of consumption in the industrialized west, which speak to particular social, cultural and desiring assemblages. The experience of acceleration, given the same tempo (which is to say quantifiable ability to complete tasks), would be different in a different political-economic context.[17]

I am not advancing the idea that particular technologies are merely passive tools, whose meaning and effects are entirely determined through human use. I am a materialist insofar as I believe that the physical forms of technology produce certain effects, which we can uncover and, if we should so choose, evaluate according to particular ethical or aesthetic criteria. But I am arguing against both a technological *determinism* (the idea that technological formations are entirely determinative of human social environments and activity) and a technological *essentialism* (the idea that any one technology constitutes a fixed, immutable form, independent of the uses and meanings which invest it). I approach technology as an open system; at least partly for the pragmatic reason that it encourages the process of investigation and experimentation which must accompany any hopeful political project. My relation to technology, then, is coloured by a guarded optimism. I follow Guattari, who says: 'It's impossible to judge ... a machinic evolution either positively or negatively; everything depends on its articulation within collective assemblages of enunciation' (Guattari 1995: 5). This is the first salvo, then, in what will be a continuing theme of this book: the critique of technological determinism, whether in the realm of politics, war, economics or social movements.

Returning to the question of social acceleration, this book accepts the assumption that the contemporary world is undergoing consistent acceleration along the three axes mentioned on pp. 27–29.[18] Now, this general social acceleration should not be confused with speed (for acceleration is a general phenomenon, whereas speed is always a singular event). However, a generalized condition of social acceleration does allow for moments of speed to proliferate. First, because as acceleration along the three axes discussed above provides more instances of change, it also provides more chances for moments of radical novelty. We touched on this point above when we noted that the speed-event is a phenomenon that occurs in the middle of a particular flow, and that the acceleration of the velocity of that flow can produce the intensive gathering of forces which can cause the change which marks the speed-event. This is due to the intertwining of speed and movement, and the fact that movement always carries with it, and borrows some, from the novelty of speed, producing the kind of accretion of quantitative change which at some point (unpredictable in principle) may transform into qualitative change.

However, there is a second point. This is that, to use the language of William Connolly, the general social acceleration of time has produced a proliferation of different 'Zones of Time' (2002: 143), which is to say zones at which different paces of action and life are pursued. These various zones of time move at different paces but periodically link up in strange ways, sometimes in sync, sometimes out of sync. Arjun Appadurai describes a similar phenomenon when he discusses the various overlapping and interacting '-scapes' travelling at different paces in modern global politics ('ethnoscape, finanscape, technoscape, mediascape, and ideoscape' [Appadurai 1990: 6–7]). The point is that with a proliferation of the various zones of time comes the increased possibility of the experience of speed, since navigating the modern world means jumping between these zones, accelerating and decelerating often at unexpected times and in unexpected ways, potentially producing politically resonant speed-events.

Speed, liberalism and *ressentiment*

Now that we have developed an ontology of speed, and shown how it relates to technological and social formations, we can return to the issue of the liberal narrative of speed, and the supposedly 'undemocratic' tendencies of the social acceleration of time. I would now argue that the functional problem of the social acceleration of time and democratic politics is a question of velocity. In other words, does the velocity of events keep pace with the velocity of our ability to respond to them? Here we must remember that, as an extensive measurement, velocity is necessarily relative. To an observer from the distant past, the current pace of politics would indeed seem bewilderingly fast. But, to an observer from the present, the pace of politics in colonial times seems unbearably slow. The question, then, is one of the relation between the tools and practices of democratic politics and the class of events to which it responds. If both are capable of moving at roughly the same velocity, then, as we know, we have a situation that can be treated as functionally identical to stasis. This does not mean that the velocities of both will necessarily accelerate in tandem (although if we assume that the pace of events increases with technological innovation, we should also be unsurprised if those innovations don't also provide a potential dividend to political practices; at the same time as the aeroplane and the mobile phone accelerate the pace of events, they can also be used to organize those events). Nor does it means that there won't be other problems produced by this social acceleration of time. What it does mean is that we should not think of ourselves as having passed some sort of natural baseline velocity beyond which democratic politics is no longer possible. Yes, we will have to be creative in our responses to this new pace of the world. We will have to develop new structures, new technologies and new ideas which will allow us to engage with this acceleration in a democratic way. But what is important is that such an engagement is possible. Acceleration is not necessarily tied to the centralization and de-democratization of politics.

So this returns us to our original question. If acceleration is not necessarily anti-democratic, why does this argument still hold so much power? Why is it that we see so many states transferring power to the executive branch, under the logic of necessity brought about by the new pace of events? My contention is that it's not purely the result of the functional threat which speed supposedly poses to the efficient functioning of government, but rather the existential threat that it poses to the smooth functioning of political identity and temporal narratives. This can be shown by returning to Scheuerman and his account of the liberal narrative of speed to see what sorts of conceptions of time and identity lie at its core.

Scheuerman argues that, as with any other political philosophy, crucial temporal assumptions underpin liberalism's account of governance (2004: 26). Scheuerman argues that the 'temporal separation of powers' assigns a branch of government to each particular tense as its sphere of interest. Therefore, the judiciary is related to the past, due to its concern with and focus on questions of precedent. The executive branch, with its reputation for energy and its ability to act in the moment, is given the present as its sphere of influence:

> The executive typically displays its distinctive temporal attributes in action designed to counteract a present threat, and its operations are 'momentary' in the sense that it swings into motion in the face of concrete or immediate dangers that appear during a contemporary temporal conjuncture of moment.
>
> (Scheuerman 2004: 36)

And finally the legislature is given to the future because 'it requires state actors to engage in a forward-looking process of trying effectively to plan or coordinate future state activities and ... future social trends' (29). This capacity, or rather requirement, for future-oriented planning is at its most extreme in the writing of constitutional laws, which Scheuerman notes that Locke expected to 'remain the sacred and unalterable form and rule of government ... forever' (33). However, even with ordinary statutory law, there is the expectation for the legislature to 'predict future state activities and future social trends' as a way of providing a stable legal environment.

However, says the liberal narrative of speed, this duty only becomes more difficult as the social acceleration of time increases the 'instability' of events and the unpredictability of the future. Note therefore that, in at least some way, the liberal narrative of speed agrees with the image of speed that was laid out on pp. 19–26, at least in terms of the radical futurity of speed. However, this throws into a relief a central shortcoming in the way Scheuerman classifies the temporality of the branches of government. Scheuerman argues that the legislature deals with the future, since it must attempt to predict and plan for the future. However, since we have defined futurity as that which is the New, i.e. that which is in principal unpredictable, this activity can't be seen as the 'future'. Rather, the goal of the legislature in the liberal narrative is not to deal with the future, but instead to extend the present as far as possible into the future, a task which acceleration makes increasingly difficult. By contrast, the executive, with its focus on 'momentary, immediate' activity is not really dealing with the present, as that which is already known, but rather with irruptions of the future into the present.

There is more at stake here than just a pedantic act of reclassification. This speaks to the central problem with the liberal narrative of speed. According to the liberal narrative of speed, the job of political governance is to maintain the stability of a political community by extending the present as far as possible into the future. It seeks not just the continued survival of its citizens, but the continuity through time of a certain way of life, of the identity of a political community.

Note that this is by no means a tendency unique to liberalism. Most, if not all, forms of political community engage in processes of projecting a narrative of identity into the future. Rather, it is important to understand that this is not a practice that liberalism *escapes*. Instead, this process of teleological projection is inflected with liberalism's particular ideals and principles. Thus we see Locke's constitutions that should last forever, Mill's slow convergence of all nations towards liberal democratic government (Mill 1998), even Francis Fukuyama's 'End of History' hypothesis (Fukuyama 1992), not to mention specific national liberal projects, such as America's narrative of itself as the 'city on a hill'. Liberalism is just as bound up in projecting the identity of a political community into the future as any other. In the context of such a project, futurity (as open futurity) must be seen as a threat and, therefore, something to be at least contained and, at most, suppressed. The temporal assumptions of the liberal narrative generate a generic hostility to the newness of the future.

This hostility to the new consists of more than the natural annoyance or anger people feel when their plans are upset. Speed is not simply to be understood in terms of the unexpected. Rather, speed must be understood in terms of an open futurity; an ateleological futurity, the breakdown of the linear progression of time. Speed makes us aware of what William Connolly calls a 'rift in time'. That is,

> A rift as constitutive of time itself, in which time flows into a future nei- ther fully determined by a discernible past ... nor directed by an intrinsic purpose pulling it along. Free time. Or, better, time as becoming, replete with the dangers and possibilities attached to such a world.
>
> (Connolly 2002: 144)

This rift in time makes the absolute linear narration of political life untenable.

The notion of a 'rift in time' and experiences of radical newness don't just challenge the validity of one particular narrative; they instead challenge the very possibility of this kind of teleological narrative of a mechanical unfolding of time. As Bergson puts it,

> Before the spectacle of this universal mobility there may be some who will be seized with dizziness. They are accustomed to terra firma; they cannot get used to the rolling and pitching. They must have 'fixed' points to which they can attach thought and existence. They think that if everything passes, nothing exists; and that if reality is mobility, it has already ceased to exist at the moment one think it – it eludes thought. The material world, they say, is going to disintegrate, and the mind will drown in the torrent-like flow of things.
>
> (Bergson 1974: 150)

Attentiveness to the rift in time produces what Rosa calls 'The *'de-temporalization of life'*, where life is no longer planned along a line that stretches from the past into the future' (2003: 19). In doing so, the rift functions as an existential threat to a community's self-understanding. Says Connolly, '[a]ttention to the rift, however, does sow anxiety in those who seek closure' in the domains of 'explanatory theories, interpretive schemes, religious identities, territorial conceptions of politics and ethical sensibilities' (2002: 146).

Speed is one of the vectors that can produce, or force, attention to the rift. And a generalized social acceleration means many more such experiences of speed, and hence more moments of anxiety.[19] Speed puts pressure on the universals and implicit teleologies of liberalism, and thus challenges its sense of identity. Connolly continues by saying, 'When the tempo of life accelerates it now takes *more political work* to protect the assumption that the identities layered into us conform to a universal model commanded by a god or decreed by nature' (158). This anxiety, this sense of existential crisis, can crystallize into what Nietzsche terms *ressentiment*, a reactive cultural dynamic which is unable to come to terms with a temporality which seems unresponsive to the demand for universal norms and a teleological narrative of political identity. This *ressentiment* against an open future, against an ateleological future, then expresses itself through an attempt to *impose* a telos on the future.

In this context, the move to increasing executive power takes on a new colouring. I read this shift to governance via executive prerogative not solely as a political manoeuvre, done for the sake of expediency, but rather as an existential manoeuvre, to secure an identity and a narrative. In times of crisis, says Connolly, there is always a tendency to 'reinstate forcefully authoritative understandings' (146). A unitary executive is ideally suited to provide a unitary account of events, one that will challenge the collective identity as little as possible, or, at the very least, re-establish the conditions of possibility for a stable narrative and identity. The executive's right of 'authority' is thus linked to a duty of author*ship*, the duty to write a new narrative. Or rather to write new events into the old narrative, to make the new gibe with the old, to extend the present into the future (which the liberal narrative of speed holds is the fundamental goal of the legislative branch anyway).[20]

At this point, one might ask, why can this job not be carried out by the legislative branch, which is to say by a democratic, pluralistic decision-making body? After all, under normal conditions this is not viewed as a threat to the collective narrative and identity. Well, the key term there is 'normal conditions'. Under the everyday functioning of government, the historical narrative and identity of the polity are relatively intact and awareness of the rift in time is suppressed. Debate and negotiation can be trusted not to upset the existential apple cart. But in times of crisis, narrative and identity are called into question, and as such there is no telling what sorts of renegotiations might emerge from democratic debate and what changes might be made to settled narratives and identities. And when a generalized social acceleration expands this time of crisis, producing a general existential anxiety, and this anxiety becomes crystallized into a general *ressentiment* against the future, a move towards government via executive fiat becomes increasingly attractive.

In the case of liberalism, then, what we see is an ideology torn between its democratic ideals and a temporal narrative which seeks to project these ideals (in the form of a particular narrative of political community) into the future. In principle, these two should work together in tandem. But in practice, the rift in time puts the second in jeopardy, and therefore puts the two at odds. In such a situation, the political community is forced to decide between its ideals and the security of a settled narrative of political identity (ironically even when that identity is rooted in those same ideals). Thus we are treated to the paradoxical image of, for example, the Bush administration authoring a narrative of advancing freedom, democracy and liberty, through a campaign premised on ignoring the rule of law, and marginalizing democratic deliberation.

The paradoxes and lines of fragmentation which the rift of time brings into relief, the sense of *ressentiment* against a future that rejects our desires to unproblematically project the present forward indefinitely is why, says William Connolly, 'so many queasy democrats want to slow the world down in the name of democracy. They are worn out by the workload imposed upon them' (158), 'the workload' here being that workload which is supposed to be the central function of democracy: the collective production of identity and community.

Sheldon Wolin: speed and locality

'Queasy Democrat' is an appellation no one could apply to Sheldon Wolin, who throughout his work has shown a reverent attachment to an engaged and robust form of democratic pluralism. The transition from Scheuerman's account of the liberal narrative of speed to Wolin's account of robust and engaged democracy is a natural one, as Wolin's work provides us with additional language to interrogate these issues. Wolin's book *The Presence of the Past* includes an essay entitled 'Tending and Intending a Constitution', which produces an understanding of time that challenges and interrogates the liberal narrative of speed. According to Wolin, the American constitution – that central, and almost scriptural, text of liberalism – is presented as an example of what he terms the 'intending' mode of politics. In addition to the more well-known meanings of this term ('to seek deliberately to bring about some desired effect or purpose' [Wolin 1989: 90]), intending also connotes 'to stretch forth' (90). Thus intending includes 'a straining towards the future' (90). An intending constitution is one which not only develops or displays an image of political community that it believes to be necessary or essential, but also seeks to produce a legal and political structure which will ensure that this image is sustained into the future. An intending constitution is always an attempt at 'the seizing of the future' (92).

According to the official narrative of the American Founding and the subsequent ratification of the constitution, the production of an American political community and its intending into an unforeseeable future represent the genius of the Founding Fathers. They created a political community when none existed before, and created it on principles robust and 'self-evident' enough to last into an unforeseeable future. The problem with this approach, says Wolin, is that, in positing this political 'new world', it repeats the errors of the discovery of the geographic 'new world', namely treating it as an uninhabited *terra nullius*. For just as the so-called Americas were actually populated by indigenous peoples organized into robust political bodies, so too was pre-1786 America populated by political bodies and organizations at numerous different levels and sites. The constitution did not create a political community *ex nihilo*. Rather, it replaced multiple competing and coexisting political communities with a new unitary image:

> Thus, when the Philadelphia Convention proposed a constitution and *The Federalist* furnished an exegesis of it, these were not solutions to a political vacuum but the superimposition of a new form of politics, national politics, on top of political life forms that, at the time, did not represent local politics because there was virtually no national politics to which they could be compared. Ratification of the new constitution necessarily signified the subjugation of other forms of politics.
>
> (Wolin 1989: 87)

The long-lasting nature of the American constitution, then, cannot solely be attributed either to its 'necessity' (a necessary unity) or its 'self-evident' nature. Rather, it is the result of political and legal machinery designed to repel attacks and challenges to the unitary narrative of political community it inaugurated. This is why Wolin describes intending as 'a straining toward the future, an effort that requires power, and hence the agent intensifies, focuses, his or her powers' (90). It is also why he states that intending inclines towards 'an authoritarian conception [of political life] as the nineteenth century understood that term: one who loves the principle of authority, that is, the right to command and enforce obedience' (88).

We see, then, how this notion of the intending constitution further under-scores the anti-democratic tendencies which we noted in the liberal narrative of speed. The intending constitution wards off the multiplicity and potential fractiousness of a democratic pluralism, and so wishes to efface this difference through the production of an artificial unity, which it then seeks to project as far as possible into the future through legal and political restraints, as well as social and cultural micropolitical techniques.

So what, then, of the 'tending' conception of politics that Wolin opposes to this politics of intending? To get at the heart of tending, Wolin begins with a simple dictionary definition: 'to apply oneself to looking after another, as when we tend a garden or tend to the sick. It implies active care of things close at hand, not mere solicitude' (89). What does this mean in a political sense? Well,

> to tend is to be concerned about something that exists, something that requires being taken care of, if it is to perdure. It represents, one might say, a concern for the historicity of things, for the preservation of pastness because the past is an important element in the narrative structure of identity attributed to the object of tendance and shared by the one who is tending. Accordingly, power is regarded as subordinate to identity and in its service.
>
> (Wolin 1989: 90)

Unlike the intending constitution, which effaces difference to produce an abstract and unitary identity, a tending politics is attentive to singularity and specificity. This is not to say that a politics of tending would simply leave everything as it is or refuse to alter or rearrange political difference. But it starts from specificities, to produce mediation and cooperation in the face of conflict, rather than attempt to resolve them into a higher unity.[21]

Now, thus far there is a rough similarity between Wolin's political values and goals and those I sketched on pp. 30–4. Both are opposed to a totalizing and unitary narrative of identity and political community which seeks to prolong itself indefinitely into the future and which is willing to efface differ-ence in order to do so, either through legal and constitutional mechanisms, or through (extra)ordinary executive authority (not to mention social and cultural narratives of identity, reinforced through micropolitical technologies of power). Both wish to encourage a politics responsive to difference, multi-plicity and singularity (all of which are interlinked), and trust a democratic political community's ability to engage with these factors. The reader will, however, notice a crucial distinction between these political orientations. Whereas in the account which I sketched out above, based in Nietzsche, Deleuze and Connolly, we see this responsiveness as at least partially rooted in an attentiveness to the future, Wolin's responsiveness to difference comes through 'a concern for the historicity of things' (90), which is dedicated to 'the preservation of pastness because the past is an important element in the narrative structure of identity' (90).[22] This exclusive focus on the past is slightly puzzling, especially since it seems as if the concept of tending is so ripe for a discussion of the future and its emergence. For just as tending must be attentive to the 'historicity of things', to a past which is carried forward into the future, it seems, at least to me, that for it to truly live up to its name tending must also be attentive to unexpected changes and occurrences in the objects of its concern. The potential for the emergence of the New in the future is just as much a site of multiplicity and singularity as is the history that Wolin is concerned with preserving. Why, then, does he seem to be uninterested in, or indeed resistant to, the question of the emergence of the new? I would posit that it has to do with his somewhat jaundiced view of speed and technological acceleration. For Wolin, and the pessimistic and disappointed narrative of the history of political thought and action which he provides (most centrally in *Politics and Vision* [Wolin 2004]), speed and accelerative technologies bear a large share of the responsibility for the totalizing and anti-democratic trends against which he struggles. Let's examine, then, Wolin's account of the effects of speed, primarily in the realms of an acceleration of the pace of political life. I will argue that Wolin's concerns are premised on an image of speed based around the obliteration of the past, and that his concerns ignore the way that speed and the coming of the New need not do so over the corpse of the past. What is more, speed can even function to activate seemingly lost or forgotten zones of the past.

Wolin deals most explicitly with the question of speed in a short essay from *Theory and Event* entitled 'What Time Is It?', where he attempts to explain the paucity of political theory in the wake of the Cold War. His argument coheres roughly with the liberal narrative of speed; namely that there is a fundamental disjunction between the time/pace of democratic politics and the time of cultural and economic life within (post)modern capitalism:

> Starkly put, political time is out of synch with the temporalities, rhythms, and pace governing economy and culture. Political time, especially in societies with pretensions to democracy, requires an element of leisure, not in the sense of a leisure class (which is the form in which the ancient writers conceived it), but in the sense, say, of a leisurely pace. This is owing to the needs of political action to be preceded by deliberation and deliberation, as its 'deliberate' part suggests, takes time because, typically, it occurs in a setting of competing or conflicting but legitimate considerations.
>
> (Wolin 1997: 4)

If, by deliberation, Wolin is referring to political deliberation by a governing body at the institutional level, then we can use the same response offered in the previous section against the liberal narrative of speed. However, since Wolin is rarely concerned with administrative matters, it is probably safe to assume that he is thinking of deliberation in a broader sense, related to the ability of citizens to develop considered, well-informed opinions about their interests and desires in the context of communal political life (as well, presumably, as their ability to lobby for those interests and desires) at a leisurely pace. Wolin claims that this is not in the sense of a leisure class. The goal here is, presumably, to separate a general discussion of the pace of modern life from a specific discussion of economic equality. But this is, in my opinion, disingenuous. In the vast majority of eras there has been a leisure class able to devote itself more rigorously to politics, and in turn a lower class of people too busy ensuring their basic survival to engage in political deliberation or participation. That countless popular political movements have arisen in the past is not a denial of this fact, but a testimony to the ingenuity and strength of human endeavour. The point is that, in terms of a constraint on the multitude's time for political deliberation, the contemporary age is by no means novel. As we have discussed above, though advances in accelerative technologies do provide challenges to the process of political deliberation, they also provide opportunities. And if we wish to investigate the lack of time for political participation on behalf of even relatively well-off segments of the population, we would be better served by looking to the general decline in real wages in the developed world, necessitating increases in the work week and multi-income families, than at abstract technological questions of speed.

To be fair, however, Wolin's complaint is not just with the quantity of time afforded to political deliberation, but also with its quality. He notes that the traditional[23] conception of political time is challenged by a new social, economic and cultural time: 'In contrast to political time, the temporalities of economy and popular culture are dictated by innovation, change, and replacement through obsolescence. Accordingly time is not governed by the needs of deliberation but by those of rapid turnover' (6). Here we begin to see Wolin's idea of a violent coming of the new, through an obliterative logic of the future. He further embellishes this discussion of the new social time with an analysis of what culture has come to mean:

> Today, however, culture is less a developed sensibility than a weapon: one speaks of 'culture wars' and can use that sort of metaphorical language knowing that, as a description, it is false. Culture can seem like war because culture is increasingly attuned to the tempos of fashion. Fashion shares with war a certain power: it forces disappearance. Fashions are evanescent, wars are obliterative. Each is in the business of replacement. Fashion produces new music, dress forms, new language or slogans. Wars produce new economies ('the German miracle'), new cities, new weapons, and new wars.
>
> (Wolin 1997: 6)

Wolin expands on this idea of a popular (and political) culture which is based on the rapid replacement of the past with the future elsewhere:

In either case culture could be treated as the enveloping ethos in which all aspects of life, including politics, are experienced in their quintessentially contemporary forms – as change. The theoretical life in a postmodern version prefers to be playful rather than contemplative: Living, acting, and exploiting change by converting it into endless novelty, accepting the production of change as the *primum mobile*, effectively assimilating revolution to a permanent condition of continuous destabilization, thereby emptying it of threat, re-presenting it as evanescence, as surface with no underlying reality.

(Wolin 2004: 581)

These quotations help us to see why Wolin did not mention futurity in his discussion of tending and intending politics. Wolin fears, or is at least uneasy about, the future. Not for the same reasons as liberalism, that it will unsettle the meaning of the extended present, but out of fear that it will erase the past. For Wolin, historicity is the thing that gives identity; a radical historicity which comes from an attunement to place and character. An acceleration of the general pace of modern life, and hence increased exposureto futurity, runs the risk of overwriting that history, and presumably replacing the difference of history with the homogeneity of capitalist (post) modernity.[24]

Such a concern is understandable, and should not be lightly dismissed. I wish mainly to moderate it through two challenges. The first is to point out that, though speed might run the risk of damaging or erasing the historicity that he so prizes, slowness too provides opportunities for the elimination of the singularity and difference which Wolin finds to be of value in historicity. William Connolly, in his analysis of Wolin's essay, notes:

A slow, homogeneous world often supports undemocratic hierarchy because it irons out discrepancies of experience through which constituencies can become reflective about self-serving assumptions they habitually use to appraise themselves in relation to others.

(Connolly 2002: 144)

William Scheuerman makes the similar point that

the deceleration of everyday existence could simply mean reducing the impressive array of choices for realizing self-chosen life plans we now enjoy. Static and homogeneous societies are less subject to social acceleration than our own, but they provide fewer opportunities for personal autonomy as well. Notwithstanding its many pathologies, social speed contributes directly to the liberties that we moderns take for granted, and a frontal assault on social acceleration risks becoming an attack on modernity's most worthwhile accomplishments.

(Scheuerman 2004: 194)

The second, more productive, challenge I wish to pose to Wolin, is the idea that there might not be a fundamental disjunction between historicity and futurity. The value that Wolin places on historicity is in its singularity, in the difference that it produces which vitalizes political life. But it is from futurity that singularity comes. And though futurity necessarily destroys or replaces some elements of the past, it is still virtually linked to that past.[25] The *Kairos* of newness is always extended in the *Chronos* of history. Indeed, there is even a historicity which is rooted in futurity, as the coming of the new has the potential to activate zones of the past (minor trends, fugitive knowledges, forgotten events) which might be lying dormant, or to interpret well-known histories in new and vital ways.

What is more, this destructive character of the future is not the destructive character of the present. The destructive present is a normalizing form of destruction, which shaves off excess and effaces difference to produce a totalitarian unity. It is a logic of destruction through substitution, which replaces difference with sameness and multiplicity with unity. In contrast to this, the destruction of the future can work according to a subtractive logic. But this is a productive subtraction, a subtraction which unbalances unity/totality, and thus produces specificity. The destruction of futurity can produce the removal of an object, event, practice or process which was presumed to be natural, transparent and eternal, and in doing so make us aware of the contingency and historicity of an entire system.[26] The destruction of the future is the destruction of '$n - 1$' (Deleuze and Guattari 1987: 6), the subtractive logic which decentres and unsettles totalizing arborescent structures.

Wolin's deepest concern is with the obliteration of difference and the past which is a characteristic of capitalist production, and not necessarily of speed or futurity in itself. But he elides the two. This is a point to which I will return in Chapter 3, when I discuss the relationship of futurity and capitalism, arguing that capitalism frequently presses against open futurity, while tending toward a kind of extended eternal present, close to the eternal 'repetition of the same' (Deleuze 1994: 76). What Wolin really fears is not the future, or a culture obsessed with the future, but rather the endless return of an empty present, rationalized and controlled by a political superpower which seeks to erase our sense of particularity (or devalue that sense until it is only a weak form of consumer identity) and replace it with a homogenized participation in one of his 'inverted totalitarian' states (Wolin 2004: 597). As our discussion of tending and intending shows, I think Wolin would certainly agree with my description of the existential desire for a unitary, authoritative narrative of identity. However, for him, speed seems to be a way to achieve this unitary identity.

On my account, Wolin need not be worried so much about speed. For speed, in its eventhood, is marked by specificity, by particularity and, hence, by an anti-totality (the n - 1). Rather, it is the techniques of movement and velocity – which homogenize and standardize, which smooth and erase – that should be his concern. The movement of the present (the present of movement) is a movement which seeks both to ward off the future and to erase the past (the past as a vital living historicity, rather than a past as reconstructed *ex post facto* teleology). A politics of the future thus also opens up the present to a politics of the past. Both require a thinking of a time out of joint, and hence a time which rejects totality. If Wolin were to tend more to the connection between a tending politics which is attentive to historicity and a tending politics that is open to futurity, he might embrace some elements of the general acceleration of the pace of modern life. He might even see a way to break the equation between speed and capitalism, which has been drawn too tightly. He might develop a program of political activity which stays true to his democratic and pluralistic commitments while not being quite so pessimistic about its space of instantiations. He might develop tools to think of a democracy that is not only local and fugitive (although these must always be elements of any democratic project). It is to this project, to seeking the possibility of a more global democratic project, that I shall return in Chapter 5.

Coda

The purpose of this chapter was twofold. First, it introduced an ontology of speed, producing a theoretical account of what speed is, and how it constitutes a particular field of forces and characteristics, which differs from the related but distinct concepts of movement and velocity. In this context, I also advanced a discussion of accelerative technologies, and their role in producing the varied zones of time which constitute the (post)modern world. Second, I challenged two bodies of thought (one the liberal democratic thought as recounted by William Scheuerman, the other the localist, radical thought of Sheldon Wolin) that see a fundamental disjunction between speed (and a generalized acceleration of society through accelerative technologies) and democratic political practice. In the first case I argued that the critique which is levelled against speed is, itself, based on subterranean anti-democratic sentiments, rooted in a fear and *ressentiment* of an ateleological future. In the second case I argued that, though I am broadly sympathetic to the critique of political life which Wolin advances, his fear of speed confuses the futurity of speed with the eternal presentification which the capital- and state-apparatuses pursue. As we will see in future chapters, it is the very characteristics of speed, futurity and exteriority which provide us with the possibility of combating the inverted totalitarian superpower, and producing a form of politics which is seated in the present, but attentive to both the past and the future.

It is, however, worthwhile to take a moment to discuss something which I mentioned only briefly in passing in a note (note 22). This is my argument that a valorization of speed does not necessarily imply a concomitant devalorization of slowness. Indeed, I would argue that there are quite a few cases in which the two can be mutually reinforcing, depending on the particular social, political and economic assemblages into which they are integrated. In principle, acceleration of technologies could provide us with more leisure time for political practice (as well as any number of other benefits). That it does not, or has not, has as much to do with the economic structures of capitalism and the consumptive structures of desire as with the schematic structures of technology. What is more, an embrace of speed, or at the very least a ferreting out of the *ressentiment* against speed that I advocate in this chapter, can also foster practices of slowness. If we return to the discussion of the ticking bomb with which this chapter began, we might notice that one of the frequent arguments for the expansion of executive power lies in what John Yoo refers to as the 'cost of inaction' (2005: x). It is important to note he does not mention a concomitant danger of action; the danger of acting too quickly. Indeed, in retrospect, in the case of the Iraq war we can see that it would have been exceedingly desirable that the 'vetoes of multiple decisionmakers' should have been allowed 'to block warmaking' (x). In this case, the political process would have been well served by a touch of inefficiency. But, if we accept the argument that was made earlier on, that the threat that speed most often poses to political community is existential, rather than functional, then a rejection of *ressentiment* against speed, and an embrace of its democratic possibilities, might make us more willing to accept bouts of 'inaction', to allow for debate and discussion over what is to be done. None of this is to deny the fact that there are not some real 'ticking bombs' in the world (though none so pure and ideal as the one laid out in the thought experiment on p. 10). But they are few and far between. And the idea that they are, universally, incapable of being dealt with through democratic deliberation is by no means an established fact or a foregone conclusion.

2 The quick and the dead

State and nomad war-machines in Deleuze and Virilio

This chapter carries forward the discussion of the relationship between speed and the state. However, where Chapter 1 focused primarily on the temporal characteristics of this relationship, investigating the ways in which speed events force attention to rifts in time, fostering anti-democratic sentiments, in this chapter we will look at the spatial implications of speed's relationship with the state, looking at how changes in the velocity of warfare underlie various reorganizations of territory and geography.

There Will Be No Time

There Will Be No Time: this is the title of William Liscum Borden's book of military strategy, geopolitics and international diplomacy, published in 1946, one year after the dropping of the first atomic bombs on Hiroshima and Nagasaki, and three years before the Soviet Union developed its first nuclear capabilities. Though written early in the life of the nuclear era, Borden's book is remarkable for the insight and prescience it brings to the subject. He identifies the status of the nuclear bomb as a strategic rather than a tactical weapon and, though he overplays it somewhat, he correctly predicts the declining importance of geopolitics as it was classically understood (Borden 1946: 169, 21). Borden also argues for the nuclear bomb's democratic possibilities, noting that its sheer power allows for the possibility of effective national defence without the need for large-scale mobilization or intensive control of the population or economy, avoiding the 'garrison state' hypothesis. In the nuclear revolution, Borden even sees an answer to Schmitt's charge of the slow and indecisive nature of liberal democracy, since the power of nuclear weapons means that mobilization for war, which has the potential to be hampered by a long drawn-out democratic decision-making process, is no longer necessary. Says Borden in regards to earlier 'industrial' wars,

> Democratic action was geared to the torturous evolution of public opinion, while the crisis called for speed and boldness. Provisional curtailment of democracy was therefore imperative for the nation to live. The atomic bomb and other weapons imply such a clean break with the past that a

completely new estimate should be placed on the survival value of both democracy and dictatorship.

(Borden 1946: 205)

He goes on to state: '[t]oday it may be that the dictator state has outlived its harsh usefulness. Perhaps totalitarianism, like the heavy bomber, is itself obsolescent in the continuing struggle for existence' (205). Borden is no naïf. He is aware of the dangers that nuclear weapons pose, and, though it is an early stage and, as such, his idea of their potential destructiveness is somewhat constrained, he is aware of the threat to human life they could pose. Still, he feels, 'the situation remains improved over one where every last adult might have been impressed into service for the state' (207).

And yet, 'there will be no time'. For all of Borden's relative optimism about the atomic future, the book carries this chilling title, which sounds more like the tagline to a horror movie than a book on international relations. Though he believes that the nuclear revolution is beneficial for both America and democracy in general, the patina of fear clings to this early evocation of nuclear acceleration. Why?

For Borden, the problem of velocity is a technical one. If he can assume that eventually nuclear weapons will be more widely possessed, then a future nuclear war will operate at such a pace that traditional strategies and tactics will be useless. What is more, the destructiveness of the battle will belie the possibility of learning via trial and error. 'There will be no time' means: there will be no time for the planning and prosecution of the war. This technical problem is met by a technical solution. If there will be no time during a nuclear war, we must do as much as we can to prepare beforehand. Thus 'the prospect of an atomic war calls chiefly for forces and stock piles in being' (207) so that the state is prepared to fight effectively at a moments notice. In terms of decision-making, the question is one of making the process as streamlined and efficient as possible. Says Borden, 'The president, along with certain congressmen, could be granted authority in advance to make all necessary decisions. An express provision in the grant might order any war to be prosecuted to a successful conclusion, irrespective of cost' (221). Presumably as the pace of a potential nuclear war accelerated, these certain congressmen would be streamlined out of the process, leaving the declaration and prosecution of the war (for in nuclear war these two things are essentially the same) solely in the hands of the Commander-in-Chief.

According to Borden, that there will be no time is a concern for the military, and not for the populace. So long as they are not actually required to fight or supply the war effort (though that they'll be required to die is, as always, a given), the general population can be freed of the burden of thinking about national security. For Borden, war is a technical matter, a special class of state activity, separate from the broader sweep of politics and popular political involvements. We see this in a particularly telling fragment when Borden once again argues for the democratic benefits of nuclear over industrial warfare. He states, 'Thought control, the most vicious of all totalitarian devices, no longer retains its old significance. From the military standpoint millions may think as they please because they will not be called upon either to work or to fight' (205–6). For Borden, this is a good thing. Without the need for large-scale industrial and popular mobilization, there is no need for large-scale *affective* mobilization (which will be either slow and torturous in a democratic state or violent and oppressive in a dictatorial one). Indeed, with the nuclear revolution, the populace can essentially be left out of the equation of warfare.

For us, however (and this 'us' is a civilian 'us'), the most compelling moment of this passage is the claim that, in the nuclear era, 'from the military standpoint' people 'may think as they please'. Here we see that with the power and velocity of the nuclear revolution comes a new world in which the military establishment need not care what a population thinks about state military action. Though the slowness and widespread mobilization of industrial war-fighting might indeed have required coercive and costly forms of affective mobilization, they, if nothing else, at least allowed for the possibility of some form of effective resistance or dissent against military activity. The authoritarian need for 'thought control' during war carries with it the necessary corollary that, in at least some small way, what the people thought *mattered*. In Borden's account, the will of the people is just a variable that can now, thankfully, be factored out of the complex technico-military problem of prosecuting a war.

There is more to this account than simply a restatement of the 'nuclear despotism' thesis. This text also serves as a useful example of the particular approach that views war as an essentially technical question (it is a political question only in the sense that it is a state matter, not in the sense that it relates to the needs and desires of a political community). In this account, velocity-induced 'nuclear despotism' isn't an unfortunate side-effect of a nuclear war; it is an explicit benefit, making the practice of war more streamlined and efficient. The pace of nuclear war allows (or rather requires of) warfare a sphere of autonomy of which, in a way, it has always dreamed. If we take Sun-Tzu at his word, when he says that 'speed is the essence of war' (1963: 134), then might not nuclear weapons function at a speed which finally allows us to experience war in its most essential form? The pace of nuclear war thus indicates a state of warfare from which people are fully abstracted, serving only as pawns or cannon fodder, but never as agents.

This is also the opinion of Paul Virilio. As we shall see, in his work he spells out a narrative similar to Borden's, although without the optimism. Virilio's philosophy describes a tight web of interrelation between speed, war and the state, where the advancement of each brings along a concomitant advancement of the others. Virilio sees in speed an autonomization (as well as an automation) of the processes of war, which in turn emboldens and secures the state (the state not as political community but as technical apparatus of discipline and control). Virilio deviates from Borden by not viewing the nuclear weapon as a victory for democracy. Rather he sees in it (and other accelerative technologies) the furthering of fascism, in terms of both intensity (the degree of totalitarian infiltration into political community) and extension (the territory over which it reigns triumphant). With the nuclear weapon, Virilio sees the finalization of a process which began with the industrial revolution – namely the development of a global military state which holds the world's population in an omnipresent state of control and terror. And counter to Borden, he sees this as the worst of all possible worlds: a military apparatus fast and flexible enough that it does not need to directly engage the populace (and hence risk their potential resistance), yet which all the same penetrates deeply into civil society, militarizing as many aspects of everyday life as it can, transforming the planet into a great clockwork military mechanism.

There is much that is of value in this account, and anyone who wants to investigate the relationship between speed and war is indebted to Virilio for tracing out some of its key characteristics. However, I believe there is also a central shortcoming in his work (a shortcoming which is also identified by Deleuze and Guattari in a brief account of his work). This is his failure to discriminate between different kinds of speed – a failure which is in turn based on his inability to discriminate between speed and velocity (Deleuze and Guattari 1987: 559). This ability to differentiate between speed and velocity will be crucial in developing a conception of resistance to war and the military state without requiring a general (and probably impossible) deceleration of the world.

Now, let me be clear: I do not defend all the effects of acceleration in the world, nor do I ignore those dangers which a general social and technological acceleration might carry; politically, socially or existentially. All the same, I do want to advance the idea that a general acceleration can, within a plausible range of outcomes, be consistent with certain goals, the very least of which is the survival of the species. It can also be compatible with democratic governance, pluralistic social formations and non-exploitative and egalitarian economic practices. Virilio's account disagrees. It draws an essential connection between speed and fascism, viewing the latter as a direct result of the former. Although I do not discount all of his claims, I do want to sever this link of necessity, arguing that there are ways to decouple social acceleration from the arrival of a fascist global military state. To do this, I will have to challenge Virilio's assumption that through accelerative technologies the military apparatus acquires a functional autonomy and omnipotence.

I will do so through an investigation of the so-called revolution in military affairs (RMA), a theory increasingly popular amongst foreign policy and military elites. RMA proponents argue, in a manner similar to Virilio, that advances in technology (especially accelerative technologies) will result in the functional dominance of advanced state militaries. Contrary to both Virilio and proponents of the RMA, I will argue that the military apparatus' immense power and velocity do not, for all that, escape the possibility of viable resistance.

This is because, whereas Virilio and the RMA treat velocity as a unitary metric (and hence a situation where the actor with the greatest velocity wins), we have advanced the idea that speed is a much more complex phenomenon, and thus, as we will see, there are speeds (a war-machine-speed, a city-speed) which can be effectively deployed against the military apparatus' velocity.

I will argue that the concepts of speed, war and the state are not locked in a tight, vicious circle. Rather, the three exist in an uneasy tension, each threatening to unbalance the others. It is this tension, and a careful discrimination between types of speed, which allows for the possibility of the deployment of speed and velocity to ward off the totalitarian military state. This is in sharp distinction to Virilio's narrative, where only slowness can be deployed as a useful weapon against the pace of fascism. For this critique to become clear, we must begin by investigating Virilio's account of the historical development of the state, noting how he links its advancement to changes in the relationship between speed and violence. From there, we will discuss the RMA and show how it mirrors Virilio's accounts (though with a more optimistic spin). However, then I will introduce an alternative account of these concepts, Deleuze and Guattari's work on the nomadic war-machine, and show how this account provides an explanation for the various weaknesses and failures which the RMA has demonstrated in Iraq, Afghanistan and beyond. I will conclude by showing how this fundamental limitation of the RMA (and Virilio's global military state) is the source of both hope and terror in global politics.

Virilio

Historical security materialism

Paul Virilio has always been a difficult thinker to classify. His work skips freely between political theory, military theory, history, architecture, urbanism, philosophy, media theory and even theology. This eclecticism of thought is exacerbated by a style which embraces a certain obscurity. In an interview with Sylvère Lotringer, Virilio states:

> I don't believe in explanations. I believe in suggestions, in the obvious quality of the implicit. Being an urbanist and architect, I am too used to constructing clear systems, machines that work well. I don't believe it's writing's job to do the same thing. I don't like two-and-two-is-four-type writing.
>
> (Virilio and Lotringer 1983: 44)

As a result Virilio's work is difficult to systematize, and it is difficult to understand what specific tradition he should be viewed in relation to. Thus, given his more explicit influences (Marx and Heidegger primarily), he tends to be lumped in with other contemporary continental philosophers such as

Baudrillard, Foucault or Deleuze (Der Derian 2001: 207). However, such groupings are always taken as contingent and, at heart, Virilio tends to be approached as a somewhat singular philosopher, not just unconnected to any existent tradition or system, but even potentially devoid of system itself. Despite all of this, I wish to argue that, in fact, Virilio is a profoundly systematic thinker, and that this system can be best understood under the rubric of what Daniel Deudney calls 'historical security materialism'.

In an article entitled 'Geopolitics as Theory: Historical Security Materialism' (1980), Daniel Deudney advances the notion that, although historical materialism has traditionally been associated with economistic accounts of history (usually Marxist), there is another body of work which roots the material progress of history in the processes of war-making. These thinkers are examples of what he terms 'historical security materialism'. Deudney pairs off the forces of production, the primary motor of historical change in the Marxist narrative of historical materialism, with the 'forces of destruction'. He argues that shifts in technological and organizational forms of war produce superstructural changes in the size, organization and composition of political units.

It is as a historical security materialist that we can best understand Virilio's writing on the history of politics and warfare. Virilio produces a grand narrative, where it is the interplay between speed[1] and warfare which has been the major historical determinant of political organization.

Virilio's account roughly segments human history into three eras of political organization, each with an attendant relationship between speed and violence. These are the 'primitive' tribe, the territorial state and the global totalitarian military state, or globalitarian state. I will now investigate each of these periods in turn.

Virilio's narrative begins with the 'chaotic' violence of the 'primitive tribe', which Virilio identifies as 'tumults' because, in his view, it does not have the organization and discipline to be considered 'wars' proper. Virilio follows anthropologist Pierre Clastres in arguing that the constitution of a regime of violence in 'primitive' society serves to ward off the coming of the state-form. Says Virilio, 'I agree with Pierre Clastres in saying that it was the "tumult" of the tribes, or if you prefer, the guerrillas, that prevented the coming of the State' (Virilio and Lotringer 1983: 11).[2] Virilio's account focuses on how the tribes' dependence on the speed of offence served to stave off the development of permanent sites of inhabitation. Sedentariness – some sort of 'territorial economy' (11) – was necessary before the state could advance its other organizational and technical projects. And so long as political violence (again, not yet war) was based on the chaotic speed and mobility of the offence, such a sedentary territorial economy could not come into being. What was needed was a form of political violence that was based on holding space, rather than passing through it. What was needed was the invention of defence – the defence of territory – and, with it, the invention of 'war' proper. The development of an idea of territorial defence carried with it the idea of territorial control:

[D]efense was not speeding up but slowing down. The preparation for war was the wall, the rampart, the fortress. And it was the fortress as permanent fortification that settled the city into permanence. Urban sedentariness is thus linked to the durability of the obstacle. Whether it's the rampart of the oppidum – of the spontaneously-fortified village in the south of Italy – or that of the ancient city, the surrounding wall is linked to the organization of war as the organization of a space.

(Virilio and Lotringer 1983: 12)

This development of a sedentary, defensive logic of war allowed for the development of a 'territorial economy' and hence a new form of political community, the state-form. This is what allows Virilio to state that '[u]p until the 19th century society was founded on the brake' (Virilio and Lotringer 1983: 50). The military form of defence (the brake of violence) produced the political form of the territorial state (the brake of movement).

This is not to say that the territorial state doesn't need speed. The territorial state uses speed in countless different ways. The territorial state does not do away with speed; rather, it aims to control it, discipline it, make it amenable to its project of acquiring and holding territory. To use the language developed in Chapter 1, the chaotic speed of the 'primitive tribe' is disciplined into the stable velocity of the state-form. This holds true most of all in the realm of warfare. For though Virilio states that the art of war is first produced through the development of the defence, he also quotes the words of military theorist Colonel Delair, who says, 'The art of defense must constantly be in transformation; it is not exempt from the general law of the world: *stasis is death*' (Virilio 1977: 13). If the State is interested in going on the offensive and acquiring more territory, then speed becomes even more important. In war, one must be capable of deploying a speed which can overwhelm the 'brake' of one's opponent. This is why '[w]ar has always been a worksite of movement, a speed-factory' (141). But this speed factory is always in the service of the territorial state. In the state-form, offence is always secondary to defence, attack always subordinated to position, and the thrust of warfare always starts from and returns to the gravitational centre of the fortress.

Dromocratic war

But there is still a paradox here (or, if we are to continue using our framework of historical security materialism, a contradiction). The territorial state is founded on sedentariness, on immobility, on the brake. And yet, to ensure its security, it must have recourse to acceleration, developing a throttle to deploy against the brakes of other states. So long as this pace of acceleration stays below a certain threshold it could be contained and integrated into the state's territorial economy of spatial order and organization. However, with the industrial revolution came a new velocity, and a new pace of technological development; an ever-accelerating curve of technological potentiality. It is for this reason that Virilio refers not to an 'industrial revolution' but to a 'dromocratic revolution', changes in the modes of production being less important for him than changes in the means of transportation, communication and destruction (46).

With the dromocratic revolution came dramatic changes in the waging of war. War had been about territory; about the control, use and acquisition of space. The defence was about holding lines, maintaining borders and protecting key centres. In turn the offence was about breaking through lines, penetrating enemy territory and gaining access to vital assets, all of which took time, during which the invading army was subject to attacks, losing soldiers, losing equipment, eventually finding itself unable to continue the advance. However, with the development of advanced accelerative technologies, distance and territory began to wane in importance. Lines and borders could be crossed much more easily (nearly effortlessly once long-range artillery as well as aerial bombardment came into play). Vital central assets were no longer so very far away. Travel through enemy territory did not take as long, and, as such, did not carry with it as many penalties. Indeed, the very concept of territory began to lose its centrality as a military asset. Says Virilio about this new form of 'dromocratic' war, 'Territory has lost its significance in favor of the projectile. *In fact, the strategic value of the non-place of speed has definitively supplanted that of place,* and the question of possession of Time has revived that of territorial appropriation' (133). What counted was no longer how much territory you controlled, but how quickly you could move. Though in the early days of the 'dromocratic' revolution this deterritorialization happened haphazardly (occasionally breaking down into hellish territorial wars such as World War I), when the 'atmospheric' theatre of war came into play, either through aerial combat, bombardment or, eventually, long-range rocket and missile technology, the obliteration of territory as the central concept of warfare began to become an accepted fact:

> With the supersonic vector (airplane, rocket, airwaves) penetration and destruction become one. The instantaneousness of action at a distance corresponds to the defeat of the unprepared adversary, but also, and especially, to the defeat of the world as a field, as distance, as matter.
>
> (Virilio 1977: 133)

As John Herz puts it, with the coming of nuclear weapons and intercontinental ballistic missile (ICBM) delivery systems, 'the "hard shell", the presumed "impermeability", "impenetrability" and, indeed, simple "territoriality" which had marked a nations borders suddenly disappears. With the air war and the nuclear revolution "the roof blew off" the territorial state' (1957: 487).

And, just as with the transition from 'primitive' tribe to territorial state, a shift in the relationship between speed and war paved the way for an attendant shift in the organization and logic of political community. With the dromocratic revolution, says Virilio, and the shift away from defensive territorial techniques of warfare, comes the decline and eventual demise of the territorial state. This is due to a tension between this new form of speed warfare and the spatio-temporal logic of the territorial state.

Virilio's idea of how speed breaks down the spatial logic of the territorial state should, I hope, be clear. As speed obliterates space, the idea of a political community bounded on a logic of territorial enclosure becomes obsolete. Virilio notes the breakdown of the territorial logic in favour of a generalized spatial '[p]roximity, the single interface between all bodies, all places, all points of the world' (Virilio and Lotringer 1983: 65). As people increasingly have the potential to live and travel globally, a political, social or cultural attachment to a territorial space becomes a less effective way of organizing political identity. In addition to this spatial challenge, the dromocratic revolution levels a challenge against the temporal logic of the territorial state as well. Virilio states that in the era of the territorial state 'political space ... existed in a given political duration. Now speed – ubiquity, instantaneousness – dissolves "political space" or rather displaces it' (63).

The speed of technology dissolves the duration of the territorial state in two ways. The first is by decreasing the time of political decision-making. As we noted in Chapter 1, with the dromocratic revolution came an acceleration of the pace of events, requiring a streamlining and centralization of the decision-making process. As Virilio puts it,

> the reduction of the margin of maneuver due to the progress of the means of communicating destruction causes an extreme concentration of responsibilities for the solitary decision-making that the Chief of Staff has become.
>
> (Virilio 1977: 148–9)

The nuclear revolution brings this process to its extreme, with a margin of decision-making so small that, even if compressed to only one person, she will still not have enough time to make up her mind. The decision must therefore be prepared ahead of time and, in a sense, automated, creating a constant deferred state of total war.[3]

Before we go thinking this is some sort of over-the-top hyperbole or elaborate metaphor, we should note that writers such as Manuel De Landa have done excellent work in cataloguing the various and continuing attempts at military automation (1991: 87). In one of the most disturbing examples of this, in Pentagon war-gaming sessions simulating nuclear conflicts (intended to develop nuclear strategies) the Pentagon replaced human participants with computer simulations because the human participants persisted in an 'illogical' refusal to 'push the button' (87). Nuclear planning and war-fighting are thus increasingly carried out without human input:

> Dynamic efficiency is the State machine's primary quality, and the nuclear State, the ultimate stage of dromological progress, ensures the concept's

cohesion thanks to the strategic calculator. Faced with and boarded by this ultimate war machine stands the last military proletarian, the henceforth will-less body of the President of the republic, supreme commander of a vanished army.

(Virilio 1977: 129)

The territorial state as political state thus becomes obsolete after the dromocratic revolution, since politics becomes a technical problem, to be solved, ideally, with as little human intervention as possible – humans being too slow and inefficient to engage in this new form of war. And this increasingly extends to all forms of war, not just nuclear war.[4] Thus, in the future of warfare, 'there will be no time' for human input. The human, political form of war loses ground in favour of an automated, technical, apolitical warfare: 'The transition *from the state of siege* of wars of space to the *state of emergency* of the war of time only took several decades, during which the political era of the statesman was replaced by the apolitical era of the State apparatus' (140).

This transition from the 'state of siege of wars of space' to the 'state of emergency of the war of time' is the second way in which the dromocratic revolution wipes out the territorial state as a form of political community. Virilio notes that, classically, a substance is defined in terms of its accidents; and an identity by its interruptions (Virilio and Lotringer 1983: 38). In the past, a state's identity was defined or produced through the interruption of war, the accident which defined its substance. The steady rhythm of the state in peacetime was interrupted by the mobilization for war, its prosecution, and then the recovery and a return to normalcy. Just as the offence was secondary to the defence, and the attack to the fortress, so too was war secondary to the state.

However, with the new pace of warfare this hierarchy is inverted. Advanced accelerative technologies make possible surprise attacks of substantial devastation, making us always aware of the background possibility of war. Hobbes says that war

consisteth not in battle only, or in the act of fighting, but in every tract of time wherein the will to contend by battle is sufficiently known. And therefore, the notion of time is to be considered in the nature of war, as it is in the nature of weather. For as the nature of foul weather lieth not in a shower or two of rain, but in an inclination thereto of many days together, so the nature of war consisteth not in actual fighting, but in the known disposition thereto during all the time there is no assurance to the contrary.

(Hobbes 1994: 76)

If this is true, then, as Herz says, with the development of the modern era, and the waning of the territorial state, we have found ourselves in a ubiquitous state of war. When even the United States, the most powerful and isolated state in the world system, is subject to either a Pearl Harbour or a 9/11, then no state can ever lay claim to feeling fully secure. War becomes primary to the state. We see the 'inversion' of the accident and the substance. The state is in a permanent state of emergency. Hence the territorial state never has the chance to settle into a rhythm, to establish its normalcy. This shatters the time which allowed identities to form and become sedimented into the territorial state. In a world of dromocratic warfare, one is never 'safe' or 'secure' inside the borders of the state. One is instead constantly subject to the insecurity and potential for violence that used to be the condition of the exile.

The globalitarian state

We should not, however, get ahead of ourselves. For Virilio says that the death of the territorial state does not mean the death of the state as such. Rather, just as the dromocratic revolution frees the military from limited, defensive, territorial wars, allowing for the production of a global 'state of emergency' of constant war, so the death of the territorial state frees the state apparatus from its limited instantiations, allowing it to re-form at the global level, producing what Virilio terms the 'globalitarian' (global totalitarian) state (2000: 42). The territorial state becomes 'outmoded by a kind of universal State, a state in its pure form which is the result of Pure War, that is, of the intensity of the means of destruction' (Virilio and Lotringer 1983: 53).

For Virilio, this new state is a sort of global military state which, through the generalized state of war and emergency, continues the state project of organizing and disciplining the world. The difference is that whereas the territorial state sought spatial control, and, with it, a logic of identity and organization based on enclosure and difference, the globalitarian military state seeks to create a universal enclosure, based not upon differentiated space, but upon the undifferentiated time of an omnipresent state-of-war (the eternal present of perpetual peace).[5] Hence, 'the goal sought by power was less the invasion of territories, their occupation, than a sort of *recapitulation of the world* obtained by the ubiquity, the suddenness of military presence, a pure phenomenon of speed, a phenomenon on the way to the realization of its absolute essence' (Virilio 1991: 44).

This globalitarian military state is not in the service of any particular ideology. Rather, it is this global state-of-war that is the order itself. 'We're no longer in a system dominated by ideology. We're in a system in which military order dominates. The only ideology is order' (Virilio and Lotringer 1983: 96). Whereas in the (territorial) past, the military was a tool to enforce a particular ideology, now war moves too fast to carry with it extra ideology. It becomes a war-virus, which can only replicate itself, and views territory only as a source of new resources for its expansion.[6]

The vision machine

This 'viral war' is the result of the particular technological characteristics of the dromocratic military apparatus. As said, this apparatus annihilates space and instead occupies the omnipresent no-place of speed, where violence is no longer blocked by territorial borders and can be effectively projected anywhere in the world. However, this omnipresence is only potential. It is not *actually* present everywhere, but rather, through various accelerative technologies, has the *possibility* of being anywhere at any time. For this virtual omnipresence to be of meaning or importance, it must be tied to an omniscient targeting system. It must know where and when to deploy violence to be effective. The dromocratic military apparatus is thus reliant on an optical apparatus, a 'vision machine' that creates a 'new harmony that blends motor, eye and weapon' (Virilio 1991: 57). Furthermore, this vision must extend along not just a spatial axis, but also a temporal axis. To effectively enact its potential omnipresence, the military apparatus must be able to predict the future. It is for this reason that Virilio states that in the globalitarian state '[t]o govern is more than ever to fore-see, in other words to go faster, *to see before*' (Virilio 1990: 87).

This 'optical' characteristic of the dromocratic military apparatus does not just serve a negative purpose. This is to say that the globalitarian state does not just see to kill. It also sees to produce, to extract and organize, to arrange civilian society in a way that is useful to the military apparatus, and make it increasingly subject to its power and control. And conversely, this new organization of civilian society makes it more transparent to the military vision machine, enhancing both the ocular and the oracular powers of the globalitarian state. Civilian society is refigured as a territory to be colonized and then militarized, its resources extracted to maintain and perpetuate the dromocratic military apparatus and the globalitarian state that it serves:

> These first attempts at penetration, clandestine 'invasion' of the social corpus, had ... a specific aim: exploitation by the armed forces of the nation's raw potential (its industrial, economic, demographic, cultural, scientific, political and moral capabilities). Since then, social penetration has been linked to the dizzying evolution of military penetration techniques; each vehicular advance erases a distinction between the army and civilization.
> (Virilio 1977: 106)

Thus, from the ashes of the territorial state rises the globalitarian state:

> The suppression of national boundaries and the hyper-communicability of the world do not enlarge the space of freedom. They are, rather, a sign of its disappearance, its collapse, before the expansion of an all-too-tangible totalitarian power, a technological control over civilized societies that is growing ever more rapid and refined.
> (Virilio 1977: 64)

The global military state freezes the world in the synopticism of its view, and in the ubiquity of its mobility. It *possesses* the globe in a way that the territorial state could only dream of. Even the fascisms of the territorial state, enlivened as they were by the early waves of the dromocratic revolution,[7] were still tied to petty nationalisms, and hence could not produce the sort of total control which Virilio sees in the globalitarian state. All of Virilio's analyses of the present and the future thus rest on this final equation: that speed equals fascism (fascism meant here in the sense of totalitarian control of a population) (64).

Speed and slowness

For all of his pessimism, Virilio does think there are actions that can be taken to resist this militarization of the world. However, this resistance must be of a very specific character, lest it run the risk of simply reinforcing the fascistic tendencies of speed.

First of all, following from his staunch pacifism and rejection of militarism, Virilio insists that all resistance to the global military state must be essentially non-violent. This is not simply an ethical injunction[8] but is primarily advanced for tactical reasons. The globalitarian state takes its power from violence, not just as a tool to enforce its will, but as a state of affairs which facilitates its global regime of control. Non-state violence merely (re)produces the global 'state of emergency', triggering the expansion of military power and control. 'One cannot use violence against what is already violence, one can only reinforce it, take it to extremes – in other words, to the State's maximum power' (Virilio and Lotringer 1983: 54). The struggle against the globalitarian state is one which is 'between civilian populations and representatives of the military techno-structure' (Virilio 1990: 60) As a result 'popular defense' must be 'a non-military entity, with specifically civilian and non-violent means and stakes' (52).

Since war brings about the globalitarian state, popular defence must challenge the make-up of the warfare system: 'The principle aim of any truly popular resistance is thus to oppose the establishment of a social situation based solely on the illegality of armed force, which reduces a population to the status of a *movable slave, a commodity*' (54).

The goal, then, is to politicize the military, to politicize war, to challenge the military from a political standpoint and return it to civilian control. However, there is an obstacle to this endeavour, since, as we've learned (both in this chapter and in Chapter 1 under the rubric of the liberal narrative of speed), there is a fundamental disjunction between politics and dromocratic war. This is because politics is rooted in what Virilio terms 'the last commodity: duration. Democracy, consultation, the basis of politics, requires time. Duration is the proper of man; he is inscribed within it' (Virilio and Lotringer 1983: 34). Dromocratic war instead employs what Virilio terms 'trans-politics', which 'marks the end of a concept of politics based on dialogue, dialectic, time, reflection' (34–5). The problem, then, is one of pace. Having taken advantage of the technological acceleration of the dromocratic revolution, the globalitarian state moves too fast to be challenged by traditional politics ('there will be no time'). Popular political resistance then must take aim at the dromocratic revolution; at the technological acceleration which provides the foundation of the globalitarian state. Virilio says in multiple instances that this shouldn't be confused with a simple Luddism, an attempt to do away with technology *tout court*. 'I'm not saying that we should revert to ancient democracy, stop the clock and all that' (34); rather, what he advocates is that '[w]e must politicize speed' (35). And though he states that he does not want a regressive rejection of technology, to politicize technology and speed is, for Virilio, to slow it down, to make it subject to debate, discussion and deliberation. Thus, he goes on to say:

> there's work to be done, the epistemo-technical work we were talking about before, in order to re-establish politics, at a time when technology no longer portions out matter and geographical space (as was the case in ancient democratic society) but when technology portions out time – and I would say: the depletion of time.
>
> (Virilio and Lotringer 1983: 34)

Virilio thus says that we must invert the material hierarchy that we find ourselves in; that we must develop an environment where technology is subject to the mandates of politics, not politics subject to the mandates of technology.

In short, Virilio argues that we must deploy slowness against speed. Popular resistance must (mimicking the old forms of war that have now been abandoned) form a brake on technology. This must happen theoretically and culturally, partly through philosophical work such as Virilio's, and more through the valorization of older forms of organization which were based on principles of slowness and territoriality (the family [Virilio 1990: 81], the nation-state [Virilio 2000: 57–8]). However, it must also happen materially, through political practice. When Virilio speaks of concrete political forms of resistance that could be put in to practice, they invariably take the form of a brake. The strike, the barricade, popular defence – political resistance, says Virilio, decelerates society (Virilio and Lotringer 1983: 40). An appeal to slowness is the only defence against the historical necessity of the vicious cycle of reinforcement between speed, war and the (globalitarian) state.

The revolution in military affairs

> [The] history of command in war consists essentially of an endless quest for certainty.
>
> (Van Creveld 1985: 264)

Thus far we have been talking fairly abstractly about war, looking at the evolution of military forms over several millennia. At this point, I wish to switch to an analysis of contemporary war-fighting doctrines, primarily to show how closely it follows Virilio's analysis. This is not to say that Virilio's account of war-fighting is necessarily correct. Indeed, in the second half of this chapter I will argue to the contrary. What I wish to show is how, somewhat ironically, Virilio holds the same view of the contemporary state of war as the state military strategists he opposes. To do this, we must talk about the revolution in military affairs (RMA). This is not because the RMA is universally accepted within the military and political establishment. In truth, there are substantial factions within both these bodies which question several principles of the RMA. Furthermore, in the wake of the various failures in the occupations of Iraq and Afghanistan (discussed in detail on pp. 71–5) crucial elements of the RMA are being critiqued, reconsidered and reconstructed. Despite all of this, the RMA is still a useful, and potentially critical, entry point to our discussion. This is because, following Virilio, the RMA constitutes a kind of faith or mythology (Virilio and Lotringer 1983: 19) about what the relationship between speed, technology and the military can do, a faith which is increasingly providing an ordering principle for warfare and politics. Indeed, the RMA is just one particular instantiation of a belief that has arrived frequently in the past – the belief in the absolute superiority of a state (and 'the State') through technology. As a result of this, the RMA has had a substantial impact on policy circles, playing a tremendous role in determining what political leaders think of as possible.

The RMA is one of those phrases which tends to mean all things to all people. However, what is agreed upon by all parties is that the RMA is centred on the use of advances in technology to change the ways in which wars are fought. Michael O'Hanlon lays out the technological assumptions which underlie most versions of the RMA:

> First, improvements in computers and electronics will make possible major advances in weapons and warfare most notably in areas such as information processing and information networks but also in communications, robotics, advanced munitions, and other technologies. Second, sensors will become radically more capable, in effect making the battlefield 'transparent'. Third, land vehicles, ships, rockets, and aircraft will become drastically lighter, more fuel efficient, faster, and more stealthy, making combat forces far more rapidly deployable and lethal once deployed. Fourth, new types of weaponry – such as space weapons, directed energy beams, and advanced biological agents – will be developed and widely deployed.
>
> (Virilio 2000: 2)

Proponents of the RMA hold that 'if properly exploited and integrated into military organizations, tactics, and concepts of operations, these technical trends can add up to a revolution in military affairs that will continue the greatest advances in warfare since the advent of blitzkrieg and aircraft carriers in the 1930s and nuclear weapons in the 1940's' (1). This analogy between the RMA and advances in mechanized warfare prior to World War II is a common one, and apt, since there a new form of war-fighting was made possible through the pairing of existing military technology (tanks) with communications technology (radios) (Der Derian 2001: 24). Though the RMA does presume advances in weapon and transportation technology, it is really advances in imaging, information and communications technologies (satellite imaging, infrared and heat imaging, GPS locators), and their effective integration with soldiers and weapons systems, that causes the 'revolution'. The importance of the acquisition and transmission of information in the RMA has led some writers to speak of a new form of info- or cyber-war. As military theorists John Arquilla and David Ronfeldt put it, 'For your forces, warfare is no longer primarily a function of who puts the most capital, labor and technology on the battlefield, but of who has the best information about the battlefield' (Arquilla and Ronfeldt 1997: 23). This often means that it is not new technology that is the most important element, but the integration of existing technology and networks to ensure that information which might previously have been retained or stored at central points is now disseminated throughout the military to ensure maximum awareness of all parties. This is why the RMA is also occasionally referred to as the 'System of Systems' approach. The idea is that new opportunities will emerge through the integration of systems providing real-time, finely detailed information about a battlespace to all levels of the armed forces. 'Today, states move from technological to strategic superiority by achieving organizational superiority' (Blank 1997: 63). This new informational awareness at all levels allows for (1) an efficiency on behalf of the armed forces, since strikes can be more effectively planned and directed, which (2) increases the flexibility of forces, capable, through advanced communications technologies, of modifying plans on the fly as situations change. This produces the idea of the new armed forces as an increasingly non-hierarchical institution, a network of interacting parts, leading some to say that '[t]he future may belong to whoever masters the network form' (Arquilla and Ronfeldt 1997: 40). The goal is to achieve what the US military calls 'full-spectrum dominance', dominance through a whole range of different war-fighting scenarios, from small-scale and covert activities up to global-scale conflicts, with the same principles of info-war at play in all levels (Graham 2004b: 12). More importantly, it is believed that the RMA allows for the possibility of this dominance with either a zero or extremely low-level casualty rate among the armed forces, thus making military action more politically viable (O'Hanlon 2000: 7). With its attention on velocity and flexibility, we could say that the guiding principle of the RMA is that whoever has the best speed wins.

In our discussion of the RMA, a special mention should be made of the role of aerial bombardment, specifically on urban terrain. In the past, aerial bombardment, aided by the memories of Guernica, Dresden, London and Laos (amongst others), was viewed as a weapon of indiscriminate destruction and chaos, creating massive civilian casualties. However, with the development of 'precision' weapons and improved targeting techniques, there is increasingly the belief that aerial bombardment can be a discriminating, 'surgical' tool of war-making. This theory seems to have been borne out by the use of so-called 'smart weapons' in the first Gulf War conflicts:

> Bombing in the Gulf war took advantage of real-time data transmission, sophisticated information technology systems, and intelligent projectiles to reinvent bombing without cold war vaporization, Vietnam War sledgehammering, or World War II inaccuracy. This event reopened the city as a viable military target, rendering urban space more vulnerable to airborne attack, if only because it could be 'contained'.
>
> (Bishop and Clancey 2004: 66)

This new aerial bombardment is an ideal weapon, since it allows soldiers to be situated tens of thousands of feet in the air, well away from danger, while at the same time producing precise and productive 'surgical' strikes. Ironically, the RMA returns to the early beliefs about aerial bombardments, when 'Britain called its air targeting of colonial cities "control without occupation"' (60).

Clausewitz

The most controversial, and truly revolutionary, element of the RMA lies in what Michael O'Hanlon calls the 'anti-Clausewitzian' beliefs of some RMA proponents (2000: 8). This is the belief that the RMA's programme of techno-organizational change allows (or will allow) the military to overcome what, since Clausewitz, had been viewed as the fundamental limitations on military actions: 'friction' and 'the fog of war'. Friction and the fog of war were the explanations Clausewitz gave as to why war is so difficult to wage (compared to other large-scale endeavours) and why war is not capable of being rationally planned and administered, despite what many military theorists up to that point had argued (and states had wished to believe).

Friction is the idea that '[e]verything in war is very simple, but the simplest thing is difficult. The difficulties accumulate and end by producing a kind of friction that is inconceivable unless one has experienced war' (von Clausewitz 1976: 119) Clausewitz goes on to state:

> Friction is the only concept that more or less corresponds to the factors that distinguish real war from war on paper. The military machine – the army and everything related to it – is basically very simple and therefore seems easy to manage. But we should bear in mind that none of its components is of one piece: each part is composed of individuals, every one of whom retains his potential of friction.
>
> (von Clausewitz 1976: 119)

He concludes by saying, 'Is there any lubricant that will reduce this abrasion? Only one, and a commander and his army will not always have it readily available: combat experience' (122). The RMA seeks to replace the psychological lubricant of combat experience with a technological one. This attempt follows along two separate, yet integrated lines. The first relies on technological advances in communications and imaging technologies to allow for the deployment of smaller, more mobile forces, which, it is believed, will decrease the inefficiencies of scale that previous forms of war-fighting produced. These smaller forces can display flexible tactical decision-making and networked efficiency. Additionally, the RMA looks towards computer automation as a way of removing the human, and hence abrasive, element from the war process (De Landa 1991). That these automated processes (and other technological fixes) are themselves frequently subject to friction-related breakdowns is viewed as a technical, rather than a fundamental, problem.[9]

In Clausewitz, the existence of friction is a check on human and military ambition, warning decision-makers that, while their complex or ingenious plans might work out on paper, in practice they will be hampered by the exigencies of real life. In contrast, proponents of the RMA 'believe that future militaries will be able to depend on highly complex and integrated communications systems that enable them to fight in cohesive and complex ways' (O'Hanlon 2000: 8). Here is the first Virilian echo in the RMA. It is the idea that increases in speed (of communication, of transportation, of information processing) lead to a fundamental shift in the form of war-fighting, to a new efficiency, a new flexibility and hence a new omnipresence. Militaries are freed from slow-moving, defensive, geopolitical, Clausewitzian war in favour of a fast-moving, offensive, chronopolitical, dromocratic war.

'The Fog of War refers to the fact that the intelligence which a military has to plan and make decisions with will be, at best, incomplete and, at worst, inaccurate. If we consider the actual basis of this information, how unreliable and transient it is, we soon realize that war is a flimsy structure that can easily collapse and bury us in its ruins' (von Clausewitz 1976: 117). This is because 'all action takes place, so to speak, in a kind of twilight, which, like fog or moonlight, often tends to make things seem grotesque and larger than they really are. Whatever is hidden from full view in this feeble light has to be guessed at by talent, or simply left to chance' (140). This unreliability of information can be the literal result of a physical occultation of events (in Clausewitz's time, the obscuring effect of the smoke from artillery batteries was a constant problem). However, it can also be a result of inadequate communication channels to transmit existing information, or the tendency of such communication channels, when present, to get clogged with simultaneous and conflicting reports, with no way to adjudicate between them.

Once again, the RMA proposes an essentially technological and organizational fix to what Clausewitz maintained was a fundamental problem. It believes that advanced sensor technology, either through satellite or enhanced personal imaging, will quite literally cut through the 'fog of war', providing accurate information on the state of the entire battlespace, and that improvements in system integration will ensure that information can be effectively vetted and organized prior to dissemination. The RMA proposes a perfection and globalization of the State's visualizing technologies, a global synoptic eye, and uses this as the foundation of politico-military activity. This is the second Virilian echo, the idea of military apparatus as vision machine.

Note also that 'friction' and the 'fog of war', in Clausewitz, serve the purpose of imposing a limitation on the potential effectiveness of war. It is a way of saying to policymakers that, when attempting to determine what they are able to do militarily, they should be humble and constrained, as elaborate and complicated plans have a tendency to break down. Proponents then see the RMA as a way of overcoming these fundamental limitations, increasing the range of activities which the military can perform, while at the same time decreasing the cost of performing them, in terms of resources, time and casualities (theirs). It makes feasible the intensive militarization of the globalitarian state (and thus the 'endocolonization' of civilian life by the military apparatus). It is this perfect melding of the military apparatus with the state organizational project which underlies Virilio's image of the globalitarian state and its omnipotence. Virilio sees a state apparatus with all-encompassing vision (along both the spatial and temporal axis) directing overwhelming, nearly instantaneous violence, productively.

Or at least such is the claim. In the second half of this chapter (pp. 61–80), we will question the supposed omnipotence of the RMA, assumed by both its military proponents and Virilio, its adversary. However, first there is more about the RMA, and the contemporary state of war, to be investigated. There are elements of both that are not revealed through Virilio's schema. To see them, we must turn to another theory, and another engagement with speed, war and the state.

Deleuze, Guattari and the war-machine

History and geography

As a starting point, it is useful to return to the historical development of the state, and discuss the question of how different modes of political organization are related to different forms of speed and violence. It is interesting to note that Deleuze and Guattari develop a historical typology of political forms which is roughly analogous to Virilio's (indeed, they acknowledge a debt to him over this). We can thus begin with their counterpoint to the 'primitive' tribe – the nomadic war-machine.[10] Deleuze and Guattari's account starts in the same way Virilio's does, by agreeing with Pierre Clastres that, amongst nomadic tribes, violence fulfils the function of warding off the coming of the state-form (Deleuze and Guattari 1987: 357). Additionally, they too take speed to be the central characteristic of this violence. However, while Virilio refuses to appraise the violence of the nomads as 'war', since it doesn't possess the element of organization and discipline that marks the war of the state apparatus, Deleuze and Guattari advance an alternative conception of war and reject the idea that war proper is only invented by the state apparatus.[11] Instead they advance the tenet that '[t]he war machine is exterior to the state apparatus' (351) and that 'the war machine was the invention of the nomad' (417). The nomad war-machine, says Deleuze and Guattari, is the 'pure' form of war.[12]

This is a crucial point of differentiation between Deleuze/Guattari and Virilio. For Virilio the war-machine is an invention of the state-form through the organization of violence into the dialectic of offence and defence (1990: 13). This is why the nomad form of organization is essentially uninteresting to Virilio. It is permanently supplanted once the state-form arises as the next r/evolutionary step. The relationship between the two is therefore diachronic and linear. For Deleuze and Guattari the relationship between the state and nomad form is synchronic and oppositional. Wherever the state-form appears, there will be nomad war-machines to challenge it, 'the local mechanisms of bands, margins, minorities, which continue to affirm the rights of segmentary societies in opposition to the organs of State power' (Deleuze and Guattari 1987: 360). The relationship is thus not historical, but geographic, not one of supplementation in time, but of conflict in space. The nomad war-machine wards off the coming of the state apparatus, and the state apparatus seeks to acquire and enclose the war-machine.

Indeed, it is only via the nomadic tribe that the state acquires a war-machine. Policing, enforcing, coercion, incarceration, punishment and execution; these forms of violence come naturally to the state-form, reinforcing, as they do, order and discipline. But to build a war-machine – to invent a collective body capable of functioning without lines and borders, of living in the heat and chaos and uncertainty and *friction* of battle – this is antithetical to the arborescent structure of the state apparatus, which demands order and discipline. Thus '[t}he state has no war machine of its own; it can only appropriate one in the form of a military institution' (351). But it is not able to acquire a pure war-machine, such as the nomad possesses. It must mutate and distort its functioning so that it can be integrated into the state apparatus. To explain what this means, we must go further into Deleuze and Guattari's account of the war-machine, a process which will allow us to discuss the war-machine's relationship to speed.

Speed and the war-machine

Just as nomads invent the war-machine, 'the war machine invents speed' (354). Here we are transitioning to speed in the specific sense which we developed in Chapter 1, as defined by the coming of the new. Its temporal axis is marked by futurity and its spatial axis by exteriority. The war-machine embodies these principles. Temporally, the war-machine always seeks to spring up unexpectedly, serving as an irruption of the new.[13] It travels in secrecy. Indeed, it invents secrecy, thus betraying and overturning the projected order of events (354). This provides us with an important insight into Clausewitz's fog of war. According to Virilio (and the proponents of the RMA), the fog of war is a technical problem, the result of the physical occultation of the battlespace, or inefficient lines of communication. Deleuze's linking of speed and futurity to the war-machine shows that the 'twilight' in which war takes place is the result of real uncertainty, of the in-principle unpredictability of the battle. The 'fog of war' is thus the fog of the New; the opacity of futurity to our knowing gaze. There is an ineradicable blindness in battle, because there is an ineradicable blindness in time (which the speed of battle brings out in explicit and violent ways).

In addition to this temporal element of the war-machine '[i]t is necessary to reach the point of conceiving the war machine as itself a pure form of exteriority' (354). The nomadic war-machine forms, and populates, a smooth space of travel. This is inherent in the very idea of nomadism. The nomad moves through space without trying to possess or enclose it. As we saw, this is the spatial logic of speed:

> Speed and absolute movement are not without their laws, but they are the laws of the *nomos*, of the smooth space that deploys it, of the war machine that populates it. If the nomads formed the war machine, it was by inventing absolute speed, by being 'synonymous' with speed.
>
> (Deleuze and Guattari 1987: 386)

The war-machine's invention of, and reliance on, speed goes against the nature of the state apparatus. Where the state desires order and control, war brings a chaos and unpredictability. Deleuze and Guattari note that war brings 'a furor to bear against sovereignty' (352). To this we should add, an exteriority against an interiority, and a futurity against a present. Sun Tzu is right. Speed *is* 'the essence of war'. But not just insofar as military adversaries are always trying to surpass each other's velocities. Rather, the practice of war requires a particular way of moving, a particular way of being in the world, embodied in the idea of speed which we developed in Chapter 1. To be good at war, one must learn to move at speed, to be comfortable with an uncertain future and with an open geometry, things which unsettle the state-form.[14]

The State recognizes the utility and power of speed and the war-machine. It therefore tries to acquire both, but in a way that is consonant with its interiorizing principles of functioning:

> Gravity, gravitas, such is the essence of the State. It is not at all that the State knows nothing of speed; but it requires that movement, even the fastest, cease to be the absolute state of a moving body occupying a smooth space, to become the relative characteristic of a 'moved body' going from one point to another in a striated space. In this sense, the State never ceases to decompose, recompose, and transform movement, or to regulate speed.
>
> (Deleuze and Guattari 1987: 386)

The state apparatus attempts to transform the speed of the war-machine, and the power and violence which are its product, into a movement and a velocity, into a relative speed (the offence secondary to the defence, the attack secondary to the fortress or the trench). It seeks to organize and discipline the unpredictable excesses of the war-machine, while retaining the element of surprise it can produce in facing an opponent. Thus we frequently see states rejecting new accelerative technologies, and returning to older more territorial forms of warfare (the lead-up to World War II provides a wealth of such examples, with the French reliance on the Maginot line for protection, and the British military's rejection of the initial components of Blitzkrieg developed at Salisbury Plain).

Deleuze and Guattari note that, while 'the war machine invents speed and secrecy … there is all the same a certain speed and a certain secrecy that pertain to the State, relatively, secondarily' (354). We might, then, derive value from a distinction between two modalities of speed: a war-machine-speed and a state-speed.[15] State-speed can be (relatively) safely incorporated into the state apparatus' organizing project, whereas war-machine-speed poses a threat to its logics. However, as we saw earlier, the unpredictability of speed is its tendential essence. In the attempt to use it, the state-form runs the risk of either (1) bending it too much to the will of the state and thus draining it of the power it was supposed to provide or (2) leaving it too unpredictable, threatening the order which is at the heart of the state apparatus. Indeed, in the long run, all states face one or another of these possibilities when they appropriate the war-machine.

From this account of the functioning of the war-machine, we can see why it is not necessarily consonant with the state apparatus, which is based around principles of interiority and enclosure. Thus, when the state attempts to acquire a war-machine, it is not a linear evolution, as it is in the Virilian narrative. There is an essential rupture and reconstitution of the war-machine:

> The State does not appropriate the war machine without giving even it the form of relative movement: this was the case with the model of the *fortress* as a regulator of movement, which was precisely the obstacle the nomads came up against, the stumbling block and parry by which absolute vertical movement was broken.
>
> (Deleuze and Guattari 1987: 386)[16]

Though this marks the same point of transition which Virilio identifies – the production of the fortress as organization of space – for Virilio this is the origination of war, the discovery which organizes primitive violence into modern war (Virilio and Lotringer 1983: 12). For Deleuze and Guattari, this is a point of mutation, a change in the fundamental rules of the game. They agree with Virilio that the beginning of the state-form of war is the introduction of the 'brake' of the fortress. However, this does not serve to organize violence into war, but rather marks a shift from war-machine-speed to state-speed, organizing excessive speeds into velocities and making war a calculation of relative velocity between armies. The fortress, and its interiorizing architecture, the phalanx and its rectilinear geometry, Frederick the Great's transformation of the mob of the army into his clockwork military, Jomini's development of scientific strategy, industrial war's rationalization of logistics; all are attempts to take the chaotic energy, the indiscipline of the war-machine, of the pack, the horde, the raiding party, and make it useful to the state apparatuses. The state military apparatus is thus a strange mutant or hybrid creature, a machine defined according to its speed, its futurity and exteriority, yet constrained and degraded into an apparatus functioning according to a velocity, and hence a temporal and spatial interiority. This, says Deleuze, is one of the reasons why the state is so leery of the military apparatus.[17]

The worldwide war-machine

The contemporary world is not organized wholly by the opposition between the state apparatus and the war-machine, however. Against the interiority of the state, Deleuze and Guattari say we also see the emergence of 'huge worldwide machines branched out over the entire ecumenon at a given moment, which enjoy a large measure of autonomy in relation to the State (for example, commercial organizations of the "multinational" type, or industrial complexes, or even religious formations like Christianity, Islam, certain prophetic or messianic movements, etc.)' (1987: 360). One such ecumenical machine is the evolution of the state military apparatuses into what Deleuze and Guattari call a 'worldwide war-machine' (421). We can begin to think of this worldwide war-machine in terms of its similarity to the globalitarian state. It too arises when the military apparatus acquires hegemony over the state apparatus:

> This is the point at which Clausewitz's formula is effectively reversed; to be entitled to say that politics is the continuation of war by other means, it is not enough to invert the order of the words as if they could be spoken in either direction; it is necessary to follow the real movement at the conclusion of which the State, having appropriated a war machine, and having adapted it to their aims, reimpart a war machine that takes charge of the aim, appropriates the States, and assumes increasingly wider political functions.
>
> (Deleuze and Guattari 1987: 421)

From one perspective, the worldwide war-machine is the re-emergence of the war-machine at the global level, having passed through the state apparatus, and having gained a taste for enclosure and interiority. From another, it is the totalization of the state-form, breaking free of its territorial specificity and recapitulating itself as a universal movement, occupying a smooth space. Thus, on the one hand, the worldwide war-machine begins to emerge 'when and where the state loses control of the institutions of war which it originally founded in order to ground its sovereignty' (Reid 2003: 82). On the other hand, the worldwide war-machine can, due to its continued attachment to the state apparatus' principles of enclosure and interiority, be considered as 'within the remit of the evolution of the state form' (82).

There are two stages to this globalization and totalization of the state military apparatus. The first is from within a particular territorial militarization of the state apparatus in the form of fascism; the state which 'makes war an unlimited movement with no other aim than itself' (Deleuze and Guattari 1987: 421). Here the military apparatus makes of itself a war-machine anew, and puts the state in its service, and in the service of war. However, this is only an early stage of this process of the inversion of the state and military apparatuses:

> [T]he second, postfascist, figure is that of a war machine that takes peace as its object directly, as the peace of Terror or Survival. The war machine reforms a smooth space that now claims to control, to surround the entire earth. Total war itself is surpassed, toward a form of peace more terrifying still. The war machine has taken charge of the aim, worldwide order, and the States are now no more than objects or means adapted to that machine.
>
> (Deleuze and Guattari 1987: 421)

We can see the symmetry with Virilio's globalitarian state, which too produces a global military state which seeks to enclose and control the earth, through the production of a complete and perpetual state of peace/terror.

This concept of a smooth space which seeks to 'control or envelop' might seem a little confusing or paradoxical, given that we have previously discussed the smooth space of speed as the space of exteriority. However, we must remember that 'smooth spaces are not in themselves liberatory' (500). A useful entryway into this idea of a controlling smooth space is through Deleuze's work 'Postscript on the Societies of Control'. That essay details the decline of Foucault's disciplinary society wherein power was based explicitly on the striation of space (Foucault 1995: 148). Deleuze argues that the static structures of the table, grid and mould are being replaced by the more dynamic and mobile – though by no means less controlling – formations of the 'modulation' and the 'code' (Deleuze 1992: 4–5). Just like Virilio's globalitarian state, which comes about through the shift from defence to offence, and from fortress to attack, the worldwide war-machine comes about by deterritorializing the state military apparatus, making it a sort of 'fleet-in-being' capable of springing up at any point on the globe, rather than being tied to national boundaries and to the black holes of sovereign power.

If we return to our discussion of the RMA, we can see how it provides a technical blueprint for the worldwide war-machine. The advocates of the RMA want to move away from conceiving of armed forces as large-scale, industrial bodies, organized at divisional levels and focused on territorial holdings, in favour of a focus on special forces organizations, small, flexible and precise war parties, suggesting a kind of re-emergence of the pack or band at the local or tactical level, thus implying the further hegemony of the war-machine over the military apparatus (Deleuze and Guattari 1987: 352). RMA theorists explicitly look to the speed, secrecy and rhizomatic organization of the nomadic tribe for inspiration.[18] Indeed, in some cases, supporters of the RMA in the military have been known to attempt to use the theories of Deleuze and Guattari on the war-machine to inform their tactical and strategic operations (Weizman 2007). This use of local packs and bands is then bolstered by the use of aerial bombardment, directed with exacting precision by an optical network of satellites, turning the whole earth into a smooth, targetable space. The RMA then produces a military apparatus capable of springing up and striking 'at any point'. The dream of the RMA is thus a dream of the complete and total integration of the war-machine into the state apparatus. They imagine a rapidly approaching time when the speed, secrecy and rhizomatic mode of organization of the war-machine are at the beck and call of the state apparatus, directed by its vision and working towards its plans for organization, control and enclosure.

It is because of this aim to organize and control that we should not think of the worldwide war-machine simply as a nomad war-machine operating at a new scale. The nomad war-machine's travel through the state apparatus changes it in fundamental ways. Its attachment to the principles of interiority and discipline put fundamental limitations on its abilities (as well as providing it with avenues for unparalleled force). For example, the worldwide war-machine can never fully recapture war-machine-speed, it can only push state-speed to its extreme. Why should I say this, when the ability to spring up at any point is exactly what defined the speed of the nomadic war-machine? Because the speed of the nomadic war-machine is tied to its unexpectedness, its secrecy, the way in which it comes from without (exteriority). The worldwide war-machine, by contrast, is able to spring up at any point because its velocity makes it *potentially omnipresent*. It is, in fact stationary, making the world move around it (a 'polar inertia' [Virilio and Lotringer 1983: 64]). It does not come from without, as the nomad war-machine does, because it is always already 'there'. It freezes the globe in the velocity of its movement, just as it does in the omniscience of its sight. And of this, it makes no secret. It is its proudest accomplishment, and much of its control comes from trumpeting this claim.

Now, the instantiation of the worldwide war-machine in a particular location may produce the surprise and newness which we associate with speed. But this is no contradiction, since speed and velocity are intertwined phenomena, and state-speed does partake of some of the surprise and newness of speed in its 'pure' form. But this surprise and newness, this speed, are only ever relative. The worldwide war-machine seeks control, and hence whatever exteriority and futurity it creates are always in the service of, and reterritorialized on, a plane of interiority and an extended present.

Indeed, as an element which seeks to escape its interiorizing drive, the nomad war-machine is as opposed to the worldwide war-machine as it is to the state apparatus. This might give us some insight into why it is that all of the RMA's anti-Clausewitzian techniques are also anti-war-machine techniques. Their attempt to cut through the fog of war is also the attempt to break the secrecy of the war-machine, to know its plans and its future. The attempt to overcome friction and produce flexible and mobile forces is an attempt to match the speed of the war-machine, to be able to meet it in its own smooth space. When discussing the worldwide war-machine, Deleuze and Guattari say, 'we have seen it put its counterguerrilla elements into place, so that it can be caught by surprise once, but not twice' (1987: 422). The only difference now is that proponents of the RMA believe that they have developed technologies that are so sophisticated they cannot be caught by surprise even once. But then, so have so many others.

The smooth space of the worldwide war-machine is not just extensive (i.e. the overcoming of state boundaries) but also intensive. It insinuates the practices of war into all elements of the social and political assemblage. It involves a progressive militarization of the state apparatus, the transition of the state's mechanisms of discipline (for example the police or prisons [418]) into extensions of the military apparatus' mechanisms of control.[19] It also means an intensification of the concept of war, of what war may be used for. When the state apparatus sought to acquire the war-machine, it was to act only in the breach, in the time of emergency, under the watchful eye of sovereignty. Deleuze and Guattari, concurring with Virilio, see the coming of the worldwide war-machine as also the coming of the permanent state of emergency, the movement beyond particular times of war, against particular enemies, to a generalized state of peace/war:

> We have watched the war machine grow stronger and stronger, as in a science fiction story; we have seen it assign as its objective a peace still more terrifying than fascist death; we have seen it maintain or instigate the most terrible of local wars as parts of itself; we have seen it set its sights on a new type of enemy, no longer another State, or even another regime, but the 'unspecified enemy'.
>
> (Deleuze and Guattari 1987: 422)

Speed, war and politics

In Deleuze and Guattari, then, we have three coexistent modes of organization, the nomadic war-machine, the state military apparatus and the worldwide war-machine. Each formation has a particular relationship to speed, velocity and movement. This, say Deleuze and Guattari, shows the limitation of Virilio's account of speed:

> Virilio's texts are of great importance and originality in every respect. The only point that presents a difficulty for us is his assimilation of three

groups of speed that seem very different to us: 1) speeds of nomadic, or revolutionary, tendency (riot, guerrilla warfare); 2) speeds that are regulated, converted, appropriated by the State apparatus (management of public ways); 3) speeds that are reinstated by a worldwide organization of total war, or planetary overarmament (from the fleet in being to nuclear strategy). Virilio tends to equate these groups on account of their interactions and makes a general case for the 'fascist' character of speed.

(Deleuze and Guattari 1987: 559)

Virilio sees a rolling acceleration of velocity from primitive war-machine to state apparatus to globalitarian state, with each expansion in level providing a concomitant increase in control, and each organizational form superseding that which came before. In this case, the globalitarian state is imbued with the weight of historical evolution and necessity; it is absolute in its hegemony and control. This is why Virilio states that 'the violence of speed has become ... the world's destiny and its destination' (1977: back cover). In Deleuze and Guattari's account each type of speed is co-eval and remains in effect today. It is even possible to deploy one speed and one formation against the others.

The greatest weakness, then, of Virilio's account, both theoretically and practically, is that he accepts – and even prefigures – the global military state's claims to omnipotence, omniscience and omnipresence. We will see in the next section that the RMA functions according to a techno-philic fantasy of control based on tying together the omniscience of surveillance technologies with the omnipotence of weapons systems. The assumption is that speed is a unitary and unifying metric, and therefore the formation with the greatest speed wins. However, if we insist on discriminating between speed and velocity, and between modalities of speed, we can happily ascribe a frightening velocity to the state military apparatus or worldwide war-machine, while still arguing that there is a speed – that there is *speed* – which escapes it and which can be deployed against it.

As we saw earlier, the power of the military apparatus lies in its ability 'to fore-see, in other words to go faster, *to see before*' (Virilio 1990: 87). It functions by combining predictive ability with a velocity which allows it to intersect the projected line of the future. However, the nomad war-machine works by bringing an open futurity to bear against the projected temporality of the military apparatus. This is why Deleuze and Guattari twin the war-machine's invention of speed with its invention of secrecy (1987: 354). The war-machine's intentions are not public, cannot be *seen*, because of its speed. It cannot, in principle, be predicted, and thus its future is a real future, a coming of the new which isn't projected in four-dimensional space. And since projection (projection in space, projection in time) is the lynchpin of the globalitarian state, it will always be incomplete, always fall short of the total control and enclosure which is its dream. We can now return to our discussion of the RMA, and begin to address the fantasies of omnipotence which fuel it.

Clausewitz's revenge

> War is an intractable problem conceptually; really the only way to know how a war is going to come out is to fight it.
>
> (Gray 2003: 204)

The end goal of the RMA is an epistemological one. It seeks to turn the state into a knowing/seeing body, the apotheosis of the state military apparatus as vision machine. However, the war-machine is unavoidably an anti-optical machine. It works in secret and functions according to the rules of surprise, bringing the unforeseen (and unforeseeable). If we are to presume, against Virilio, that the war-machine can still be viably deployed against the globalitarian state, this puts a fundamental challenge to the omniscience of the RMA's vision machine. We must argue that the globalitarian state cannot in principle see, and fore-see, everything. We must argue for the ineradicability of the fog of war.

In his discussion of the anti-Clausewitzian supporters of the RMA, Michael O'Hanlon provides a technological critique as to why, for at least the foreseeable future, the state apparatus' dreams of absolute vision will be incomplete. He notes that advanced sensor technologies, the lynchpin of the RMA, are limited by two central factors: (1) the laws of physics and (2) enemy countermeasures (O'Hanlon 2000: 45). The first refers to the fact that, no matter how good sensor technologies become, they are checked by the fact that much of the world is not transparent to sensors, no matter how refined they are. There are many things which inhibit the supposedly all-seeing eye of satellite cameras: atmospheric formations such as cloud cover; natural formations, such as dense forest, or mountain regions; and, most importantly, artificial structures such as buildings, vehicles and underground bunkers. This is a major limitation as over the past half-century wars have increasingly been fought in cities, in buildings, in mountains and in forests. Thermal imaging may do something to decrease the opacity of these locations, but we are still nowhere near the transparency which a truly synoptic war-machine would require. And as potential enemies 'come to recognize the capabilities of U.S. signals intelligence' (116) they will increasingly organize their activities to travel through those blind-spots in the synoptic war-machine's view. They will also seek to construct new ones.[20] Stephen Graham notes the rise in the use of underground bunkers as a way of escaping the synoptic view of the state apparatus:

> 'Without having the ability to hold those [underground bunker] targets at risk,' suggested JD Crouch, Bush's assistant secretary of Defense, in February 2002, 'We essentially provide sanctuary'. USA Today reports that deep bunkers 'have become rogue nations' weapon of choice for putting their weapons beyond the reach of the world's mightiest military force. The inability of the US to destroy Saddam Hussein's deep bunkers

during Gulf War II is clearly a powerful driver of this sense of palpable anger that globe-spanning US power can be defeated by the simple act of digging and pouring concrete.

(Graham 2004b: 19)

In addition to passive evasion of surveillance, there is also the possibility of actively confusing, confounding or misdirecting the synoptic war-machine. During the Kosovo war Serbian troops used tricks such as rubber tank models and microwave decoys to confuse visual and radar imaging technologies (Ignatieff 2000: 104). This was one of the factors which contributed to the fact 'that the mightiest air forces in the world were unable to destroy Milosevic's army in the field' (106). All of this produces an image which shatters the RMA's account of the present and the future. It shows that there are numerous ways in which actors can avoid, subvert or confuse the RMA's targeting abilities, and 'the United State cannot attack enemy targets it cannot locate' (O'Hanlon 2000: 27).

The city

> Some people say to me that the Iraqis are not the Vietnamese! They have no jungles or swamps to hide in. I reply, 'Let our cities be our swamps and our buildings our jungles.'
>
> (Tariq Aziz, Iraqi Foreign minister, quoted in Graham 2004a: 18)

When we realize that cities are becoming the world's battlefields, then the opacity of buildings becomes more than an incidental point. Hence, '[a] military unprepared for urban operations across a broad spectrum is unprepared for tomorrow' (Peters 1996: 43). And yet urban terrain is the greatest check on the surveillance and imaging technologies central to the RMA. Indeed, more than this, military operations in urban terrain (MOUT) produce a whole host of new challenges to the military apparatus:

> Cities represent a complex blend of horizontal, vertical, interior, and external forms, superimposed on natural relief. Ground maneuver becomes multidimensional. Structural density requires precise small-unit location capabilities within a three-dimensional puzzle. Such terrain provides cover, concealment, and sustainment but it also limits observation distances, engagement ranges, weapons effectiveness, and mobility. Electronic interference and interrupted lines of sight typically reduce the value of overhead sensing systems and Global Positioning Systems (GPS), complicating communications and targeting. Industrial hazards abound and the flammable nature of building materials, combined with the widespread use of propane or natural gas, creates a fire risk. Poor or non-existent sanitation often threatens health.
>
> (Hills 2004: 236)

This intransigence of the city serves to 'stop the US military gaining the full benefit from the complex, expensive and high-tech weapons that the military industrial complex has spent so many decades piecing together. Annoyingly, cities simply get in the way of the US military's technophiliac fantasies of omnipotence' (Graham 2004b: 15).

The return of friction

Virilio too is aware of this challenge which the city sets to the globalitarian state, saying that that is why in the coming future cities 'have to die' (Virilio and Lotringer 1983: 113). The city confounds the vision machine's targeting power, and this is why, Virilio says, the future will bring the 'end of cities'.[21]

However, this is where the limitations of Virilio's historical security materialism become apparent. For Virilio, 'the city is the result of war, at least of preparation for war' (11). According to the logic of historical security materialism, if the form of war shifts, the form of the city will, on this account, also shift, or even pass away. Such a theory, again, assumes the omnipotence of the RMA, and the globalitarian state. This ignores the crucial role that cities play in articulating the global economy,[22] as well as the deep cultural, social and political attachments which surround them, making cities intransigent to all but the most violent attempts at their disaggregation.

Of course, the undesirability of cities as a battleground has been known since the time of Sun Tzu, who said, 'The worst policy is to attack cities. Attack cities only when there is no alternative' (Sun Tzu 1963: 78). This is why aerial bombardment has become such a favoured way of dealing with cityscapes in recent years, in wars such as the First Gulf War and Kosovo. It was at the heart of the initial American attack on Baghdad, in the so-called 'Shock and Awe' campaign. Indeed, its success in helping with the relatively quick occupation of Iraq by American forces suggested that concerns over the city's opacity were somewhat overstated. The early implication that was drawn from the 'battle for Baghdad' was that 'the urbanization of terrain may not necessarily inhibit US military and geopolitical hegemony as much as was thought – at least not in the formal times and spaces of war when the systems for distanciated, verticalised killing are in full murderous flow' (Graham 2004b: 16).

However, though high altitude bombing of a city might be *part* of a war-fighting strategy, it is very rarely a goal unto itself. The Americans did not enter the Second Gulf War with the intention of destroying Baghdad (or indeed all of Iraq) but of controlling it. The early successes of aerial bombardment 'have been followed by complex, uneven, guerrilla-style resistance campaigns against occupying ground forces. Such forces have to move down from their GPS targeting from 40,000 feet, or out from behind armored plate, to occupy urban sites, and have thus become immensely more vulnerable to political opponents and bitter local civilians alike' (Graham 2004a: 5) And it is here where things become more problematic:

now that Basra, Baghdad and other Iraqi cities are occupied, the US and British military have now emerged, ironically, as much more vulnerable targets. Now that they are forced to occupy the streets of Baghdad – a 'megacity' of six million people – and other Iraqi cities over an extended period, the US military have to overcome their first instincts to project power and kill at a distance that is safe (that is, safe for them).

(Graham 2004b: 16)

What we see in late-modern warfare, time and again, is that the globalitarian state's military apparatus of synoptic vision and instantaneous violence is good at destroying; but it is severely limited in its ability to achieve productive political results, regardless of what Virilio says about its organizing and disciplining powers. This may have been acceptable for older military apparatuses, which were only expected to conquer or destroy territory, rather than control and administer it. However, implicit in the RMA (and explicit in the account of the globalitarian state and worldwide war-machine) is the promise that the military can now take over the task of imposing political order (the 'inversion of the Clausewitzian dictum'). In the Second Gulf War, America did not just want to defeat an enemy, but to enact a 'regime change', producing the Iraq which they desired. Clausewitz once more rears his ugly head. 'War is policy achieved by other means' is not just a way of justifying war, but also a normative injunctive. War that does not achieve such a result is a pointless, or foolish, endeavour. Thus, for example, from the state apparatus' perspective, the real problem with the decision to fight the Kosovo war entirely through aerial tactics is not that it resulted in indiscriminate civilian casualties, but rather that *it did not work*, which is to say that it did not achieve the stated policy goals of stopping the genocide. What is fascinating is that Virilio has written a book on the subject of the Kosovo war (2000's *Strategy of Deception*) and does not notice this fact. In focusing on the power, velocity and vision of the globalitarian state, he fails to see its insufficiency as an agent of control.

Ironically, this failure of the worldwide war-machine is, in many ways, due to its velocity. The jets, satellites and missiles that are its backbone travel too fast to productively affect the rhythms and duration of the city. They can only obliterate it, rather than productively control it. The idea of 'control without occupation' mentioned above is little more than a technological fantasy. To take political control, to achieve policy ends, the military apparatus must voluntarily decelerate, enter the city space and attempt to tame it by hand.

However, the city resists these attempts, because of what Weizman terms its 'verticality':

In fully urbanized terrain … warfare becomes profoundly vertical, reaching up into towers of steel and cement, and downward into sewers, subway lines, road tunnels, communications tunnels, and the like ... the broken spatial qualities of urban terrain fragments units and compartmentalizes [sic] encounters, engagements, and even battles.

(Peters 1996: 45)

Here, vertical space is similar to smooth space. This is not to say that the city must be read as a smooth space, but that the city can be used as smooth space by a resistance force familiar with it. The guerrilla in the city functions as a kind of fleet-in-being, travelling through the smooth space of the city, popping up in unexpected and dangerous places.[23] The verticality of the city is a crucial element in this fluidity; the ability to pop out of a basement or a sewer grate, to hide on a rooftop. This ability to 'spring up at any point' is what defines the war-machine and the smooth space it inhabits/creates. The verticality of the city leaves it opaque to the vision machine and thus leaves the state military apparatus open to the coming of the new. The city serves as an architectural fog of war. Increasingly, military analysts understand the reality that in urban combat '[s]oldiers will die simply because they were looking the wrong way' (46).

The city's density makes it resistant to velocity, but conducive to speed, the speed of those who know how to use it. There is a certain bizarre bivalency to the city here. On the one hand it is too slow to submit to the globalitarian state's attempts to pacify it, too jagged, fragmented and potentially striated to be integrated into the worldwide war-machine's smooth space of enclosure. But on the other, when the military apparatus seeks to striate and control it, the city reproduces itself as a smooth space of unpredictability. The city is a duality; a smooth space at the micro level, a striated space at the macro level and resistant to enclosure and interiority at both.

Thus Ralph Peters, a theorist with the US military, describes the city as a space of confusion, unpredictability and, most importantly, speed:

Noncombatants, without the least hostile intent, can overwhelm the force, and there are multiple players beyond the purely military, from criminal gangs to the media, vigilante and paramilitary factions within militaries, and factions within those factions. The enemy knows the terrain better than the visiting army, and it can be debilitatingly difficult to tell friend from foe from the disinterested. Local combat situations can change with bewildering speed. Atrocity is close-up and commonplace, whether intentional or incidental. The stresses on the soldier are incalculable. The urban combat environment is, above all, disintegrative.

(Peters 1996: 45)

The city is a space of 'bewildering speed'. Its opacity is the secrecy of the nomadic war-machine and its verticality the exteriority of its speed. As we said earlier, the RMA's devolution of the hierarchical military apparatus into smaller, more flexible packs or bands with tactical adaptability was supposed to provide the answer to this problem of the bewildering speed of the urban environment. And there is little doubt that it has helped. But in the end, the worldwide war-machine can only ever develop its 'counterguerrilla elements' to the point that 'it can be caught by surprise once, but not twice' (Deleuze and Guattari 1987: 422). Though the worldwide war-machine and the nomadic war-machine both seek to produce a smooth space, the nomad's is local, whereas the ecumenical machine's is global. The worldwide war-machine may have the ability to spring up at any point on the globe, at the macro level. But at the micro level it will always be one step behind. This is because the nomadic war-machine is the 'constitutive element of smooth space', and seeks to inhabit it, to 'make the desert, the steppe grow ... not [to] depopulate it, quite the contrary' (417). The worldwide war-machine seeks only to use smooth space as an instrument of control, and, as such, it is always at one step removed.

The nomad war-machine versus the worldwide war-machine

This is the central point as to why Deleuze and Guattari say that the state apparatus is unable to invent a war-machine of its own, and can only appropriate one. It is not because the State is lacking in intelligence or creativity; it has great reserves of both. It is because the war-machine and the state apparatus do fundamentally different things. The war-machine is based on the principles of speed. It brings futurity where the state seeks continuity. It brings exteriority where the state seeks enclosure and interiority. Cities must, in the end, be administered, by the slow-moving, time-consuming, resource intensive practice of political organization, which the technological fluidity of the RMA (the worldwide war-machine) had hoped to leave behind.

You cannot organize and control a city through the mechanisms of war. In the past, this was not necessary, since enemy territory was either (1) destroyed or (2) conquered and assimilated into the state apparatus. The former is still an option for the state military apparatus, though an increasingly unpopular, and finally unproductive, one. However, since at least Vietnam, we see the beginning of a new era, wherein territory resists conquest and assimilation through military means. The assimilation of cities and their war-machinic formations was possible when there was a dramatic disjunction between the sheer power of the nomad war-machine and the state military apparatus. However, in the past half-century, to make a conservative estimate, we have experienced what Daniel Deudney terms the 'Kalashnikov Revolution'. In this new world, '[t]he diffusion of easy-to-operate automatic weapons and other conventional weaponry has made conquest and assimilation vastly more expensive than before. Territory inhabited by extensive populations is very difficult to conquer and nearly impossible to absorb' (Deudney 1995: n.p.). The war-machine can now be armed, if not as well as the state military apparatus, at least well enough so that its innate talents of speed and secrecy do the rest. Thus, the Pentagon's 'Analytical Review of Low Intensity Conflict' states: 'The availability of technologically advanced weapons and communications equipment has increased the lethality, mobility, and security of terrorist and insurgent groups. Rapidly changing technology has benefited insurgents and terrorists' (Gray 1997: 35). Ironically, the coming of the worldwide war-machine, with its vast arms industry, has provided the means for the nomadic war-machinic formation to produce potentially effective resistance to the state military apparatus.[24]

This is not to say that conquering and assimilating territory is impossible, especially given the dramatic asymmetry of force available to different actors in the global order. However, doing so requires a substantial investment of resources and time, going against the claims of the RMA and the worldwide war-machine.[25] For example, had the US followed certain pre-war planning arguments and deployed 300,000 to 350,000 troops, as opposed to the 150,000 troops sent, it's likely that the pacification of Baghdad and Iraq would have gone much more smoothly. However, in doing so they would have lost the character of being a worldwide war-machine. War-machines, as we've said, need the quality of being able to 'spring up at any point'. Nobody would believe that the US military would be able to muster that level of troops and resources in more than one theatre (or even in multiple subsequent conflicts occurring close together in time). That advanced militaries, and advanced military technologies, can win wars is not up for question. The question is whether they can do so quickly and cheaply enough to be able to make the claim to be able to project violence and control throughout the world, instantaneously without regard for borders. The Iraq war was as much a symbolic show of force as it was an actual engagement. Its failure (in the sense that it devolved into a slow-moving, resource intensive war that the United States will not be able to replicate any time soon) shows the fundamental limitations and ultimate failure of both the RMA and also the worldwide war-machine.[26]

Nuclear war

> Now I am become death, destroyer of worlds.
>
> (Robert J. Oppenheimer)

> Now we are all sons of bitches.
>
> (Kenneth Bainbridge)

The intransigence of the city and the rebellion of various war-machinic, guerrilla, nationalist and terrorist organizations are a source of constant frustration to the worldwide war-machine. As Virilio recounts in exquisite detail, the Cold War, and its coupled deterrence machine, served to provide the foundation for a global order of control: 'Absolute unity is what deterrence aims toward. Deterrence has begun to realize this Pure State' (Virilio and Lotringer 1983: 161). The Cold War and deterrence took us out of the first phase of the worldwide war-machine, the fascist machine, and into 'a form of peace more terrifying still' (Deleuze and Guattari 1987: 421), where control was achieved through a bivalent unity. The grand meta-narrative of east versus west, overshadowed by the constant threat of mutually assured destruction, provided an order of control and organization throughout the first, second and third worlds. With the end of the Cold War, this sheen of duality was no longer necessary, and the unitary worldwide war-machine of the 'New World Order' took over, supported by the technological narrative of the RMA, and the politico-ethical narrative of the new military humanism.[27] The success of the First Gulf War was hailed as the beginning of a new era in global military politics. However, the Gulf War was not the test of the new regime that it appeared to be. First of all, as Chris Hables Gray points out, '[h]igh technology can be defeated, but it takes organization, loyalty, patience, political acumen, intelligence (in both senses), popular support, and allies. Saddam had few of these' (1997: 40). The first test of the New World Order had been a rigged one, technologically speaking. What is more, the goal of the Gulf War was not a complete supplanting of the Iraqi state. At this stage the worldwide war-machine was still content to have its actions mediated through more traditional state apparatuses. However, in recent years, in Kosovo, in Palestine, in Iraq, in Afghanistan, in Somalia, in Chechnya and in countless other places, the worldwide war-machine has attempted to reach its highest potential, to fully subsume the work of the state apparatus into itself, to completely reverse 'Clausewitz's formula' and make politics entirely a continuation of war by other means. And it has been repeatedly frustrated in its attempts to do so. This is not to say that it has been defeated. The worldwide war-machine is simply too powerful to be defeated (at least in the classically Clausewitzian sense of being disarmed and unable to fight anymore [von Clausewitz 1976: 77]). Nor is it to say that countless people have not died in conflicts since the end of the Cold War. Nor is it even to say that the worldwide war-machine has failed to establish military political control throughout wide swaths of the world. Rather, it is to say that the worldwide war-machine continues to fail, in an absolute sense, to create 'a smooth space that now claims to control, to surround the entire earth' (Deleuze and Guattari 1987: 421). It seeks absolute control, but everywhere resistance crops up:

> [T]he very conditions that make the State or World war machine possible, in other words, constant capital (resources and equipment) and human variable capital, continually recreate unexpected possibilities for counter-attack, unforeseen initiatives determining revolutionary, popular, minority, mutant machines. The definition of the Unspecified Enemy testifies to this: 'multiform, maneuvering and omnipresent … of the moral, political subversive or economic order, etc.,' the unassignable material Saboteur or human Deserter assuming the most diverse forms.
>
> (Deleuze and Guattari 1987: 422)

At root, war and the tactics of the war-machine are ill suited to do the things which the worldwide war-machine wants them to do. The worldwide war-machine wishes to use a technology of exteriority to achieve a state of interiority. Again, this is not to say that this endeavour will fail all the time. As we know, state formations can acquire a war-machine and use it to their own ends. The worldwide war-machine does succeed occasionally (indeed, perhaps most of the time) in using these techniques as a means of control. However, unlike the state, whose logic of interiority is also tied to a logic of particularity, and thus can allow some lines of flight to escape, the worldwide war-machine is totalizing. It, by definition, cannot allow escape. And yet it does not have the tools to stop it. The more tightly it grasps, the more it ensures something will escape.

However, there is still a terrifying hope for the worldwide war-machine. The worldwide war-machine has enormous power and velocity at its disposal, and yet is consistently frustrated in its attempt to 'reform a smooth space that now claims to control, to surround the entire earth' (421). And if it cannot achieve this smooth space in the form of a productive political control, it might decide to seek it in the form of a destructive annihilation. This is the push towards total war, which is concomitant with the move from the state military apparatus to worldwide war-machine. Total war 'is not only a war of annihilation but arises when annihilation takes as its "center" not only the enemy army, or the enemy State, but the entire population and its economy' (421). At various lower-level conflicts we see the use of destructive mechanisms to annihilate areas where productive political control is unfeasible: defoliation in the Vietnam War, aerial bombing in Kosovo, the use of helicopter gunships and clusterbombing in urban terrain in Fallujah and Basra (Hills 2004: 242). Increasingly, the motto of the worldwide war-machine has been that old Vietnam slogan-cum-Zen koan 'We had to burn the village to save it'. And as various enemies continue to discover more and more ways to evade and resist the worldwide war-machine's efforts at total control, the frustration mounts, and destruction is increasingly considered an appropriate tactic to achieve supposedly productive ends.

In returning to our discussion of the blind-spots in the RMA's synoptic vision, we see how frustration can turn to destruction. Graham describes the sense of frustration inherent in the military at the befuddlement of its advanced technologies: 'How unfair for the enemy to withdraw into protected capsules deep underground when the United States has so expensively developed the technologies of geosynchronised annihilation for surface and open warfare!' (Graham 2004b: 19). And thus, if the people of the world will not submit to surveillance and control, the worldwide war-machine will do whatever is necessary to drag them kicking and screaming into the light, even if that means crossing thresholds of destruction which up until now had been considered sacrosanct:

> George Bush's 2002 Nuclear Posture Review suggest that the US will soon restart nuclear testing and that it is also considering a first strike

nuclear policy. Frustrated that their conventional 'bunker busting' bombs cannot penetrate deep into the protected underground spaces built deep into the bedrock within alleged 'rogue nations', the US regime is planning a new range of nuclear weapons.

(Graham 2004b: 19)

Graham goes on to say that '[w]ith such legitimization a major R&D programme is now in full swing to develop nuclear "bunker busting" bombs that will allow instant annihilation of any (alleged) bunker complex, any-where in the world, within a very short time of targeting' (19–20). The increasing support for the idea of nuclear weapons as a viable tactical weapon can be seen in a variety of different conflicts.[28] And though this rise in the US's willingness to use nuclear weapons was undoubtedly influenced by the downfall of the Soviet Union, at the same time nuclear proliferation should, in principle, have taken up the deterrent slack, as it were. However, whereas the US–Soviet deterrent dyad served to maintain a global space of control, the current proliferation of nuclear weapons merely increases the possibility of resistance to the worldwide war-machine and the striation of the smooth space it desires. In this case, nuclear war may be more useful to the worldwide war-machine than a state of uneasy deterrence.

We noted earlier that, according to Deleuze and Guattari, the first phase of the worldwide war-machine is the fascist phase, which prefigures a second, post-fascist phase of global-level 'peace' (1987: 421). This notes the way in which the fascist state and the worldwide war-machine are conceptually linked, because in both cases the war-machine, or its equivalent in the form of a state military apparatus, inverts the relation of power and subordinates political control to military control. Elsewhere, in their writing on fascism, Deleuze and Guattari describe the way in which the fascist state can become the suicidal state, an unreterritorializable line of flight, preferring to destroy itself rather than see its vision of purity and control be lost.[29] Now, the war-machine also builds itself lines of flight; it is a deterritorializing machine. But it is also metamorphosis machine. It engages in an absolute deterritorialization, but it then engages in a reterritorialization (Patton 2000: 116). Its comfort with the smooth space of exteriority allows it to do that. (We will discuss the war-machine's status as metamorphosis machine further on p. 82.) But the coming of the worldwide war-machine initiates a line of flight with no resources to reterritorialize it. Its totalizing and interiorizing drive makes it incapable of metamorphosis. In this case, the worldwide war-machine always runs the risk of becoming subject to a pure death drive:

The line of flight crossing the wall, getting out of the black holes, but instead of connecting with other lines and each time augmenting its valence, *turning to destruction, abolition pure and simple, the passion of abolition* … like suicide, double suicide, a way out that turns the line of flight into a line of death.

(Deleuze and Guattari 1987: 229)

This is the result of '*a war machine that no longer has anything but war as its object* and would rather annihilate its own servants than stop the destruction' (231).

Deleuze and Guattari note the interesting fact that it is Virilio himself who 'puts us on this trail' with his account of the suicidal state (231). However, by creating the connection between the suicidal fascist state and the post-fascist worldwide war-machine, Deleuze and Guattari make us aware of a bleaker situation than even Virilio envisioned. For Virilio, the globalitarian state is in a sort of steady terminal state. In contrast, Deleuze and Guattari describe an essential tension in the worldwide war-machine, which seeks to create a smooth space of interiority and produce a productive political organization through violent destructive means. Deleuze and Guattari see the spectre of the line of flight becoming a line of death, of absolute deterritorialization without the possibility of reterritorialization.

Nuclear war provides a way for the production of a global and totalizing smooth space. If the worldwide war-machine cannot have the peace of order, then it might very well be willing to accept the peace of death. The worldwide war-machine is, or always has the potential to be, a broken meta-morphosis machine, which can only transform us into one thing: corpses. 'It is precisely when the war machine has reached the point that it has no other object but war, it is when it substitutes destruction for mutation, that it frees the most catastrophic changes. Mutation is in no way a transformation of war; on the contrary, war is like the fall or failure of mutation' (230). In this sense, the worldwide war-machine can achieve the goal of turning the earth into a zero degree Body without Organs. No longer an organism. No longer anything.

Table 2.1

Primary formation	*Form of war in Clausewitz*	*Mechanism of action*	*Secondary formation*
Nomadic war-machine	Pure war	Absolute deterritorialization/ reterritorialization (line of flight)	Metamorphosis machine
State military apparatus	Limited war	Relative deterritorialization/ reterritorialization	Disciplinary apparatus
Worldwide war-machine	Total war	Unreterritorialized absolute deterritorialization (line of death)	Corpse machine (zero degree BwO)

Resistance

And so we see that the case of the worldwide war-machine is both more terrifying and more hopeful than Virilio advances in the theory of the globalitarian state. Virilio's globalitarian state is totalizing and absolute, encompassing the world through a state of pure war. It is perfect and perfecting. It can, in principle, continue indefinitely. Virilio is aware of the totalizing destruction that the globalitarian state can unleash, but it is not his central concern, nor does he think that it is inherent to its functioning (indeed, one gets the feeling it would be the result of a breakdown or failure of the system). According to Virilio, '[t]he [nuclear] weapon's serious danger is not that it could explode tomorrow, that there could be five million deaths, but that for thirty years it has been destroying society' (Virilio and Lotringer 1983: 58). Contrary to this, Deleuze and Guattari conceive of the worldwide war-machine as inherently unbalanced. It carries within it a central tension, a paradox which can only be resolved, in principle, through utter destruction. It is a (dys)functioning line of flight that can really only end in death. However, while this contradiction is what makes it so dangerous, it is also what gives us hope. This tension means that there are holes in its armour. It means it may be possible to combat it.

What is more, we gain some hope if we look at the role that speed plays. In Virilio's account, the relationship between speed, the state and war is a circle of mutual reinforcement. This is why the only avenue of defence is through a deployment of slowness against the speed of the globalitarian state. Projects of popular defence, strikes, local forms of pacifism, challenging technological acceleration, barricades, brakes; these are the weapons which Virilio solicits. In at least a circumscribed way, my account touches his. Slowness, the brake, is a powerful weapon against the velocity of the global war-machine (as we saw in our account of the city on pp. 71–5) and we would be fools to not find a political value in it. However, by noting how the speed of the nomadic war-machine can unsettle and challenge the state, as well as be deployed against the velocity of the state military apparatus, we begin to see how speed can be an important element in stopping the worldwide war-machine's totalizing project. We thus return to Deleuze and Guattari's central critique of Virilio, that he assimilates 'groups of speed that seem very different' (Deleuze and Guattari 1987: 559) By failing to appropriately discriminate between speeds – between a state-speed and a war-machine-speed – Virilio thinks that the only way to challenge the globalitarian state is through slowness. Deleuze and Guattari inform us that we can unleash a nomad-speed against a state and ecumenical velocity, although in ways that must be carefully thought out. Speed can be a weapon against speed, just as surely as slowness can.

Before we go on to discuss the use of nomadic war-machines against the state of war, let us be precise about what is and is not a war-machine; or rather, clarify the fact that the war-machine, like the state apparatus, is an ideal historical type, a sort of symptomology of tactics and mechanisms, which can (and must) appear to a greater or lesser degree in admixture with other machines and formations. We can therefore have non-state formations which use the tools of the war-machine without being a nomad war-machine. I mention this because in my account of war there has been an elephant in the room that I have not discussed: terrorism. Terrorism unquestionably employs the mechanisms of speed and the war-machine. Its very nature is to bring the new: a horrible new, a violent new. To be effective it must operate in secrecy and be able to spring up at any point. It subverts and uses the velocity of modernity and turns it against itself in unexpected and unpredictable ways. It brings 'a secrecy against the public, a power against sovereignty' (Deleuze and Guattari 1987: 352). And yet, we should not confuse terrorism with a war-machine. It may use the weapons of the war-machine against the state. (Terrorists are, again, by definition, weak in comparison to the state, and the weapons of the war-machine are the most powerful ones the weak have at their disposal.) However, many terrorist organizations incline away from the war-machine in that they do not use its technologies as a way to ward off the state (both externally and internally). Terrorist groups from Al Qaeda to American Survivalists seek to ward off particular states, but with the goal of taking their place and forming themselves as a state or state-like terrorist formations. Rather than becoming minoritarian (Deleuze and Guattari 1987: 379) they are a kind of becoming-majoritarian, seeking to only to replace the head of sovereign power, rather than rejecting it entirely. If anything, terrorists groups have less in common with the nomadic war-machine than they do with the ecumenical global war-machine. Frustrated in their attempts to establish themselves as a state, to enclose the space and time which they desire and identify with (either historically or ethnographically), they take war as their primary object (the exact opposite of the war-machine). They become broken war-machines, and hence inscribe an unreterritorialized line of flight. We thus see an isomorphism at all levels: the suicide bomber, the suicidal state, the suicidal globe.[30]

Indeed, the relationship of the nomad war-machine to war and violence is a crucial one to our discussion of resistance. As Deleuze and Guattari are insistent in pointing out, war is not the essence of the war-machine. The essence of the war-machine is metamorphosis, transformation, exteriority and futurity, and it only employs war as a means to promote this, either through fighting the externally territorializing forces of the state apparatus or through warding off internal formations which produce a passage to the state-form: 'The war machine is that nomad invention that in fact has war not as its primary object but as its second-order, supplementary or synthetic objective, in the sense that it is determined in such a way as to destroy the State-form and city-form with which it collides' (Deleuze and Guattari 1987: 417).

War is thus a means to an end, and we can question whether its status as a useful means has changed or not. And the question of the use of violence and war as a mechanism of resistance (to the state apparatus, to the interiorizing drive of the ecumenical war-machine) becomes even more pressing when we take in mind the development of the worldwide war-machine. This is for two reasons. The first comes from the work of Virilio, when he notes that '[o]ne cannot use violence against what is already violence, one can only reinforce it, take it to extremes' (Virilio and Lotringer 1983: 54). There is a tendency for violence and the fear of violence to contribute to the worldwide war-machine, and reinforce its regime. Hardt and Negri describe 'the tragic asymmetry of the many forms of contemporary violence that do not threaten the current order but merely replicate a strange new symmetry: the military officer is infuriated at the dishonest tactics of the suicide bomber and the suicide bomber is indignant at the arrogance of the tyrant' (2000: 346). The reinforcing duality of the Cold War is recreated, but in a terrifying spiral of accelerating violence rather than the terrifying peace of deterrence. This fear and uncertainty of non-state violence are deployed by the state apparatus and the worldwide war-machine as a way to legitimate extending their control and power. Here we can look back to our discussion in Chapter 1 and see how non-state violence can be used as a way of producing a *ressentiment* against the future, encouraging the growth of the fascistic desire for control.

The second reason to be concerned about the use of violence in the age of the worldwide war-machine lies in its tendencies to go to extremes, to the limit. It is the frustration of the worldwide war-machine that leads it to consider global destruction as an option. Any effort at resistance must ensure that it is not simply baiting the worldwide war-machine into retaliation. Though tempting an enemy into reprisal has frequently been a tactic of resistance movements in the past, with the new power of the worldwide war-machine this produces a whole new level of danger. Such a war-machine would be, if not a suicide machine, then at least a martyr machine. And in a world of violence, resistance needs no more martyrs.

Hardt and Negri note that 'Leon Trotsky learns his lesson in the Russian Revolution of 1917 – "A revolution," he says "teaches you the value of a rifle" – but a rifle does not have the same value today as it did in 1917' (345). With the development of the worldwide war-machine, it is possible that the synthetic link between war and the nomad war-machine is broken, since war is no longer capable of achieving those things which the nomad war-machine wants. But this is the beauty of the nomad machine. It is at heart a metamorphosis machine. And thus, it can do what the worldwide war-machine cannot:

> If guerrilla warfare, minority warfare, revolutionary and popular war are in conformity with the essence, it is because they take war as an object all the more necessary for being mere 'supplementary': *they can make war only on the condition that they simultaneously create something else,* if only new nonorganic social relations.
>
> (Deleuze and Guattari 1987: 423)

The coming of the worldwide war-machine changes this condition. It makes it so that that war can only lead to the extremes, and not to creation. We can therefore perhaps begin to articulate the coming of an anti-war-machine, not solely because it is more ethical but also because it is more effective. The nomad war-machine still has resources at its disposal, a way of being (or rather becoming), a way of occupying space, a way of moving, all of which can be used against the worldwide war-machine. In some cases the anti-war-machine, the metamorphosis machine, might function by subverting or *détourn*-ing the mechanism of warfare.[31] One example of such a movement might be the Zapatistas in the Chiapas region of Mexico, who seek to occupy territory and ward off the state apparatus, but do so in a way that does not use weapons, but rather many advanced communications and transportation technologies, subverting the tools of the worldwide war-machine (the internet as a product of the Defense Advanced Research Projects Agency [DARPA]) to challenge it.[32] The global protests which sprung up against the Second Gulf War contain many interesting possibilities. David Graeber describes the subversion of military techniques for the purposes of non-violent protests in the form of either elaborate street theatre which mocks the militaries forces of control[33] or the actual material use of war-fighting techniques as a way of eluding control.[34]

More than just an expression of popular discontent and solidarity, the form of these protests also serves an important role. In his article on Nuclear One-Worldism, Daniel Deudney speaks of the importance of 'nuclear education and remembrance' amongst the world's population as a way of maintaining political pressure in favour of disarmament (1995: 9). The same sort of educational programme has to be levelled against the state apparatus as a way of making those captured by it aware of the impossibility of total control. I have argued, alongside Deleuze and Guattari, that the shift from the state apparatus to the worldwide war-machine, and its attendant militarization of civilian society, is by no means a historical necessity. It comes about, in fact, through a belief on behalf of the state apparatus that the power and velocity of the worldwide war-machine can provide it with the universal control that it craves. I have sought to provide an argument as to why the worldwide war-machine can never provide that universal control; it can only provide universal destruction, a fact which is being played out in numerous conflicts all over the globe. Though global anti-war protests undoubtedly spur the state apparatus' desire for control, they also serve to remind it that that control is unattainable. They make it aware of the intransigence and potential opposition of the global population, and its ability to come together in unexpected and surprising ways. They make it aware that if it completely succumbed to the line of militarization it would only serve to militarize this opposition. It makes the state apparatus aware that, no matter how fast it goes, it will never escape resistance.

3 The acceleration of inertia

Towards a political economy of speed

> Constant revolutionizing of production, uninterrupted disturbance of all social conditions, everlasting uncertainty and agitation distinguish the bourgeois epoch from all earlier ones. All fixed, fast-frozen relations, with their train of ancient and venerable prejudices and opinions, are swept away, all new formed ones become antiquated before they can ossify. All that is solid melts into air.
>
> (Marx 2000: 248)

Who says capitalism, says speed. Who says speed, says capitalism. From high theory to popular commentary, capitalism and speed tend to be seen as closely related – almost synonymous – terms. Capitalism encourages the social acceleration of time, while that acceleration in turn advances capitalism's social integration.

It is this relationship with speed that is often said to be capitalism's great merit; that while past social formations remained hopelessly tied to tradition and the reproduction of the past, capitalism encourages constant innovation, engendering the steady progress of human knowledge and power. Capitalism's cheerleaders never tire of describing its dynamism:

> As a matter of fact, capitalist economy is not and cannot be stationary. Nor is it merely expanding in a steady manner. It is incessantly being revolutionized *from within* by new enterprise ... Any existing structure and all the conditions of doing business are always in a process of change. Every situation is being upset before it has had time to work itself out. Economic progress, in capitalist society, means turmoil.
>
> (Schumpeter 1950: 31–2)

We see this connection between speed and capitalism as much in capitalism's critics as its supporters. Indeed, it is Marx who provides one of the most extensive accounts of the relationship between speed and capitalism. For Marx, capitalism is understood fundamentally not as a series of discrete moments of exchange and production, but rather as continuous and foundational movement:

> Capital is now posited, however, as not merely sustaining itself formally, but as the *realizing of itself as value*, as value relating to itself as value in

> every one of the moments of its metamorphosis, in which it appears at one time as money, at another time as commodity, then again as exchange value, then again as use value ... Capital is thus posited as *value-in-process*, which is capital in every moment. It is thus posited as *circulating capital*; in every moment capital, and circulating from one form into the next.
>
> (Marx 1973: 536; emphasis added)

Capital is thus never value *tout court*, but only ever 'value-in-process'. It is not *in* any particular commodity, or means of production, or even currency, but is instead realized in the movement between these states. As a result of this, moments of stasis in the realization process, which is to say moments in which capital is stuck in any one facet of the production–circulation–exchange process, serve to devalorize value (through depreciation, through inflation, through wasted storage space).[1] Acceleration thus plays a central role in capitalist production. The more quickly and efficiently capital circulates, the more total is the realization of its value.

This impetus to accelerate is manifested in particular technological and organizational innovations which increase the velocity of central processes such as transportation and communications:

> The more production comes to rest on exchange value, hence on exchange, the more important do the physical conditions of exchange – the means of communication and transport – become for the costs of circulation. Capital by its nature drives beyond every spatial barrier. Thus the creation of the physical conditions of exchange – of the means of communication and transport – the annihilation of space by time – becomes an extraordinary necessity for it.
>
> (Marx 1973: 524)

If we to return to the account that was given in Chapter 1 by William Scheuerman of the three components of the social acceleration of time, we see how this accelerative drive coincides with the first: technological acceleration, 'the speeding up of intentional, *goal-directed* processes of transport, communication and production' (Scheuerman 2004: 6). Here we see that this acceleration is not purely the result of an abstract process of human innovation, but is tied to the particular needs of capitalist circulation and expansion.[2]

The drive to increase the velocity of the circulation of commodities is not, however, the only accelerative drive within capitalism. There is also the push for the acceleration of the production process itself. Marx describes the goal of innovation within the production process as the decrease of time necessary for the production of a commodity. This is because in doing so it necessarily increases the ratio of surplus labour time to necessary labour:

> The increase in the productive force of living labour increases the *value* of capital (or diminishes the value of the worker) not because it increases the

quantity of products or use values created by the same labour ... but rather because it diminishes *necessary* labour, hence, in the same relation as it diminishes the former, it creates *surplus labour* or, what amounts to the same thing, surplus value.

(Marx 1973: 339)

Thus even innovations which may not take the form of an increase in velocity are undertaken because they increase the relative surplus labour extracted from the production process, and are therefore, at root, about increasing the velocity of production (what in non-marxian terms is called pushing the production possibility curve outward).[3] This push for innovation in the production process contributes to the first component of the social acceleration of time as well as the second: 'social change and transformation', which refers to the rate at which we see major (or minor) changes in social, political and economic patterns (Rosa 2003: 7). The constant push for innovations within the capitalist process means a continuous shift in the mechanisms of production, circulation and exchange, forcing workers and owners to adapt to accelerating change in their jobs and lives. The acceleration of social change and transformation is thus also not a wholly independent process, but is at least partly determined by capitalist drives for relative surplus value and for a more intensive and extensive commodification of the world. The need for acceleration in both these cases of production and circulation leads to the third component of social acceleration, the 'heightened tempo of everyday life', the ability (and pressure) to perform an increasing number of tasks and activities in a decreasing period of time (8–10).

We now have an introductory schema of how social acceleration and capitalism are interrelated. Indeed, at this point, we might be tempted to conceive of capitalism and speed as, if not synonymous, then at least intimately linked. Marx provides an almost ontological account of the relation of capital to limits, saying:

> However, as representative of the general form of wealth – money – capital is the endless and limitless drive to go beyond its limiting barrier. Every boundary is and has to be a barrier for it. Else it would cease to be capital – money as self-reproductive. If ever it perceived a certain boundary not as a barrier, but became comfortable within it as a boundary, it would itself have declined from exchange value to use value, from the general form of wealth to a specific, substantial mode of the same. Capital as such creates a specific surplus value because it cannot create an infinite one all at once; but it is the constant movement to create more of the same.

(Marx 1973: 334)

Here we see the image of the initial definition of speed given in Chapter 1, as a force marked by both futurity and exteriority. Capitalism accelerates society through technological innovations which make the future uncertain and unpredictable, while at the same time moving to overcome established spatial boundaries and limits. In a Deleuzo-Guattarian register we see the image of capitalism as a deterritorializing force, producing lines of flight which overcome rigid, striated lines of containment, and break up traditional codings.

This perceived connection between speed and capitalism is then deployed in different ways. For boosters of capitalism, this acceleration is taken as a central merit of capitalism, in that it encourages technological innovation and the progress of human productive capacity. Indeed, even when a commentator acknowledges the inequality of capitalism's regime of distribution, this inequality is frequently justified by the progress that it engenders (it does not divide the pie evenly, but does ensure the pie's continual growth). Conversely, critics of capitalism see in technological acceleration the intensification of its processes of exploitation and oppression.[4] This critique of capitalism's accelerative drive frequently lapses into a kind of technological determinism, as people view capitalist oppression as a function of this acceleration.[5]

However, this reminder of capitalism's exploitative character should now give us pause in terms of how closely we align it with speed, as speed phenomena tend to relate uneasily to apparatuses of capture and control. We saw in Chapter 2 how an apparently reinforcing circle of speed, the state and war in fact devolved into an uneasy state of tension.

And let us make no mistake, for all of the talk of dynamism, acceleration and innovation, capitalism is an apparatus of capture. This is why Deleuze and Guattari state that while capitalism may produce a deterritorialization of flows, it then 'maintains the energy of the flows in a bound state on the body of capital' (1983: 246). This is to say that there is a relative limit to the deterritorialization of flows, and this limit is the coherence of capitalism. Marx, too, is aware of this, for, following his comments about capitalism's ability to overcome barriers, he states, 'Capitalist production constantly strives to overcome these immanent barriers, but it overcomes them only by means that set up the barriers afresh and on a more powerful scale. The *true barrier* to capitalist production is *capital itself*' (1981: 358). This is a way of saying that, though capitalism has a drive to accelerate, this drive is by no means absolute or unqualified. If an accelerated flow begins to threaten the limit conditions of capitalism, then there are mechanisms internal to capitalism ('axioms' in Deleuzo-Guattarian language) which seek to channel, redirect, slow down or even stop that flow.

Nonetheless, speed, as we have seen, tends break through barriers, to bring forth an uncertain and uncontrollable future. What begins as a steady increase in velocity can result unexpectedly in an intensification of speed. In this regards there is an inherent tension within capitalism between a need to accelerate flows (whether of commodities, money, capital, knowledge or people) to ensure its proper functioning and expansion, and a fear that those flows might escape the attempt to capture and contain them within the cycle of capitalist production. Thus Antonio Negri, in his commentary on Marx's *Grundrisse*, states: 'Capital's expansion seems to be a power expressing itself, but it is, instead, a hostile relation which has to be resolved each time' (Negri 1991: 116).

This chapter will attempt to map out the tension, the uneasy partnership, between speed and capitalism. In doing so it will be fighting a war on two fronts. Against those boosters of capitalism who see in it only acceleration and progress, I will argue that because of the danger that speed poses to capitalism's control it is frequently pressed to inhibit that speed; to channel, decelerate and in some cases reverse it. Conversely, to those critics who see in technological acceleration only the further perfection of capitalist exploitation, I argue that speed and accelerative technologies present potential sites of resistance and possibility which can be deployed against exploitation and inequality. I will argue that more important than acceleration itself is the way in which it enters into particular political-economic assemblages, and how it can be *détourned* into new assemblages. In short I will argue against both the idea that capitalism *is* accelerative and the idea that acceleration *is* capitalist. The point is to challenge both economic and technological determinism. Neither economic nor technological necessity determines the character of the social assemblage (which is not to say that they are without impact on its formation). Because of the tension inherent in the relationship between speed and capitalism, any given social formation will form an aleatory and contingent stabilization of forces, replete with potential lines of flight.[6]

This chapter will deal with the temporal elements of this relationship, whereas Chapter 4 will map out its spatial consequences, through an in-depth discussion of globalization. I will begin by investigating the work of Joseph Schumpeter. We see, even in Schumpeter, that prophet of capitalist innovation and entrepreneurship, the outline of capitalism's conservative tendencies. I will then discuss how these insights can be enriched by translating them into Deleuze and Guattari's conception of capitalism as both a machine of deterritorialization and an apparatus of capture. Having developed this theoretical language, I will I then discuss this tension with reference to the issue of developments in information technology and intellectual property rights. This case study will show how the battle over intellectual property rights demonstrates capitalism's simultaneous desire to accelerate technological flows, and then decelerate them via legal and economic controls. At the same time, we will also see how acceleration, innovation and experimentation can provide us with a host of tools and opportunities for resistance to capitalist exploitation, and potentially open up spaces of non-capitalist production and consumption.

The acceleration of inertia: capitalism and innovation

Innovation and entrepreneurship

Joseph Schumpeter, the theorist of capitalist dynamism *par excellence*, claimed that capitalism is 'not and cannot be stationary'. He is the great thinker of technological innovation in capitalism, through the image of 'creative destruction' and the entrepreneur which is its bearer. However, for our purposes, what is most useful about Schumpeter is that he also theorizes a collection of what he terms 'restrictive practices' which function within capitalist production to constrain, channel and decelerate innovation. In this discussion, he shows the ambivalence which exists between capitalism and speed, and the tension between capitalism's accelerative and conservative drives. However, before we get to these restrictive practices, an analysis of Schumpeter's account of innovation is necessary.

Technical innovation, for Schumpeter, takes place against the backdrop of day-to-day capitalist production that occurs in a relatively stable, static and circular fashion (Schumpeter 2002: ch. 1). In day-to-day activity, the processes of production and exchange maintains a relatively steady equilibrium, organized through market pressures according to basic laws of 'supply and demand'(11). This is not to say that change doesn't take place. But such change is either steady and incremental (the kind of change 'which may, in time, by continual adaptation through innumerable small steps, make a great department store out of a small retail business' [62–3]) or as a result of exogenous upheavals (such as wars or natural disasters) which will eventually be adapted to. Within this 'accustomed circular flow',

> every individual can act promptly and rationally because he is sure of his ground and is supported by the conduct ... of all other individuals, who in turn expect the accustomed activity from him. ... While in the accustomed channels his own ability and experience suffice for the normal individual, when confronted by a new task.
>
> (Schumpeter 2002: 79)

As a result, rational prediction and planning can take place, and the future can (barring exogenous change) be projected from the present.

However, on top of this process of circular flows (and where, Schumpeter is quick to point out, much classical economic theory is happy to complete its analysis), Schumpeter then directs our attention to the processes of technical innovation, which produce 'a change in the channels of economic routine or a spontaneous change in the economic data arising from within the system' (82–3).

These two types of processes find their roots in two very different kinds of economic 'conduct'; the circular processes coming from the steady, rational and predictive activities of a managerial class, and the spontaneous, systemic change coming from the intuitive and creative activity of an 'entrepreneurial' class (ibid.). Here we can see a precursor of the distinction we made in Chapter 1, between a teleological, predictable, orderly movement and an abrupt, discontinuous and creative speed. This point of connection will become even more robust as we look further into how Schumpeter conceives of the entrepreneur, and the creative innovations she brings.

According to Schumpeter, the entrepreneur is the figure who is able to shake off the accumulated strictures of habit and the narrow focus of economic rationality, and see possibilities that elude the managerial class:

> Here the success of everything depends upon intuition, the capacity of seeing things in a way which afterwards proves to be true, even though it cannot be established at the moment, and of grasping the essential fact, discarding the unessential, even though one can give no account of the principles by which its is done.
>
> (Schumpeter 2002: 85)

Jon Elster, in his discussion of Schumpeter's account of technical change, notes its particular power and novelty:

> Here the key explanatory idea is that of the *entrepreneur* – a unique historical figure, of supernormal will and energy. Rather than gloss over the creative and unpredictable aspects of innovation, he made these into the cornerstone of this theory. Innovation is essentially a disequilibrium phenomenon – a leap into the dark, requiring abilities found only among the few.
>
> (Elster 1983: 112)

Economic innovation carries with it the characteristics that we identified in the ontology of speed; a leap or swerve, a creative coming into being of a future which could not have been predicted beforehand. Schumpeter's account of economic time even touches Bergson's notion of creative duration discussed in Chapter 1:

> We must cease to think of [progress] as by nature smooth and harmonious in the sense that rough passages and disharmonies present phenomena foreign to its mechanism and require special explanations by facts not embodied in its pure model. On the contrary, we must recognize that evolution is lopsided, discontinuous, disharmonious by nature – that the disharmony is inherent in the very *modus operandi* of the factors of progress.
>
> (Elster 1983: 122)

The genius of the entrepreneur comes from the ability to figure out how to carry on when the circular flows of economic life are interrupted:

> While in the accustomed channels his own ability and experience suffice for the normal individual, when confronted with innovations he needs guidance. While he swims with the stream in the circular flow which is familiar to him, he swims against the stream if he wishes to change its channel. What was formerly a help becomes a hindrance. What was a

familiar datum becomes an unknown. Where the boundaries of routine
stop, many people can go no further, and the rest can only do so in a
highly variable manner.

(Schumpeter 2002: 79–80)

Once again, innovation in the economic sphere has the same, or similar,
ontological effects as the sudden swerve of the speed-event. Old certainties are
lost, teleological predictions are useless, and we find ourselves having to find
our way in a new world.

When these innovations work, economic life is thrown out of equilibrium, and new rules have to be invented and economic laws have to reassert
themselves. Old practices, processes and technologies which are less efficient
or profitable than those which the innovation brings are replaced, and
those firms caught by surprise, unable to adapt or no longer competitive,
are replaced by those most amenable to the entrepreneurial spirit (66). It is
this process which produces the 'perennial gale of creative destruction'
(Schumpeter 1950: 84) that sits at the heart of Schumpeter's analysis of
capitalism. 'Creative destruction' is the process by which that which is
old, antiquated, not profitable, inefficient or just plain slow is destroyed in
favour of that which is new, efficient, lively and, most importantly, profitable. Through creative destruction capitalism's unique qualities as an
economic formation are expressed. It encourages innovation, it ensures that
old ways of doing things – however comfortable and traditional – when they
are shown to be inefficient, are discarded. In this process, the human potential
for production and achievement expands and accelerates, seemingly without
limit.

It is important, however, at this point, to note that the criterion of whether
an innovation is conserved or not is its profitability. It is necessary to point
this out, since it points to the limits of innovation within capitalism, a fact
which Schumpeter is perfectly aware of:

> Economic reality does not necessarily carry out the methods to
> their logical conclusion and with technological completeness, but sub-
> ordinates the execution to economic points of view. The technological
> ideal, which takes no account of economic conditions, is modified. Eco-
> nomic logic prevails over the technological. ... The economic best
> and the technologically perfect need not, yet very often do, diverge,
> not only because of ignorance and indolence but because methods
> which are technologically inferior may still best fit the given economic
> conditions.
>
> (Schumpeter 2002: 14–15)

Innovation within capitalism is advanced more by the logic of profitability
than technological optimization as an end in itself. As we will see, this sets the
foundation of capitalism's conservative tendencies.

Restrictive practices

Now, many accounts of Schumpeter (and of capitalism in general) end here, with this model of innovation. The steady and circular flow of economic life, slowly expanding due to demographic shifts, is occasionally bent or accelerated by innovations introduced through entrepreneurial intuition. This gives the impression of a healthy equilibrium alternating between times of static circular flow and times of rapid, discontinuous change. However, this description misses the way in which these two moments are in tension. Indeed, the only equilibrium to be found is *within* the circular flow of economic life, which innovation, in the Schumpeterian sense, shatters, destroying old certainties and forcing a new equilibrium to be painfully and erratically (re)composed. Schumpeter is well aware of how upsetting the upheavals of innovation can be within economic life. Indeed, just the *possibility* of such innovations diminishes the ability to act rationally and plan effectively in economic life.[7] This is why Harvey states that '[p]erpetually accelerating technological change can be extraordinarily destructive for capitalism – it is ... a major source of instability' (2006a: 117). Schumpeter goes on to draw out how the 'perennial gale of creative destruction' can affect the day-to-day functioning and decision-making processes of economic production:

> Practically any investment entails, as a necessary complement of entre-preneurial action, certain safeguarding activities such as insuring or hedging. Long-range investing under rapidly changing conditions, especially under conditions that change ... is like shooting at a target that is not only indistinct but moving – and moving jerkily at that.
>
> (Schumpeter 1950: 88)

The 'destruction' of creative destruction, then, is not just levelled against older forms of economic activity. It is the destruction of all the certainties of the economic system, which actors use to make decisions, plan and organize production. Actors within the capitalist system thus have a vested interest in the maintenance of the system as it is and 'will cling as tightly as possible to habitual economic methods and only submit to the pressure of circumstances as it becomes necessary' (Schumpeter 2002: 9).

As a result the 'circular flow of economic life' does not exist simply as a passive backdrop for technical innovation. Rather, it is an active, at times outright hostile, agglomeration of expectations, predictions, knowledge and habits which seek to maintain the status quo. The entrepreneur must therefore not only intuit what others cannot and lead where others don't think to go. She must also break through the weight of expectation which the 'circular flow of economic life' produces as 'all knowledge and habit once acquired becomes as firmly rooted in ourselves as a railway embankment in the earth' (84).

This conservative element within capitalism is, however, not just expressed through a baseline intransigence to novelty. In addition to this passive resistance, capitalist production is marked by a collection of what Schumpeter terms 'restrictive practices', practices which function to decrease the rate and velocity of technological innovation, as well as channel and redirect it in systemically acceptable ways. These restrictive practices include 'patents or temporary secrecy of processes or, in some cases, long-period contracts secured in advance' (Schumpeter 1950: 88) as a way of controlling the path of technical innovation; and more generally what Schumpeter calls 'monopolistic practices' (102), whereby a firm, corporation or industry uses economic power to ward off technical innovation, despite it being useful/profitable. We will discuss each of these sets of practices in more detail shortly. For now it is useful for us to realize that

> restrictive practices of this kind, as far as they are effective, acquire a new significance in the perennial gale of creative destruction, a significance which they would not have in a stationary state or in a state of slow and balanced growth. In either of these cases restrictive strategy would produce no result other than an increase in profits at the expense of buyers ... But in the process of creative destruction, restrictive practices may do much to steady the ship and to alleviate temporary difficulties.
>
> (Schumpeter 1950: 87)

This is to say that these restrictive practices are not failures or distortions of the market. Rather, they serve a necessary and central function in the reproduction of the capitalist system. We will now look at these arrangements in detail.

Patents

It is odd at first that Schumpeter identifies patents as one of his restrictive practices that inhibits technical innovation, since it is usually argued that the purpose of patents it to encourage innovation (Boyle 1996: 43). Of course, in a narrow sense, patents are essentially restrictive since they serve to put legal limits on the use of a practice or technology. As Christopher May and Susan Sell describe,

> Intellectual property [of which patents are one form] constructs a scarce resource from knowledge or information that is not formally scarce. Unlike material things, knowledge and information are not necessarily rivalrous, and therefore coincident usage seldom detracts from social utility. Whereas two prospective users must compete to use a material resource (and this competition may be mediated through markets and the setting of a price), two or more users of any particular item of knowledge or information can use it simultaneously without competing.
>
> (May and Sell 2006: 5)

The logic of this restriction is that, by creating an artificial monopoly around a form of knowledge, the law ensures that the creator will be able to make money selling it. By doing this, the law provides an increased incentive to create and innovate. Alternately if 'information is not property, the incentives to create it will be lacking' (22).

So why identify patents as a restrictive practice if, in theory, they serve to encourage innovation and change? Well, at the very least, for Schumpeter, patents serve as a restrictive practice since they give the company introducing the innovation a level of certainty and stability, allowing them to determine how and to what extent the innovation will be introduced, rather than having to react to the competitive pressures of the market as a whole. This can frequently mean that the innovation will be introduced and utilized (at least for the life of the patent) in a sub-optimal manner. May and Sell describe how James Watt refused to license his steam engine's patent, requiring that all engine construction and sales go through him. 'By doing so he may have "held back the development of the metalworking industry for over a generation". Had his monopoly expired in 1783, England might have had an extensive railway system much sooner' (38). If a single patent can have such an effect on technical innovation, it is not surprising that businesses begin to look at the acquisition of patents as a way of controlling the market.

We will discuss shortly the interrelation between patents and monopoly (in the sense of large-scale control of an entire market, rather than a single technology). For now it is pertinent to note how patents create a bottleneck in the production of technical knowledge, potentially slowing its introduction and use. It allows a single entity to plan out the life of a technological innovation. Though the introduction of the innovation may have an unsettling effect on the current market equilibrium, it will be a muted one by comparison to the free distribution of the innovation on the open market, with multiple actors employing it in different ways. More than this, the legal structure of patents creates a barrier to entry as the process of defending them tends to discriminate against smaller and weaker entrepreneurs, in favour of stronger interests.

This function of patents as a way of inhibiting, rather than encouraging, technical innovation becomes even more acute as contemporary post-industrial economies become more dependent on intellectual property as a source of value (Perelman 2003: 35). With the rising value of intellectual properties, we increasingly see what Arti Rai and Rebecca Eisenberg term 'upstream patenting', which is to say patenting not just 'end products' but also 'fundamental discoveries that provide the knowledge base for future product development' (2003: 289). Scientific and technological progress has always depended on a certain amount of openness and free exchange of ideas, especially in the realm of pure research. New patenting strategies, however, seek to curtail this openness, because of the fear developers have of losing control of the potential value of a discovery. This is limiting because 'patents on upstream discoveries hinder subsequent research by permitting owners to charge a premium for the use of discoveries that might otherwise be more cheaply available in a competition market or in the public domain' (295). Furthermore, '[u]pstream patents may also hinder subsequent research if they give a single entity monopoly control of basic research discoveries that enable subsequent investigation across a broad scientific territory' (296).

As a result of this, the traditional underpinnings of scientific discovery and progress such as '[e]xchanges of DNA sequences, laboratory animals, reagents, and data that were once subject to a normative expectation of free access are today subject to license agreements, material transfer agreements and database access agreements' (297). The open space of scientific discussion and debate has been replaced by a 'patent thicket' where researchers are frequently incapable of affording access to necessary forms of knowledge and afraid to act out of threat of legal ramifications. This leads some writers to speak of the creation of an 'anti-commons' (Maskus and Reichman 2004: 3) where the collective knowledge of human effort is increasingly parcelled to individual owners. And as economic actors push the extent to which knowledge becomes privatized, political actors have supported them, seeking to expand intellectual property rights regimes both intensively and extensively.[8]

Software development constitutes another area (and a particularly crucial one in the context of the contemporary information economy) where patents can serve to inhibit innovation. Patent laws in the US allow developers to patent not just entire applications, but any component part of the program, including tools, algorithms, or even a particular combination of existing technologies or ideas.[9] As all the individual building blocks of computer code begin to be patented, it becomes almost impossible to write a computer program that doesn't infringe one patent or another.[10] For the large corporations this isn't a problem, as they each tend to possess large patent portfolios, which they can then cross-license against one another, ensuring that they are able to make software unobstructed. For smaller developers, however, the choice is either to pay the licence, which can frequently make the software unprofitable, or to work around the patent, which is time consuming and might not even be possible.

The effect on software development therefore is much the same as that of 'upstream patenting' on scientific research, namely, the existence of a monopoly over the *tools* for the production of new knowledge:

> Imagine the young software engineer, trying to start a new software company in the approved iconoclastic, entrepreneurial manner. He finds that many of the programming tools he wants to use have already been patented by large companies, some of which now make *more money from litigating patent claims than they do from actually producing something new* (a result that could only make a lawyer happy). What would Shakespeare do if the Stationers' Company owned the alphabet? In the end, our software engineer ends up working for Microsoft, and the tendency towards oligopoly continues.
>
> (Boyle 1996: 178)

We will discuss the problem of oligopoly and monopoly shortly. For now it is only important to see that patents can create an anti-commons on the building blocks of software development, which acts as a barrier to entry to young and 'entrepreneurial' developers.

In patents we thus see an instrument which nicely expresses capitalism's ambiguous relationship with technological innovation. It provides a legal structure for the ownership of knowledge, a way of encouraging innovation, while at the same time providing a measure of control over that innovation. Patent law turns what is essentially a public into a private property, making scarce what is not by nature. It turns the unruly progression of human knowledge into another commodity to be privately held, controlled and deployed for profit. And as human knowledge becomes increasingly public (contemporary technological innovation is rarely the work of one lone genius toiling in isolation, as with, say, James Watt or Philo Farnsworth), the mechanisms for its privatization become harsher and more all encompassing.

Monopolistic practices

Patents are a way for powerful economic interests to use legal power (and quasi-legal power) to control the pace and direction of technological innovation. Schumpeter also identifies a more general mechanism of control – monopolistic practices. Monopolistic practices refer to those sorts of economic powers which a large-scale concern is able to wield over the market. In Schumpeterian language, a firm need not be a full monopoly, which is to say in complete control of a particular commodity or market, to employ monopolistic practices. It must simply be able to exert a certain amount of autonomous control over the market, either alone or in concert with a few other concerns (it might be more accurate to call these practices oligopolistic, but for simplicity's sake we will stick with Schumpeter's terms). The two are not entirely unrelated, as patents confer a sort of monopoly, and large corporations are able to more effectively acquire, enforce and contest patents. Large-scale concerns are able to use their power to inhibit technological innovation where it might threaten the existing forms of production. Thus, says Schumpeter,

> In perfect competition the old investments must be adapted at a sacrifice or abandoned; but when there is no perfect competition and when each industrial field is controlled by a few big concerns, these can in various ways fight the threatening attack on their capital structure and try to avoid losses on their capital accounts; that is to say, they can and will fight progress itself.
>
> (Schumpeter 1950: 96)

When the innovation is the result of the firm's own research, it can be introduced slowly, after current fixed capital investments have already been written off (98). If the innovation comes from a smaller competitor, the concern can use patents and legal challenges to delay the introduction. And if this doesn't work, large companies can switch lines to something more profitable without the loss in fixed capital completely destroying them, or at least can afford to continue producing at diminished return until they too can integrate the new innovation.

Though these large corporations are capable of delaying technical innovation in the short term, Schumpeter is not concerned about their overall ability to diminish or block progress:

> The power to exploit at pleasure a given pattern of demand – or one that changes independently of the monopolist's action and of the reactions it provokes – can under the conditions of intact capitalism hardly persist for periods long enough to matter for the analysis of total output.
>
> (Schumpeter 1950: 99)

Monopolistic practices thus serve as way of slowing down or smoothing out the abrupt and destructive consequences that technical innovation can have. This is useful not just for the individual concerns, says Schumpeter, but for the market in general, which can be thrown out of equilibrium or drop into a depression through the destruction of capital attendant on technical innovation.[11]

However, though Schumpeter may be relatively unconcerned with the effects of monopolistic practices, seeing them as a way of providing a break against the 'perennial gale of creative destruction' and hence reducing shocks to both individual firms and the market in general, later theorists would argue that this is because he was writing before the true ascendancy of the large-scale concern or corporation. He had yet to see what real monopolistic practices could be deployed in the market.

According to Paul Baran and Paul Sweezy, in Schumpeter's time there were still enough small-scale economic firms to ensure that new technical innovations would eventually, if slowly, work their way into the market. However, with the rise of what they term 'monopoly capitalism', which is to say the rise of the market being primarily dominated by large corporations which are able to express monopoly-like control (and which relate to one another according to principles of 'corespectivity', rather than traditional economic competition), there is no longer the same competitive pressure to innovate, or to take account of innovations produced by others.[12] Once the 'largest-scale unit of control' has taken over, 'the new commodity, the new technology, the new source of supply, the new type of organization' all tend to be monopolized by a handful of giant corporations (Baran and Sweezy 1966: 74). As a result of this,

> innovations are typically introduced (or soon taken over) by giant corporations which act not under the compulsion of competitive pressures but in accordance with careful calculations of the profit-maximizing course. Whereas in the competitive case no one, not even the innovating firms themselves, can control the rate at which new technologies are generally adopted, this ceases to be true in the monopolistic case. It is clear that the giant corporation will be guided not by the profitability of

the new method considered in isolation, but by the net effect of the new method on the overall profitability of the firm. And this means that in general there will be a slower rate of introduction of innovations than under competitive criteria.

(Baran and Sweezy 1966: 94–5)

Baran and Sweezy argue that 'this means that Schumpeter's perennial gale of creative destruction has subsided into an occasional mild breeze' (74).

The ability of large corporations to exert monopoly-like economic power in the market effects both the pace and direction of technical change. In a most basic sense this can mean the general production of sub-optimal technology (sub-optimal both in terms of what is available according to existing technologies and in terms of inadequate research and development). One example of this is what is commonly known as planned obsolescence. This is the situation where it's possible to produce longer-lasting, 'better' products, but products with shorter life spans are produced for the sake of increased profitability.[13]

More than just lifespan, the power of monopolistic practices is such that they can affect the *type* of technical innovation which is introduced. Thus for the sake of profitability 'a monopolist might consciously forego development of a socially desirable technology in order to develop and utilize a socially undesirable alternative. In so doing, he effectively prevents development of the socially desirable technology' (Adams and Encaoua 1994: 664). And, once again, to exert this kind of control the corporation need not be a perfect monopoly. It can, through the use of patents and economic power, still avoid competitive market pressures to innovate properly: 'Firms positioned to behave strategically might spend bountifully on R&D, develop radically new technologies, and innovate rapidly; in so doing, however, they might simply be engaged in strategic suppression of technologies which better serve the public interest' (671). And in the case where a smaller firm does develop a technological innovation that the larger does not control, it always has the option of buying them out. This is not to say that these tactics will work every time, and that technical innovations which escape the hands of large concerns won't occasionally work their way into the market. But it is to say that there are general mechanisms in place within the market that serve to channel and control the pace of technical innovation, despite the image of freewheeling dynamism which capitalism promotes. As an example of how large-scale corporations can crush smaller competitors and quash technical innovations that threaten their established interests, we might take the case of RCA and the invention of FM radio, as recounted by Lawrence Lessig (2004).

FM radio, invented and patented by Edwin Howard Armstrong in 1933, was vastly superior to AM radio. According to the competitive logic of the market, FM should have quickly supplanted AM for radio broadcasts. However, at the time of his invention Armstrong was working for RCA, the dominant player in the AM radio market. The development of FM radio at the time would have threatened RCA's AM empire. RCA, and its president

David Sarnoff, thus devised a strategy that deployed the full power of their restrictive practices, using both legal and economic means to crush Armstrong and FM radio:[14]

> For six years, Armstrong fought an expensive war of litigation to defend the patents. Finally, just as the patents expired, RCA offered a settlement so low that it would not even cover Armstrong's lawyer's fees. Defeated, broken, and now out of money, in 1954 Armstrong wrote a short note to his wife and then stepped out of a thirteen-story window to his death.
>
> (Lessig 2004: 6)

The RCA–FM story demonstrated vividly the way that large concerns can employ their legal and economic power to inhibit the development and deployment of technical innovations which threaten their established interests.

However, capitalist reticence towards technical innovations need not be based solely on a fear of being supplanted in the market. New technical innovations, even when developed by a one of the large concerns, might still be deemed undesirable due to the way that they subvert principles of capitalist organization and property regimes. Take, for example, the development of certain information and communication technologies. New communication technologies allow a more fluid and decentralized distribution of information and decision-making, thus making numerous processes within production and exchange potentially more efficient and profitable:

> One of the potential consequences of the new technologies is to create a technological basis for alternative ways of organizing economic activity, for pushing further some of the embryonic efforts to decentralize economic activity ... Since these technologies facilitate rapid communication over long distances, it now is possible for widely separated enterprises to coordinate their activities. Moreover, since they are also able to provide individuals and/or enterprises with sophisticated, up-to-date information about markets, the behavior of other actors within the technological network and other relevant matter, those individuals and/or enterprises no longer need to be confined within rigid, prescriptive plans and procedures set well in advance. Instead, with an understanding of what is expected of them, they can react autonomously and creatively to the information provided through the technological link.
>
> (Meiksins 1996: 99)

The trouble is that decentralizing information and autonomous decision-making exacerbate elements of uncertainty and unpredictability that are uncomfortable for capitalist enterprises, as well as subverting the hierarchies of control at work in most corporations. As such, moments of autonomy and creativity are to be kept to a minimum. Indeed, capitalist enterprises frequently use these new information technologies as a way of surveilling and controlling the actions of workers and consumers, rather than empowering them, even when this is less efficient. The capitalist is thus torn between two drives, the first the drive to innovate, to change, to make things more flexible and efficient, the second the drive to conserve, to maintain stability, control and capture.

In the service industry, banking provides a key example of this:

> In the case of banking, the contradictions are ... obvious. Systems are installed with the explicit purpose of reducing teller discretion, replacing middle-level management, and increasing centralized control over information flow and the behaviour of employees. Yet, at the same time, under pressure from external markets to extend the range of banking services available to customers, banks are forced to 'upgrade' tellers; the new technology is used to provide tellers with information and abilities that they can use to sell a wider variety of banking services and products to customers. Banks are clearly uncomfortable with this contradiction, and do whatever they can to limit and 'program' away teller discretion. Nevertheless, the underlying contradiction does not disappear and the possibilities of the new technology cannot be entirely suppressed.
>
> (Meiksins 1996: 5)

Tensions

This tension between technical innovation and established interests, between creative destruction and restrictive practices, between acceleration and slowness, lies at the heart of the capitalist assemblage. Deleuze and Guattari map this tension in their image of the capitalist axiomatic as both a machine for decoding/deterritorializing and an apparatus of capture. By pursuing this tension through their concept of the 'capitalist axiomatic' we can go beyond the duality of Schumpeter's account, uncovering a more volatile and multifarious capitalism than even the prophet of creative destruction imagined.

Deleuze and Guattari's concept of axioms (bound together in an axiomatic) is a way of distinguishing the capitalist form of organization and control from the 'codings' and 'overcodings' of other forms of social organization (usually affiliated with the state-form). A good starting point to understand the axiomatic is found in Moishe Postone's account of 'abstract social domination'. Says Postone, in opposition to, for example, the concrete domination of the state-form, 'social domination in capitalism does not, on its most fundamental level, consist in the domination of people by other people, but in the domination of people by abstract social structure that people themselves constitute' (2003: 30). This is to say that, as opposed to the close coding of other forms of social domination, where transgression is policed through hierarchical (and occasionally sovereign) force, the socio-economic order in capitalism relies more on a distributed set of interdependencies which immanently produce a social order and hierarchy. Thus, for example, whereas the relationship of domination between lord and serf, or between judge and defendant, is a coded one, where neither party is free to abandon their role without consequences, the relation of capitalist to proletariat is less strictly coded as, in principle, no one is officially bound to their role and they are free to move between positions. That they, in general, fail to do so is less the result of sovereign power, or some sort of explicit caste system, than of generalized and ambiguous forms of social and economic control, of immanent mechanisms (axioms) which put abstract pressures on people to conform to a set of investment, labour and consumption practices.

What this means is that capitalism is less a hierarchical system of discipline than a networked structure of control (Deleuze 1995). Although it is an apparatus of capture that produces an order as well as hierarchies, stratifications and relations of dominations, it does so without the systematic logic of a centralized organization. Again, this goes back to its character as an abstract form of social domination. In sovereign overcoding, domination is hierarchical, as control radiates outwards from a central authority and foundational rules (the body of the king, the will of god, the document of the constitution). The capitalist axiomatic is less centred. It is a supple and flexible inter-coding of diverse axioms; axioms of production and consumption, distribution and commodities, finance and capital, labour and knowledge, and state intervention. No single axiom is fundamental, and as the context changes any axiom may become more or less important.[15] New axioms can be added or subtracted as circumstances require (Deleuze and Guattari 1983: 461). To the extent that we can describe a set of core axioms, it is a very small list, which includes the principles of free labour, enforceable contract law and capital investment.[16] (And even then, the coming of the global capitalist axiomatic allows the integration of regions and economies that lack these axioms, as we will see in Chapter 4.)

This is why we see so many different kinds of capitalism: from American evangelical cowboy capitalism[17] to European social democratic capitalism, to southeast Asian quasi-authoritarian capitalism, to Russian mafia-style capitalism.[18] This multiplicity of capitalism(s) can also be discussed in terms of diverse capitalist *assemblages*, which describes how the capitalist axiomatic enters into assemblage with different social, political, cultural and legal milieus. These multiple capitalisms bear family resemblances to one another, with the axioms of capital, labour, profit and the commodity form assuming a somewhat different shape in different times and places. The capitalist axiomatic thus functions according to the logic of minor essentialism that we discussed in Chapter 1.

This immanent distributed character of the social domination of the capitalist axiomatic creates the interesting phenomena that, though it produces orders of hierarchy, it can refuse responsibility for them, because it does so in indirect ways. Deleuze and Guattari term this the 'unavowable' character of the capitalist axiomatic; it does not, cannot, acknowledge itself as an apparatus of capture and domination:

It is with the thing, capitalism, that the unavowable begins: there is not a single economic or financial operation that, assuming it is translated in terms of a code, would not lay bare its own unavowable nature, that is, its intrinsic perversion or essential cynicism.

(Deleuze and Guattari 1983: 247)

This is to say that, whereas codings and overcodings are willing to speak the truth of their relations of domination (the King *is* inherently superior to the subject, the lord *is* better than the serf), the bearers of the capitalist axiomatic view the stratifications it produces as exigencies or accidents, the result of personal faults or failures, rather than systemic, coded hierarchies. Furthermore, we see the supporters of capitalism exult in its dynamism and 'creative destruction', but remain silent on the issue of its restrictive practices. To acknowledge these restrictive practices would be to lay bare the axioms of control and domination which are necessary for the axiomatic to function.

This strange duality of the capitalist axiomatic, an order that shuns sovereign overcodings and direct social domination while at the same time creating an order and hierarchy as thorough as any other, is partly rooted in the two drives which we have identified within capitalism: the accelerative and conservative drives. On the one hand, it decodes and deterritorializes flows, freeing up stocks of goods, people, knowledge, money, etc. that might be otherwise frozen or immobilized by tradition, insufficient technological advances or lack of creative intuition. Acceleration is a crucial element of this process, since it allows capital to exist more fully as value-in-process, rather than forcing it to sit, bound and sequestered at some particular point in the production process (land as family inheritance, labour unfree to travel). The capitalist axiomatic, as Marx says, drives to break every barrier, to loosen every fetter and to create constant movement. In this regard, it subverts the sovereign overcodings which necessarily territorialize and block these flows.

And yet, just as this deterritorializing movement pushes towards the 'infinite' (Marx 1973: 334) towards an absolute deterritorialization, the larger capitalist assemblage must function as an apparatus of capture to reterritorialize these flows back 'on the full body of capital,' (Deleuze and Guattari 1983: 225), which is to say immanently reintegrate them into the orderly process of capitalist production (which, as we saw earlier, is willing to tolerate surprisingly little in the way of novelty, disorder and dynamism).[19] It therefore creates axioms which are more supple and flexible than the state-form's codings and overcodings. They are less totalizing and allow for a greater multiplicity of form. But for all that, they are no less a technology of capture and domination.

Thus, in contrast to the image we saw in the introduction, capitalism is not synonymous with speed, is not defined purely by an inherent dynamism, because it only ever effects '*relative* breaks, because it substitutes for the codes an extremely rigorous axiomatic that maintains the energy of the flows in a bound state on the body of capital as a socius that is deterritorialized, but also a socius that is even more pitiless than any other' (246). Axioms are introduced which tie these flows back to the capitalist milieu, channelling their speed into regularized rhythms of movement. At the same time as it has a tendency to overcome limits, 'capitalism only functions on condition that it inhibit this tendency, or that it push back or displace this limit, by substituting for it its own *immanent* relative limits, which it continually reproduces on a widened scale. It axiomatizes with one hand what it decodes with the other' (246). Deleuze and Guattari describe this tension in terms of the development of blocks of antiproduction. The axiomatics of antiproduction 'double the capital and the flow of knowledge with a capital and an equivalent flow of *stupidity* that also effects an absorption and a realization that ensures the integration of groups and individuals into the system. Not only lack amid overabundance, but stupidity in the midst of knowledge and science' (246).

Thus the capitalist axiomatic relatively deterritorializes only to effect a relative reterritorialization. It accelerates only to slow down once again. It seeks out the speed-event for its power, its possibility and its uncertainty, only to then try to subordinate this speed-event to a comfortable, orderly velocity-state (in this regard, we see a process very similar to the state apparatus' attempts to appropriate the war-machine). It desires the quantitative change of acceleration, while minimizing the danger of a qualitative change in its mode of functioning. It goes as near the edge, the absolute limit, as it can, only to begin backpedalling furiously, seeking to return to the territory that it has just left. The capitalist axiomatic is thus, in the words of Jean Baudrillard, an 'accelerator of inertia' (1994: 92).

What we have is a tension between two opposing – yet interdependent – forces, one accelerative and deterritorializing and the other conservative and reterritorializing. However, let us not make the mistake of conceiving of this duality of forces as some manner of dialectical contradiction to be resolved diachronically in a future synthesis. This duality of forces is constitutive of capitalism, and therefore cannot be resolved by it. All that can happen is the contingent and aleatory stabilization of the struggle somewhere between the two ideal poles of speed and control. What we therefore have is a struggle played out not in historical terms, but in geographic terms, as the play of forces which carves out diverse territories and equilibria.[20] This is one of the roots of the multiplicity of capitalism discussed on p. 102. Different capitalisms, and different sectors within each capitalism, are produced by different negotiations between these warring forces. Where the balance between these forces is established is the result of multiple factors within the capitalist assemblage in which they take place, including cultural practices, legal structures, political formations, business and management cultures, natural events, material conditions, etc. Note that this assertion of the contingent and aleatory negotiation of these two forces constitutes a substantial break with economic determinism. This is because these two forces are internal to the economic sphere. Therefore, the negotiation between them, the *decision*[21] between them, is often produced, and overdetermined, by 'outside' elements.

Different capitalist assemblages, placing emphasis on different needs, desires and norms, will influence the social decisions on how to negotiate this tension.

For example, in the realm of industrial manufacturing, Robert Brenner argues that the major global economies have been seeing a steady decline in economic performance over the past half-century (2006: xxiv–xxv), as a result of the failure to enact the process of creative destruction in major manufacturing sectors. His argument is that established concerns, when faced with more innovative, efficient competition, have not withdrawn from production (as Schumpeter would predict), but have continued to produce even at a lower profit margin, thus lowering the overall value produced. This intransigence comes from the larger concerns' refusal to give up the fixed capital already spent (31), and the intangible assets which come from experience in a particular line.[22] From the perspective of an economic and technological determinism which assumes a singular logic of economic rationality (that capital will eschew unproductive sectors in favour of more productive lines) this appears to be a breakdown of market forces. However, from a perspective which acknowledges the existence of a conservative pole within the capitalist axiomatic, this can be seen as a decision (a decentralized, distributed decision performed by multiple actors and institutions) to forgo the possibility of higher rates of value in favour of greater stability. In this case, the conservative desire for certainty and control outweighs the desire for capital to escape traditional, potentially less profitable lines and seek out new entrepreneurial pastures.

Alternatively, we see cases which list towards the pole of deterritorialization. Let us take the example of the introduction of new information and communication technologies in the technological and financial sectors. The development of advanced communications technologies has allowed for substantially increased speed and flexibility on behalf of firms. And yet, that demand for speed and flexibility frequently serves to unsettle some more fundamental (and slower) processes necessary for business to function. For example, Sean O Riain (2006) discusses how the increasing push for flexibility amongst tech firms, the move to more, and shorter-term, contract work, means introducing a new level of uncertainty, decreasing the ability to plan and predict, and therefore the ability to act in a future-oriented way (i.e. allocating funds or encouraging training for employees).[23]

Additionally, the rise of flexible, fragmented and frequently multinational product cycles means the increasing destruction of what O Riain terms 'relational assets', intangible goods which result from 'embedded social relations', which is to say the existence of a locally organized community of producers. This is especially true in a creative sector such as tech, since the development of a community (even between firms) means the opportunity for the dissemination of new ideas, technologies and even basic problem-solving techniques. Thus:

> The pressures of the market and the embedding of social relations exist in a dynamic and symbiotic tension: the market cannot operate without

> embedded social relations but unchecked market relations attack those very social relations which sustain them, producing a defense of social cooperation and solidarity on the part of those integrated into the market.
>
> (O Riain 2006: 511)

Once again, we have here a situation which can appear like a breakdown of market forces, the failure of the capitalist axiomatic to ensure the conditions of its own reproduction. But from the perspective of the duality of forces, we can see a capitalist assemblage that has 'chosen' to pursue the accelerative and deterritorializing possibilities of new technologies, even if these new lines of flight potentially endanger the certainty and stability of traditional modes of production.

These stabilizations, these assemblages, are always contingent, contingent both because they are the result of complex decisions made at a variety of levels (and hence not the result of an immutable economic or technological logic unfolding in teleological time), but also because they do not fundamentally resolve the tension between these opposing forces; they merely negotiate between them, and produce a temporary equilibrium. As time progresses, these opposing forces will require new negotiations in response to new dangers. In the first example we gave, the declining rate of value runs the risk of increasing the frequency and intensity of recession cycles if capital isn't freed up from increasingly unproductive manufacturing. In the second example, there's the possibility that, at a certain point, these deterritorializing lines of flight might become un-reterritorializable 'lines of death' (Deleuze and Guattari 1987: 229–31). Embedded social relations might become so distended that production cannot be efficiently carried out, resulting in an economic breakdown (indeed, we can look to the global economic meltdown which began in 2008, with its roots in 'innovative' banking practices and instruments which sought greater and faster capital circulation and investment). Conversely, the capitalist axiomatic might establish new ways to reterritorialize these lines, transforming their abrupt speed into the meter of a regularized velocity.

Deleuze and Guattari remind us, however, that there is another possibility for the lines of flight that capitalism produces. In addition to spiralling off into nothingness, or being relatively reterritorialized onto the body of capital, there is also the possibility that they might be absolutely reterritorialized onto another plane of immanence.[24] These lines of flight might open up a new plane of immanence, a potentially non-capitalist space either within capitalism or beyond it. This is of interest to those of us who see in speed a potential challenge to capitalism, the possibility of taking advantage of those deterritorialized flows which capitalism produces and turning them against it, exacerbating them, using them as lines of flight and escape which might lead us to new and different worlds. Rather than seeking to slow down the acceleration of capitalism, Deleuze and Guattari ask the question whether we might not 'go still further, that is, in the movement of the market, of decoding and deterritorialization?':

For perhaps the flows are not yet deterritorialized enough, not decoded enough ... Not to withdraw from the process, but to go further, to 'accelerate the process,' as Nietzsche put it: in this matter, the truth is that we haven't see anything yet.

(Deleuze and Guattari 1983: 239–40)

We will continue this investigation of how speed can turn against capitalism in the next section, in the context of the development of new information technologies and how they challenge existing property regimes. Here we will see a line of deterritorialization that poses a challenge to the capitalist axiomatic, and which has the potential of turning into a line of flight that might be absolutely reterritorialized on a different plane of immanence. This is to say that we see how a deterritorialized flow might, if pushed beyond the comfort level of the capitalist axiomatic, produce a non-capitalist regime or practice.

Information technology and intellectual property rights

The development of information technologies is a particularly germane case for us since it is one of the major driving forces behind all three components of the social acceleration of time. We can start by looking at one particular form of information technology, the drive for the increased digitalization of information: 'Digitalization has removed the quality/copy trade-off, by allowing generational copies to be, for all intents and purposes, exact copies of the original digital artifact.' This produces '[a] "frictionless environment" for content, where successive copies do not degrade' (May and Sell 2006: 183) There are countless ways in which this digitalization has been useful to business, both in terms of production and day-to-day operations. From the ability to speed up internal communication, to making the production and delivery of music, books and film cheaper and more efficient, digitalization perfectly serves capitalism's internal drive to decrease production and circulation time, and accelerate capital as value-in-motion.

The problem, however, is that as digitalization produces a 'frictionless environment' where information can move freely, increasingly producers are incapable of maintaining control over content. Digitalization 'immediately raises the potential threat that once a digital good is distributed, unauthorized copies can compete throughout its market for consumer use' (183). In the past, when one wanted to pirate a particular content, one needed to either gain access to a master copy, which would be restricted, or make inferior second- and third-generation copies, which would not stand up to the original. However, 'whereas in the past the users of copied goods would receive an inferior product, and thus the price discrimination between unauthorized copies was clearly reflected in the quality of the product, digital copies have removed this distinction' (183).

Though copying was around long before digital technology, digital piracy entered a new phase with widespread access to high-speed information networks. With higher-speed dial-up modems – and later broadband internet – it became feasible to share digital content with people anywhere in the world. This meant that there was now no limit on the number of times a piece of digital content could be copied and shared. This ability to share information led to the rise of 'Peer-to-Peer' software (P2P).[25] P2P programs such as Bittorrent and Soulseek allow individuals to search the collections of all other users on the network and download from them. These programs made simple the distribution of digital content. This ability to freely distribute information was seen as a deep threat to corporations' ability to control their product. According to the Recording Industry Association of American (RIAA), the 'estimate for worldwide losses in 1994 was $2.245 Billion' (Boyle 1996: 121). And according to the Business Software Alliance (BSA), 'losses to the worldwide software industry caused by the use of unlicensed software were said to amount to US $10.97 billion in 2001' (Deibert 2003a: 506–7).

Of course, the actual monetary losses through online piracy are somewhat difficult to determine. Part of this has to do with the non-rivalrous nature of information, i.e. when I 'steal' a song online (unlike, say, a car) the company does not as a result have one less song to sell. There is really no way of telling how many downloads precluded the pirates from actually buying the music. The real problem is one of control. With digitalization and access to high-speed internet access, corporations can no longer maintain reliable control of the information that they develop.[26] In response the content owners (and their group organizations such as the RIAA, the Motion Picture Association of America and the BSA) have sought to employ the restrictive practices with which we are now familiar.

In the first instance, the media concerns sought to use legal power against illegal copying. The RIAA, for example, in 2003 began a campaign of tracking down and suing music downloaders for copyright violations.[27] In concert with this increased enforcement there has been a push for increased scope and power of copyright laws. For example, '[o]ne of the more notorious measures is the Digital Millenium Copyright Act (DMCA), an act of US congress that was signed into Law on 28th October 1998 … and whose purpose is to update US copyright laws for the digital age' (Deibert 2003a: 507–8). The DMCA allows for quicker enforcement of copyright law through the use of DMCA 'take-down notices'. If an owner feels that material infringing their copyright is being hosted somewhere on the internet, they need only send a 'take-down' notice to the internet service provider (ISP) which hosts the site, and they are legally obliged to take it down. The crucial point is that all this happens without the owner having to go to the court to get an injunction. The ISP is required by law to comply simply on the owner's assertion of violation.[28] The law thus begins to move to automatically favour the copyright owner, allowing them to enforce almost unilaterally.

This deployment of legal power is then backed up by a deployment of economic power to decrease the speed and flexibility of information technology. One way this was done was through the introduction of what is termed digital rights management (DRM) technology, the introduction of code into digital content and media programs to limit their ability to be used for piracy purposes. What it is important to understand is that the use of DRM technology exists solely for the purpose of increasing the ability of copyright holders to control their content. It results in the production of sub-optimal technology. DRM decreases the speed, flexibility and ease of use of information technology, making interoperability more difficult, and even disabling the ability to use it in non-infringing, but also non-authorized ways (such as fair use, or using digital technology to produce and play independent media created and distributed for free). Indeed, DRM technology frequently makes digital technology less functional than the non-electronic equivalent, inhibiting the ability to do such things as make back-up copies, use small portions for personal use or even lend it to a friend. DRM necessarily makes information technology worse.[29] It attempts to reverse the effects of the 'frictionless environment' that digitalization introduced. (Here, we can think back to Deleuze and Guattari's reference to doubling the flow of information with a flow stupidity.)

This is particularly important in the context of a culture where media consumers are frequently becoming media producers. Remixing, mash-ups, self-publishing, micro-low-budget filmmaking. All of these new forms of independent media production are aided by the increasing fluidity of digital media. Technologies such as DRM make it more difficult for these independent producers to use new media technologies, and hence potentially to ensure the monopoly of large media concerns over producing content.

In response to this purposeful sub-optimalization of digital technology, individual users all over the world have taken to trying to overturn DRM technology. Hackers figure out how to break encryption technology on DVDs, strip DRM out of music files, crack software, open up music and video players for unrestricted use. Some (possibly most) of this activity is undertaken out of a desire for access to free content. However, this activity must also be seen as an expression of what Stephen Levy terms the 'Hacker Ethic', a set of principles, not necessarily always articulated, shared by many hackers which prizes optimization, hands-on access to technology, freedom of information and decentralization above all else (Lessig 2004: 193).

In response to this, media conglomerates have returned to legal powers as way of protecting their sub-optimal technology. Another, and perhaps more disturbing, aspect of the DMCA discussed above is that it 'prohibits circumvention of any technological protection against copying and prevents the production of any device or provision of any service designed to defeat protection mechanisms' (May and Sell 2006: 181). Thus not only is it illegal to break the copyright, it is illegal to circumvent technologies put in place to protect the copyright (even if the circumvention does not result in copyright infringement, i.e. if the circumvention is for the purpose of fair use of copyright materials, or of producing and broadcasting one's own content). Indeed, it is even illegal to publish information that might aid in doing so. This is one more way in which a drive to control information and maintain intellectual property rights serves to suppress technical innovation and inhibit research and development: 'Industry has used the DMCA to prevent the dissemination of information about circumventing encryption technologies; for example, "Professor Edward Felten of Princeton University was asked to withdraw his paper from a scholarly conference, lest he be prosecuted under the DMCA"' (181–2). Indeed, the DMCA has been used by entrenched media as a club to inhibit advancements that might threaten their power and control:

> the DMCA has been employed as a tool of anti-competition, has stifled legitimate research into cyber-security and encryption technologies, and has undermined 'fair use'. To give just a few egregious examples, a garage door opener company has employed the DMCA to prevent rival companies from developing universal remote controls that operate on its system. Computer scientists working on encryption systems have been scared away from their research by legal threats from industry groups who claim proprietary ownership over the codes employed to prevent piracy. The DMCA and other laws have also impinged on academic databases and the circulation of electronic journals, once one of the unmistakable positive elements of the Internet. Many believe the restrictions are leading to the suffocation of works in the public domain for scholarship and a wholesale erosion of the global commons of information.
>
> (Deibert 2003a: 507–8)

This has led to at least one situation where a researcher, Dmitry Sklyarov, a Russian computer scientist, was arrested while in the US giving a talk because he had produced and distributed a software program that could be used to circumvent DRM technology.[30] This threat of legal action for the sake of protecting property rights and market share has produced a chilling effect in research in computer science, cryptography and mathematics (once again, the capitalist axiomatic's 'flow of stupidity').[31]

This tension between the potential of information technologies and the attempts to circumscribe them, through both legal and economic means, has lead to a struggle between producers and users of technology and content. As media corporations try to close Pandora's box and reacquire the control over information that they lost with the development of digital technology, users have become increasingly enchanted with the possibilities that these technologies provide, and frustrated with attempts to block their use and development. We have already discussed the work of hackers who seek to subvert attempts at technological control and free up information for all. Such efforts are just one element (and probably the most illegal) of a more generalized push to take advantage of the speed and flexibility of digital technologies, and take control of the possibilities that they offer. Indeed, these individual acts of technological subversion, frequently undertaken for self-interested reasons (not that that makes them illegitimate), have begun to percolate into broader social and political positions. As people see how digital technologies allow for information to be easily shared and remixed, used and combined, they begin to question the current structure of intellectual property and the types of control it seeks to exercise. As a result certain groups have begun to develop new ways to think about intellectual property.

One example of the attempt to develop a new intellectual property regime is seen in the 'Creative Commons' licence:

> The Creative Commons is a non-profit corporation established in Massachusetts, but with its home at Stanford University. Its aim is to build a layer of *reasonable* copyright on top of the extremes that now reign. It does this by making it easy for people to build upon other people's work, by making it simple for creators to express the freedom for others to take and build upon their work.
>
> (Lessig 2004: 282)

Creative Commons licensing allows creators to give away, up front, the right to use their work in specific ways.[32]

The most interesting thing about the use of 'Creative Commons' licensing for our purposes is the way in which it begins not from the primacy of the singular author as the agent of creativity, but instead from the commons. As knowledge producers (whether in the arts or sciences) become aware of the ease with which communications technologies can facilitate collaboration, and as users become increasingly used to forms of knowledge production based on the explicit use and repurposing of old knowledge objects (everything from software development to music remixing), the idea of creativity as the gift of a sole artist begins to wane in favour of an image of vibrant commons of intellectual labour.[33] The Creative Commons licence is not 'anti-capitalist' *per se*. What it does do is reintroduce the notion of the commons as a central figure in the innovation of human knowledge.

A similar set of challenges to the maximalist form of intellectual property rights, and perhaps an even greater commitment to the intellectual commons, comes from the Free Software foundation and the idea of Free Software/ Open-Source Software (FS/OSS): 'FS/OSS is software whose source code is shared. Anyone can download the technology that makes a FS/OSS program run. And anyone eager to learn how a particular bit of FS/OSS technology works can tinker with the code' (46). To call it 'free' software does not mean that it is given away for no charge. What it does mean is that the software is 'free' of any copyright rules or restrictions which would inhibit your ability to use, change or even share the program. Free Software is distributed on a very special copyright licence which producers call 'copyleft':

> Copyleft uses copyright law, but flips it over to serve the opposite of its usual purpose: instead of a means of privatizing software, it becomes a means of keeping software free. The central idea of copyleft is that we give everyone permission to run the program, copy the program, modify

the program, and distribute modified versions – but not permission to add restrictions of their own. Thus, the crucial freedoms that define 'free software' are guaranteed to everyone who has a copy; they become inalienable rights.

(Stallman 2002: 20)

The use of copyleft turns copyright against itself. It not only releases information into the public domain, but ensures that anyone who wants to use that information will also have to contribute to the public domain. It is thus an engine for growing the intellectual commons.

This move to produce free software as part of a vibrant intellectual commons is based on two sets of beliefs. First of all, that innovation, especially in the field of software development, is best achieved through a generalized program of collaboration and cooperation, rather than proprietary knowledge and software patents. However, even if this didn't provide better conditions for knowledge production, some defenders of FS/OSS support it on the basis of ethical convictions. Richard Stallman, founder of the Free Software Foundation and Free Software programmer, speaks frequently and movingly about the ethical need for commonality and cooperation:

Many programmers are unhappy about the commercialization of system software. It may enable them to make more money, but it requires them to feel in conflict with other programmers in general rather than feel as comrades. The fundamental act of friendship among programmers is the sharing of programs; marketing arrangements now typically used essentially forbid programmers to treat others as friends. The purchaser of software must choose between friendship and obeying the law.

(Stallman 2002: 32–3)

The FS/OSS movement, though constrained to a narrow (but increasingly important) sector of production, challenges the current property regimes, and instead seeks to encourage a mode of production based on ethical and intellectual beliefs in collaboration and community.

In addition to those trying to promote alternative intellectual property regimes, there are multiple groups trying to affect the functioning of the current regime. Groups like the Electronic Frontier Foundation provide legal support to groups and individuals trying to defend themselves against lawsuits brought by large corporations, levelling the legal playing field. The Association for Progressive Communication 'attempt[s] to influence the global communications policy agenda from a civil society perspective' (Deibert 2003a: 525). In addition to these specific organizations, 'Major Foundations, such as the Ford Foundation, Markle Foundation, and George Soros' Open Society Institute, have supplied critical funding and encouragement to bring civil society actors interested in information and communication technologies together' (525).

Though none of these organizations or ideas is 'anti-capitalist', all advance ideas which challenge the current intellectual property regime, and seek to modify axioms of capitalist production, consumption, labour and organization. In the case of the alternative intellectual property regimes we have discussed, though they do not separate themselves from the capitalist market (indeed, they build on the current existing intellectual property regime), they challenge it by opening up new spaces, showing new possibilities for production (the essential nature of the Creative Commons is to give away your property rights, to allow others access to that which is supposedly yours). Indeed, we should not conceive of the idea of absolute reterritorialization as the over-turning of all capitalist principles (or, even more so, as a revolutionary over-throwing of the capitalist regime), nor should we conceive of a non-capitalist plane of immanence as one that is completely separate from and unconnected to the capitalist axiomatic. Such a duality between the capitalist and the non-capitalist is unnecessary. For a line of flight to be absolutely reterritorialized on a new, non-capitalist plane of immanence, it need only function in such a way as to challenge one or more of capitalism's central axioms and open up a space for alternative production or consumption. It may continue to enter into assemblage with the capitalist axiomatic (indeed, given the capitalist axiomatic's scope and intensity in modernity, it would be almost impossible for it not to). However, in doing so, it forces a change in the capitalist territory of the capitalist assemblage, expanding or contorting its borders and challenging its axioms.

In this case, we see a collection of actors and organizations that advance the idea that innovation and progress are better served and encouraged through some element of common ownership of human knowledge, rather than exclusive private property. Indeed, more than that, they advance the idea that the public good of innovation and the advancement of human knowledge are *more important* than the private good of exclusive ownership. Note that this is a fairly radical set of claims. It is one thing in this day and age to challenge the justice and equity of capitalism. But to charge it with inefficiency and conservatism is to strike where it is supposed to be strongest.

These organizations have seen the opportunities that these new information and communications technologies provide, how much easier they make col-laboration and cooperation, how they make possible the leveraging of mass collective action for problem solving and production. They have given us a glimpse of what the commons can do (in truth, one more glimpse of what the commons can do).

The speed of new communications technologies provides a new way of going about the world, one which unsettles the structures and orders of the capitalist regime. Entrenched business interests seek to do what they can to restrict these possibilities and reterritorialize these escaping lines of flight. In many cases they will succeed. What is important, however, is that these lines exist, and are never fully closed off. Capitalism's need to accelerate, to break boundaries, ensures that they will always send off at least some lines that will resist reterritorialization. These lines open up new spaces of production and consumption. And when the capitalist axiomatic produces new axioms to incorporate these pockets into capitalist production, it produces changes in that axiomatic, pushing what capitalist production means and how it is carried out. These lines function as experiments of what economic production can be like, and hence open us up to the possibilities of the future.[34]

Speed and capitalism

The purpose of this investigation into struggles around media content ownership is not to suggest that digital technologies are the gateway to a glorious post-capitalist utopia. Nor is it to argue that, if we manage to overcome DRM technology, capitalism will have been defeated.[35] Rather, it is to point out that, in the face of all of the discussions about the wonders of post-industrial info-capitalism, capitalism and digital technologies (capitalism and innovation, capitalism and acceleration ...) do not fit together perfectly, but rather exist in an uneasy tension.

This, to a certain extent, then, can be our response to those who see in the social acceleration of time – and the technological innovations which characterize the (post)modern era – purely the mechanisms of capitalist oppression and exploitation. From the analysis composed here, we can instead see in this acceleration lines of flight which are reterritorialized back onto the full body of capital by the capitalist axiomatic. Those who resist capitalist exploitation through an unequivocal rejection of technology, or through a broad process of deceleration as a way to return to an older mode of social organization,[36] will potentially miss out on important opportunities. We must look not at any particular technology or acceleration as the source of capitalist strength and exploitation (or as the silver bullet to defeat it). Rather, we must see how it enters into assemblage with the capitalist axiomatic to produce exploitation, and how we might deform it, *détourne* it to a new assemblage.

This is not to say that there are never situations in which a wilful political deceleration or the rejection of a particular technological innovation might not be politically useful. What it does mean is that we should attempt to investigate politically the deterritorialized lines which capitalism throws off to determine their trajectories, their possibilities and their modes of reterritorialization. And then we should begin to ask how we might use them to break through the barrier of the capitalist axiomatic, how we might enact an *absolute* reterritorialization of those lines onto a new plane.[37] Deleuze and Guattari state that at the root of both the capitalist axiomatic and other, more rhizomatic,[38] minoritarian and potentially more egalitarian social formations is the decoded flow, but

> not in the same way; they are not at all the same thing, depending on whether the decodings are caught up in an axiomatic or not; on whether one remains at the level of the large aggregates functioning statistically,

or crosses the barrier that separates them from the unbound molecular positions; on whether the flows of desire reach this absolute limit or are content to displace a relative immanent limit that will reconstitute itself further along; on whether controlling reterritorializations are added to the processes of deterritorialization; and on whether money burns or bursts into flames.

(Deleuze and Guattari 1983: 247)

The problem, then, is not simply one of accelerative technologies, but of how we intervene in those technologies, what assemblages we allow them to enter into. Thus we see hackers investigating how digital technologies can subvert the surveillance power of new information technologies;[39] activists using those same technologies to coordinate resistance, circulate information and strengthen organization and solidarity;[40] cryptographers attempting to produce better encryption technology which allows citizens to bolster their privacy;[41] computer scientists acknowledging the power of the commons for problem solving and knowledge production and thus inculcating practices of collectivity and cooperation. And lawyers and artists come together to try to develop new property regimes for new forms and times of artistic creation.

Not all of these attempts will work. Some will fail. Some will be successfully reterritorialized onto the body of capital. The capitalist axiomatic has proven itself resilient and adaptable and it will always seek out ways to reincorporate dissident elements. But what gives us hope is that it also never ceases in deterritorializing new lines, in providing opportunities for subversion, creativity and the production of new futures. This can give us hope that 'in this matter, the truth is that we haven't seen anything yet'.

4 Regimes of (im)mobility

Towards an international political economy of speed

Neoliberalism and the new map of the world

Thomas Friedman is a financial journalist, a bestselling author, a trend-watcher and a trend-setter; a jet-setting cosmopolite, travelling the world, tracing the contours of global trade and finance (Friedman 2006). Thomas Friedman has made an amazing discovery. Thomas Friedman has returned from his world travels (more specifically, the now not-so-mysterious Orient) with the realization that the map of the world which has been in existence for the last 600 years is wrong. Thomas Friedman has discovered that the world is flat.

It wasn't always flat of course. There was a time when the world closely resembled the geographical variegation of our maps and globes. But since then it has been flattened and smoothed out by the rise of advanced communication transportation and information technologies – accelerative technologies. When Thomas Friedman says that the world is flat, he means 'the playing field ha[s] been leveled' (7); the barriers (spatial, economic, social, political or cultural) between geographic locations have steadily fallen before the inevitable logic of globalizing capital and its technological innovations. This, says Friedman, is the world of 'Globalization 3.0'. Globalization 1.0 came with the 'discovery of the new world', and was an era of states in a global world. Globalization 2.0 was the era of firms and companies competing at the global level. And:

> [Globalization 3.0] is the newfound power of individuals to collaborate and compete globally ... the phenomenon that is enabling, empowering and enjoining individuals and small groups to go global so easily and so seamlessly is what I call the *flat-world platform* ... the flat-world platform is the product of a convergence of the personal computer (which allowed every individual suddenly to become the author of his or her own content in digital form) with the fiber-optic cable (which suddenly allowed all those individuals to access more and more digital content around the world for next to nothing) with the rise of work flow software (which enabled individuals all over the world to collaborate on that same digital content from anywhere, regardless of the distances between them).
>
> (Friedman 2006: 11)

Friedman is, of course, not the first to notice the importance of these accelerative technologies, or the effect that they are having on global economic (not to mention political, cultural, social, etc.) activity. However, Friedman has become a kind of high priest of this change. Indeed, his work has become shorthand for the processes of globalization. In a recent IBM commercial one businessman answers another's question about what he means by a 'global action plan' by stating, 'You know. The world is flat. That whole thing.'

Thomas Friedman's map is a world collapsed into a point, a virtual, non-spatial space of interconnection and interactivity:

> [W]hat the flattening of the world means is that we are now connecting all the knowledge centers on the planet together into a single global network, which – if politics and terrorism do not get in the way – could usher in an amazing era of prosperity, innovation, and collaboration, by companies, communities and individuals.
>
> (Friedman 2006: 8)

This is Friedman's map of the world, a world where companies, communities and individuals are all connected; where the alienation and isolation of geography and politics are overturned in favour of a pre-babelian sense of undifferentiated unity.

However, let's look at another new map of the world, this one developed by Professor Miguel Angel Centeno along with the 'International Networks Archive' (INA) at Princeton University.[1] The INA, too, is built on the awareness that, given new accelerative technologies, geographic space is no longer what it once was. That is why they sought to develop a non-geographic mapping system. The system that they ended up producing is an interactive and dynamic map of the world, based around the relative locations of 23 cities, measured by travel time.[2] To use the map, the viewer picks one city as the central hub, and the others are dispersed spatially according to how long it takes to travel between them. Set the hub city as New York and the other cities cluster around it; first London, at a mere four hours away, then Vancouver at six, Tokyo at 12, etc. Conversely, if we pick Jakutsk, Russia, as our hub city, we are given a visual representation of the middle of nowhere, as the rest of the cities spring desperately away, none closer than a seven-day trip.

What quickly becomes apparent with this map is the disjuncture between the relative temporal difference of travel time and the absolute spatial difference between cities. Though they are only 1,670 miles apart, there are 59 hours of travel between Gaborone, Botswana and Kisangani, Congo (requiring three plane trips, a bus ride and a long walk into the jungle). Compare this with the relatively brief 23-hour trip between Gaborone and New York, despite the ocean and 7,800 miles which separate them.

The INA's project agrees with Thomas Friedman that our traditional geographies are inadequate to describe life in the space and time of (post) modernity. However, the map they develop in response looks substantially different. Their map is not flat, nor does their world collapse into a central point. Rather, their map reveals a rough, variegated world, replete with expansions and contractions, wormholes and tunnels, flows and blockages. (And all this before the question of access is introduced. For the INA's map only describes technical possibility; it in no way takes into account potential restraints on individuals' ability to travel, due to either inadequate wealth or legal obstructions such as entry visas, immigration quotas, etc.) The problem of living in this space of flows is made even more problematic by the question of access to information technologies. Despite Friedman's enthusiastic account of digital technology, access to the internet – not to mention expensive computer technologies – is far from universal. In this case, the playing field seems far from level and the world far from flat.

Or perhaps we might take Friedman at his word, in the most exacting and pedantic of manners. For we know that, topologically speaking, when the world becomes flat it does not level the playing field, nor bring everyone closer together. Unlike a sphere, which has the unique property of producing the least surface area for a given volume, a circle has an edge, and will therefore necessarily create a hierarchy of distance between those on the rim and those in the centre – between the core and periphery of the map. Flattening the world, in fact, drives people apart. On such a map the core would be Friedman's collapsed world of instantaneous connectivity (New York/London/Tokyo on the INA's map). But this inner circle would be ringed by a wider, slower, more dispersed circle (Gaborone/Kisangani/Jakutsk).

Now, many advocates of neoliberal economic policies acknowledge that there are substantial inequalities in the world – of development, of resources and of interconnectivity. However, such inequalities are seen as a result of insufficient integration of certain zones into globalizing capitalism's sphere of influence. Neoliberal economist and Nobel laureate in economics Jagdish Bhagwati acknowledges that, '[f]or example, tribal areas in India where poverty is acute may not be connected sufficiently to the mainstream economy where growth occurs' (2004: 57). Friedman himself believes that 'Globalization 3.0' is an ongoing project which has not yet reached completion. Neoliberal economics describes these differentials as a result of an incomplete historical process of integration, frequently made more difficult by the intransigence of 'backward' or less 'developed' global zones. Bhagwati, for example, explains the poverty of inner-city populations as the result of 'structural problems such as the allure of drugs, transportation bottlenecks, and the lack of role models in broken and single-parent families struggling against terrible odds' (57). He also criticizes indigenous groups who refuse to 'confront the fact that the old yields to the new' (116). Friedman, in the quotation above, notes that Globalization 3.0 will carry on, unless blocked by 'politics and terrorism' (2006: 8). Underdevelopment, or 'backwardness', is thus not the result of capitalism, or globalization, but of their lack, and of internal forces that block or slow their fulfilment. This produces what David Harvey terms a 'historicist diffusionist' model of geography (2006b: 71), which views differentials between regions or zones of space as the result of an incomplete diffusion of system and practices from the core to the periphery. Such a model serves to overcode the INA's map of concentric circles with a map of zones of time ('advanced' or 'backward', 'developed' or 'underdeveloped') and speed ('fast' or 'slow', 'connected' or 'isolated').

This map of globalization is not just the purview of neoliberal economists. In an article published in, of all places, *Esquire*, Thomas P. M. Barnett, the head of the US Naval War College laid out a similar image of the world. The article, titled 'The Pentagon's New Map', made a connection between integration into globalizing capitalism and security threats to America, separating the world into three broad regions: the 'Functioning Core' of advanced capitalist countries, 'where globalization is thick with network connectivity, financial transactions, liberal media flows, and collective security'; 'the non-integrating gap', where 'globalization is thinning or just plain absent' and people are plagued by 'politically repressive regimes, widespread poverty and disease, routine mass murder, and – most important– the chronic conflicts that incubate the next generation of global terrorists'; and, finally, the crucial 'seam states' that 'lie along the Gap's bloody boundaries' (Barnett 2003). I say that seam states are crucial because, according to Barnett, '[i]t is along this seam that the Core will seek to suppress bad things coming out of the Gap' (ibid.). Barnett uses this 'new map' to support the American invasion of Iraq. The invasion of Iraq is seen as an attempt to bring Iraq from the Gap to the Core, to integrate it, forcefully, into the circuits of globalization. Says Barnett, the United States must 'export security' to Iraq so that '[f]reedom [can] blossom', globalization can take hold, and it will no longer be a security threat. (It is, I suppose, nice to know that there is still something that the US can export to rectify its trade imbalance.) In this account, the developing world's intransigence to proliferating globalization is not just a threat to itself, through poverty and disease, but also to the developed world, making such countries breeding grounds for terrorism. The peripheral zone of this global map is coded as stagnant water, producing dangerous disease, which needs to be irrigated through connection to the fast-moving flows of the core zones.

This approach to mapping falls into the traditional pattern of what John Agnew calls 'geographing history', the identification of 'blocks of space' with 'the essential attributes of different time periods relatively to the realized historical experience of one of the blocks' (Agnew 2003: 35). The danger of this approach is that it supports the image that '[a]ll the world [is] united in a single, one-way history' (46), the history of western capitalist globalization, with states typed according to where they fall along that trajectory. Time and space become neatly bound up in the simple formula that 'here (the West) [is] now and there (the Rest) [is] then' (46). Such an image ignores the possibility of novel or unique paths to development, or indeed even different conceptions of what 'development' might look like. Historical progress is only defined through deviation from, or fidelity to, the highest point of western 'development' ('Backwards' or 'Advanced', 'Developed' or 'Underdeveloped'). The greater danger in this approach, however, is that it leads 'towards an absence of "coevalness": the sense of societies affecting one another at one and the same time' (46–7).

In neoliberal economics, the variegation of the map of the world and its separation into zones of time (development) and speed (interconnectivity) is viewed as a function of the unfinished project of globalization and the intransigence of those more backwards zones. These zones are isolated, left behind, they are 'not … connected sufficiently to the mainstream economy where growth occurs' and thus globalization is 'thinning or just plain absent'. Such an approach ignores the possibility that this variegation of zones is a result not of globalizing capitalism's failure or insufficiency, but of its proper and orderly functioning.[3]

Counter to this, Neil Smith, argues that 'uneven development is the hallmark of the geography of capitalism' (1984: xi). This is to say that the variegation of global geography between developed and underdeveloped, core and periphery, is not a result of the incompleteness of globalizing capitalism, but its expected outcome. What is more, underdevelopment in peripheral zones is a necessary counterpart to the development of core zones, as the enrichment of the centre is based on the impoverishment of the edge. This theme is developed extensively both in Marxist geography (Harvey 2001) and in World Systems Theory literature (Wallerstein 1974; Arrighi 1994; Amin 1976). It is from the latter that we get the evocative concept of the 'development of underdevelopment', the idea that underdevelopment is the result not of inadequate globalization – of capitalism's inattention – but rather of its intimate structural workings (Frank 1969).

Though this concept of the development of underdevelopment refers specifically to economic development, it is my contention that this also holds for the question of speed and velocity. By this I mean that just as uneven global development is not the result of the inadequate diffusion of global capitalism, but is an effect and integrated component thereof, uneven global access to mobility, in whatever form, is not the result of a failure to integrate geographic regions into the circulating flows of globalization, but rather a way of controlling the global mobility of certain flows in ways that ensure the functioning of global capitalism. The central thesis is that the extreme velocity and mobility of certain actors and processes in globalization is premised on the forced immobilization of other actors, processes and populations. Thus the INA's map of travel times is also a map of global exclusions and structural inequalities.

Some of these exclusions and immobilizations are questions of infrastructure and access to infrastructure, while others are rooted in legal, social, cultural and political obstacles to movement. We must therefore discuss how certain apparatuses (be they states, international bodies, legal systems, cultural practices, physical infrastructures, technologies or political movements) serve to coordinate the processes of globalizing capitalism. We will develop this understanding in the next section, through a discussion of Deleuze and Guattari's concept of the global capitalist axiomatic. From there we will look at the ways in which global flows are organized according to what I term 'regimes of (im)mobility'. In the final section we will look at reactions to these regimes of (im)mobility, and how the response to the violence and exploitation of globalizing capital is misplaced, and how it frequently and paradoxically serves to bolster them.

The global capitalist axiomatic

One of the presuppositions of neoliberal economics is the fundamental opposition of the political and economic spheres. This enables the call for the removal of political 'obstructions' from the natural functioning of markets. As an example of this neoliberal position, Manfred Steger provides an account of the work of Kenichi Ohmae, who projects 'the rise of a 'borderless world' brought on by the irresistible forces of capitalism' and argues:

> the nation-state is becoming irrelevant in the global economy. Seen from the perspective of real flows of economic activity, Ohmae asserts that nation-states have already lost their role as meaningful units of participation in the global economy. As territorial divisions are becoming increasingly irrelevant to human society, states are less able to determine the direction of social life within their borders.
>
> (Steger 2005: 33)

This separation produces a spatial imagery whereby the political sphere consists of static territories and the economic sphere consists of flows (flows of capital, knowledge, resources, people, etc.). Neoliberal economics thus maps a binary opposition between economics as a productive space of flows and the state as a potential obstruction (an obstruction which is becoming, thankfully, increasingly weak and ineffective).

In contrast to this image of a weakening state structure, in Chapters 1 and 2 we surveyed accounts of the increasing power of the state in the context of globalization (a more unitary executive state, a more violent military state). How are we to reconcile this apparent rise of the state apparatus when the prophets of neoliberalism are already preparing their eulogy for the state's eventual demise? We can, I suppose, seek recourse in the separation of spheres and argue that the state apparatus' growth is restricted to its territorially bound role of supplying security, while in the economic sphere it is still 'vulnerable to the discipline imposed by economic choices made elsewhere' (33).

However, to do this is to ignore the possibility that the growth of the state is *necessary* to globalizing capitalism and that, rather than simply being an obstruction, the state plays a critical role in the production and organization of global flows of money, goods, people and knowledge. In this section I will look at Deleuze and Guattari's theory of the global capitalist axiomatic, as a way to think about how the state functions within globalizing capitalism, specifically as regards the question of regulating speed and mobility. Deleuze and Guattari's account of the emergence of the state and capitalism shows that, rather than being opposed forces, the state was necessary for the emergence of the capitalist axiomatic, and the capitalist axiomatic is dependent upon the state's role as an apparatus of capture.

The state and the deterritorialization of flows

The first problem with the neoliberal mapping of the economic and the political is that it presumes that capitalism and the state belong to different spheres of functioning. It produces a spatial ontology whereby the state-form embodies a static territoriality and capitalism is defined by an ever-expanding space of flows. Such a position deflates the crucial role the state-form played in the decoding and deterritorialization of flows that eventually helped compose and organize capitalism.

For Deleuze and Guattari, all life is flow, and variations in the speed, direction and organization of that flow; flows of desire, energy, power, production, distribution (1983: 1). In the first forms of human political organization, what Deleuze and Guattari term the 'Territorial Machine',[4] particular codes channel these flows into set processes and social organizations (production, distribution, hierarchies of control, etc.). In this case, the coding is primarily territorial, tied to an understanding of the earth. The earth 'is the surface on which the whole process of production is inscribed, on which the forces and means of labor are recorded, and the agents and the products distributed. It appears here as the quasi cause of production and the object of desire' (141).

This conception of the earth as a binding structure, a plane of consistency on which the inscribing socius lays out social organization, produces a different sense of territoriality than that which underpins the state-form. The territoriality of the territorial machine is singular and ontogenetic:

> The people, as part of nature, are intimately linked to the land. To belong to a territory or place is a social concept which requires first and foremost belonging to a societal unity. The land itself is in the possession of the group as a whole. It is not privately partitioned and owned. Moreover, it is alive with the spirits and history of the people, and places on it are sacred.
>
> (Smith 1984: 69)

For the territorial machine, the earth functions not as an empty vessel filled or occupied by human activity. It is a kind of 'immobile motor'. It gives meaning and order to human activity, provides identity and unity to a community; it is a producer and consumer of flows, rather than a stage for their play. Territory is valued not for its size, its quantity, but rather for its quality, its function as a location of history, culture and power. Life cannot be separated from it.

Contrary to this fundamental connection to the earth is the abstract territoriality of the state-form. In the state-form, one resides on a territory, but one is not united with it:

> Far from seeing in the State the principle of a territorialization that would inscribe people according to their residence, we should see in the principle of residence the effect of a movement of deterritorialization that divides the earth as an object and subjects men to the new imperial inscription, to the new full body, to the new socius.
>
> (Deleuze and Guattari 1983: 195)

With the coming of the state-form, people are no longer tied to a particular, singular earth, but rather reside in an empty homogenous space (or at least a space which can be theoretically modelled as homogenous). The earth is stripped of its specificity, and becomes a commodity, potentially interchangeable. This primal moment of deterritorialization produces the condition of possibility for globalizing capital. This foundational moment of separation between humans and the earth unconsciously paves the way for a coming globalization, millennia down the road.

In the territorial machine, codes are local, never global, always particular and singular, never abstract and potentially generalizable. Flows of goods (and hence of labour and energy involved in their production) between groups and individuals exist, but never as capitalist exchange or market (186).[5] Exchange is coded as gift, as debt, as duty, as reciprocity. These exchanges produce a surplus value of code, but they circulate between definite and determined poles. The specific and personal surplus value of these exchanges can never (or was never allowed to) mutate into the abstract surplus value of capital.[6]

With the coming of the state-form, there is a need to break these local webs of debt and exchange, to overcode local codes with a global organization, with the Despot (ruler, sovereign) as the head. This is why the introduction of the state-form brings the introduction of the money-form; partly as a method of simplifying the procuring of taxes, but also as a way of generalizing the concept of debt, of making it transferable and abstract.[7] Indeed, until the bonds of a form of political community premised on particularity, locality and reciprocity are broken, the possibility of the state (as an order of universal rule, as 'sovereignty') is impossible. The abstract overcodings of the state are only possible once the particular codings of the territorial machine are stamped out.

The deterritorialization of flows of people from the plane of the earth is doubled by the freeing of flows of debt (and hence of labour, goods, energy, *capital*) from the local creditor. All these flows are reterritorialized by (on) the state apparatus, overcoded and reinscribed by a new socius. The important point for our purposes is that it is the state-form above all that generates this deterritorialization of flows. It is because of the state apparatus that flows become abstract and generalizable enough to give rise to capitalism.[8]

The capitalist axiomatic

The state apparatus both decodes the flows of the territorial machine and overcodes these flows into a hierarchy of resonance, capture and control. Hence '[e]ach state is a global (not local) integration' (Deleuze and Guattari 1987: 433). The state-form seeks the absolute reterritorialization of flows onto the 'full body of the Despot' as the plane of consistency which orders and drives the social machine (Deleuze and Guattari 1983: 146). The despotic state-form produces a decoding of flows as a way of converting what is a web of intercoded flows of debt, filiation and territoriality, and replacing it with an hierarchical structure where the primary political structure is the singular overcoded relationship of the subject to the sovereign.

However, this process of overcoding and reterritorialization is always incomplete. Decoded flows always escape the state apparatus of capture. Freed of the dense, communal web of relational intercodings present in the territorial machine, the sovereign overcoding can only maintain a tenuous grip on the vast flows of power it unleashes. These flows can pose a threat to the State, even as it is the state apparatus that produces or inaugurates them: 'It is evident that all decoded flows, of whatever kind, are prone to forming a war machine directed against the State' (Deleuze and Guattari 1987: 459). Flows of religious migrants freed from territorially based religions can produce a fervour against the state (i.e. the Knights Templar, or the Fraticelli in medieval Europe). Flows of knowledge and artisans can produce alternative structures of governance in the form of guilds which challenge the authority of the state. Most importantly for our discussion, so can flows of goods and wealth, via early (very early) merchant capitalist structures.[9] The flow of merchant wealth along trade routes tended to be reterritorialized in urban centres, creating internal oppositional structures to the state-form.[10]

Now this might seem to prefigure the neoliberal image of a binary opposition between a static, overcoding state and an amorphous, free-flowing capitalism. However, this is to ignore how the escape of these deterritorialized flows predates capitalism and is present in the very irruption of the state-form. Capitalism proper does not come about until a distinct organization of these flows arises. Thus:

> the pressure of the flows draws capitalism in negative outline, but for it to be realized there must be a whole *integral of decoded flows*, a whole *generalized conjunction* that overspills and overturns the preceding apparatus.
> (Deleuze and Guattari 1987: 452)

The basic principle here is one that Fernand Braudel developed earlier, and which Deleuze and Guattari draw upon: that there were capitalist formations predating the arrival of capitalism, in the form of market exchange and trade processes. As Braudel puts it,

Far in advance, there were signs announcing the coming of capitalism: the rise of the towns and of trade, the emergence of a labour market, the increasing density of society, the spread of the use of money, the rise in output, the expansion of long-distance trade or to put it another way the international market.

(Braudel 1992: 620)

These early flows were the result of the deterritorializing movements of the state machine. However, these flows were not, in themselves, constitutive of the capitalist system. As a result, Giovanni Arrighi notes that 'the really important transition that needs to be elucidated is not that from feudalism to capitalism but from scattered to concentrated capitalist power' (1994: 11). This transition only occurred after a series of structural changes transformed these scattered capitalist processes into a general, dominant order of production. Say Deleuze and Guattari,

> capitalism doesn't begin, the capitalist machine is not assembled, until capital directly appropriates production, and until financial capital and merchant capital are no longer anything but specific functions corresponding to a division of labor in the capitalist mode of production in general.
>
> (Deleuze and Guattari 1983: 226)

For capitalism – as a dominant social formation rather than an anomalous or local activity – to come into being something else is necessary. For this proto-capitalist activity to percolate into a broader social formation, it is necessary for blocks of antiproduction and organization to come into play, blocks which can discipline these flows and make them 'productive'. (Productive here in the sense of a universal and generalized process of integrated value production, rather than the individual and singular flows of value and capital which merchant capitalism produces.)[11] It is not enough that the flows are decoded. Indeed, as we saw in Chapter 3, an unrestricted deterritorialization of flows can be disastrous for the capitalist axiomatic. Having been deterritorialized, these flows must then be reterritorialized on the full body of capital. The flows must be disciplined, channelled, differentiated and conjoined. The state apparatus, functioning as an apparatus of capture, is very adept at this organization of flows. In Giovanni Arrighi's discussion of the emergence of capitalism, he describes Braudel's account, saying:

> The conventional view in the social sciences, in political discourse, and in the mass media is that capitalism and the market economy are more or less the same thing, and that state power is antithetical to both. Braudel, in contrast, sees capitalism as being absolutely dependent for its emergence and expansion on state power and as constituting the antithesis of the market economy.
>
> (Arrighi 1994: 10)

This is because the state and capitalism both have a vested interest in the control and discipline of decoded flows which a market economy unleashes.

However, whereas the state attempts to overcode them, disciplining them and robbing them of much of their energy and power, capitalism as a mode of production allows these flows to remain decoded and (relatively) deterritorialized, organized via a more supple *axiomatic*. Capitalism, counter to the state, 'substitutes for the codes an extremely rigorous axiomatic that maintains the energy of the flows in a bound state on the body of capital as a socius that is deterritorialized' (Deleuze and Guattari 1983: 246). We discussed this in Chapter 3 in the account of the capitalist axiomatic as an abstract form of social domination, opposed to the concrete social domination of the state-form's sovereign overcoding.

Here, however, we can go further. Despite this distinction between forms of social domination, the axiomatic is not opposed to the state apparatus. Rather, the state apparatus is a crucial part of the capitalist axiomatic (or here we might more accurately say the capitalist assemblage): 'Thus the States, in capitalism, are not cancelled out but change form and take on a new meaning: models of realization for a worldwide axiomatic that exceeds them. But to exceed is not at all the same thing as doing without' (Deleuze and Guattari 1987: 454). Deleuze and Guattari go on to say:

> The state was first this abstract unity that integrated subaggregates functioning separately; it is now subordinated to a field of forces whose flows it co-ordinates and whose autonomous relations of domination and subordination it expresses. It is no longer content to overcode maintained and imbricated territorialities; it must constitute, invent codes for the decoded flows of money, commodities, and private property. It no longer of itself forms a ruling class or classes; it is itself formed by these classes, which have become independent and delegate it to serve their power and their contradictions, their struggles and their compromises with the dominated classes. It is no longer the transcendent law that governs garments; it must fashion as best it can a whole to which it will render its law immanent.
>
> (Deleuze and Guattari 1987: 221)

Within a capitalist state (which is to say a state where the dominant social formation is capitalism), the state performs multiple services to the capitalist axiomatic. Of course it provides a disciplinary apparatus to tame potentially intransigent parts of the population (a concrete social domination to back up an abstract social domination). However, this apparatus – the state's police, army, welfare, bureaucracy – also serves as a node of antiproduction, to absorb and mediate the threat of the crisis of overproduction (Amin 1976: 180–1). It's important to note, however, before we replicate the neoliberal division of categories (capitalism as production, state as antiproduction), that '[t]he apparatus of antiproduction is no longer a transcendent instance that opposes production, limits it, or checks it; on the contrary, it insinuates itself everywhere in the productive machine and becomes firmly wedded to it in order to regulate its productivity and realize surplus value' (Deleuze and Guattari 1983: 235). Just as we saw in Chapter 3 that the deployment of restrictive practices was not a failure of market forces, but a crucial element in their reproduction, so here the state as producer of blocks of antiproduction is not an inhibitor of the capitalist axiomatic, but a crucial element within the assemblage that makes capitalism a viable social formation. It mediates, moderates, disciplines and channels flows in ways which tame the wild speed of diverse and conflicting capitalist practices, making a capital*ism* possible.

What is more, we shall shortly see that this mutual imbrication of state apparatus and capitalist axiomatic holds even at the global level, where a global capitalist axiomatic is again not hindered by states, but works in assemblage with them.

The global capitalist axiomatic

At this point the theory of the capitalist axiomatic, and its interactions with the state apparatus, may seem akin to Marx's conception of the state as the 'committee for managing the common affairs of the whole bourgeoisie' (Marx 2000: 247). And in some situations it is. But it exceeds it in others, since, as we will see, the capitalist axiomatic is capable of incorporating state apparatuses housing non- and extra-capitalist modes of production, and hence incorporating non-bourgeois social formations.[12] Indeed, the power of the capitalist axiomatic is that it is able to modulate and mould its functioning to the particular environment and milieu it finds itself in. (Hence our discussion of the multiplicity of capitalisms in Chapter 3.) The axiomatic is able to develop particular axioms for each state apparatus, mode of production or social formation which it seeks to integrate into capitalist production. This is the flexible power that the axiomatic holds over the sovereign form of overcoding. Furthermore, it is this ability to proliferate axioms that allows us to take account of the global capitalist axiomatic to supplement our discussion of the capitalist axiomatic from Chapter 3. For we see how Deleuze and Guattari are able to develop a conceptual language to describe the integration of even non- and semi-capitalist territories into the global capitalist axiomatic.

The deterritorialization of flows marks capitalism with an inherent exteriority; an attempt to overcome boundaries and encompass more territory. We discussed this primarily in relation to temporality in Chapter 3, but it holds just as much in spatial considerations. Thus the decoding and reterritorialization of flows via the capitalist axiomatic at the local or state level extends its reach, eventually producing a *global* capitalist axiomatic. The construction of a global capitalist axiomatic is premised on the attempt to reterritorialize deterritorialized flows at the global level, integrating more and more territory into its assemblage, even territory not fully bound up in capitalist social formations. This means that 'the process of deterritorialization goes from the center to the periphery, that is, from the developed countries to the underdeveloped countries, which do not constitute a separate world, but rather an essential component of the world-wide capitalist machine' (Deleuze and Guattari 1983: 231).

This projection of capitalist relations to encompass the globe should not, however, be confused with neoliberalism's account of making the world flat. For reasons that will be developed further on pp. 131–146, such a homogeneity would be disastrous for a global capitalism that relies on a system of uneven development (in the same way that, as we saw in Chapter 3, a runaway innovation would be catastrophic for capitalism). Instead, the capitalist axiomatic modulates itself, or rather develops additional axioms, to integrate different forms and levels of capitalist production – and even non- and extra-capitalist state-economic formation – into global capitalist production without necessarily transforming them into 'capitalist states' or ensuring their eventual progress to a first world level of 'development'. This concept of the global capitalist axiomatic challenges the idea (whether lauded or criticized) that capitalism is a purely homogenizing force. Says Samir Amin, 'The world capitalist system is not homogenous; ... it cannot be seen as the capitalist mode of production on a world scale' (Amin 1976: 147). (Thus, to the multiplicity of capitalisms that we saw in Chapter 3, we can now add a continuum of levels of capitalist development, as well as a multiplicity of non-capitalist assemblages that can be functionally integrated into global capitalist production.)

It is true, say Deleuze and Guattari, that, within the core, 'developed' areas there tends to be a certain isomorphy between states. However, even here 'it would be wrong to confuse isomorphy with homogeneity. For one thing, isomorphy allows, and even incites, a great heterogeneity among states' (Deleuze and Guattari 1987: 436). Thus, as we saw in Chapter 3, there can be an axiom for the evangelical, corporate-cowboy capitalist state of contemporary America, another axiom for Scandinavian social democratic capitalism, another for the quasi-authoritarian 'Confucian' capitalist state of Singapore; all of them participating in the web of global flows and global production.

This multiplicity of political-economic assemblages becomes even more diverse as we begin to move out of the core of developed countries. The global capitalist axiomatic, because of its supple and diverse axiomatizing of flows, is able to produce and organize a global division of labour, which incorporates states of countless different compositions. Thus the global capitalist axiomatic

> tolerates, in fact it requires, a certain peripheral polymorphy ... this explains the existence, at the periphery, of heteromorphic social formations, *which certainly do not constitute vestiges or transitional forms* since they realize an ultramodern capitalist production (oil, mines, plantations, industrial equipment, steel, chemistry), but which are nonetheless precapitalist, or extracapitalist, owing to other aspects of their production and to the forced inadequacy of their domestic market in relation to the world market. When international organization becomes the capitalist axiomatic,

it continues to imply a heterogeneity of social formations, it gives rise to
and organizes its 'Third World'.

(Deleuze and Guattari 1987: 436–7)

The capitalist system can have extensive, productive contact with non-capitalist
economies without thereby needing to transform them into capitalist social
formations, and with 'underdeveloped' states without thereby needing to develop
them. Or, rather, the capitalist axiomatic can produce axioms to integrate non-
and semi-capitalist formations, extracting surplus value from them without
including them in the isomorphy of the core countries. Indeed, in many cases
it is essential that these states do not reach the same level of capitalist development, for then they would not be of use as a source of unequal exchange
(Amin 1976: ch. 3). This is the dark side of the ability of the capitalist axiomatic to enter into assemblage with non-capitalist formations. In Chapter 3, we
saw how the development of non-capitalist economic formations can challenge,
and force changes in, the capitalist axiomatic. Here, we can also see that the
axiomatic can force, or forestall, changes in a non-capitalist social formation
for its own benefit, and to the detriment of the formation in question.

This challenges the geographization of history which we saw in the first
section (as is only right of Deleuzo-Guattarian theory, which works very hard
to keep history and geography in their respective places). Rather than seeing
zones of 'underdevelopment' as temporal lags in a global trajectory of globalizing capitalism, we see a geographic struggle between core and peripheral
countries, mutually constituting each other. The 'isolation' and 'non-integration'
of peripheral zones into the capitalist globalization is, in many ways, illusory.
These peripheral zones are perfectly well integrated into the global capitalist
system, in the sense of fulfilling the function of either producing or receiving
flows of capital (Harvey 2001). The axiomatic simply does not require these
zones to be fully 'developed'. Indeed, it specifically rejects this end result. As Neil
Smith puts it, '[c]apital has no choice whether to expand into pre-capitalist
societies, but it does have a "choice" about how it does this' (1984: 140–1).

The rise, fall and rise of the state

Contrary, then, to the neoliberal image of a state in conflict with the flows
and passages of capitalism, the global capitalist axiomatic imagines the state
(whatever kind of state) as fundamentally folded in to processes of global
capitalist production. Describing the development of the global capitalist
axiomatic, Deleuze and Guattari state that '[n]ever before has a State lost so
much of its power in order to enter with so much force into the service of the
signs of economic power' (1983: 252). Notice the dual articulation of that
sentence. At the same time as the state gives up its power in relation to the
capitalist axiomatic, it gains a new force in its service. This is to say that,
contrary to the narrative (alternately lauded by proponents and disparaged
by critics) of neoliberal economics that the state is shrinking in the face of

globalization (or should, or will), the state gains more power as an axiom of capitalism than it had as an apparatus of overcoding. The image of a minimal state retreating in the face of globalizing capitalism is a myth. The state has always played a role in organizing the flows of capitalism. The world of 'Globalization 3.0' is no different:

> And capitalism, despite what is said to the contrary, assumed this role very early, in fact from the start, from its gestation in forms still semifeudal or monarchic – from the standpoint of the flow of 'free' workers: the control of manual labor and of wages; from the standpoint of the flow of industrial and commercial production: the granting of monopolies, favorable conditions for accumulation, and the struggle against overproduction. There has never been a liberal capitalism.
>
> (Deleuze and Guattari 1983: 252–3)

This provides the answer to the paradox, noted by many commentators on globalization, that as the power of the state seems to weaken in relation to the global economy, 'the *intervention* of state authority and of the agencies of the state in the daily lives of the citizen appears to be growing' (Strange 2000: 4). This is because 'capitalism makes use of the [state] for affecting its reterritorializations' (Deleuze and Guattari 1983: 262). (This relationship once again displays the dual articulation of the capitalist axiomatic as apparatus of capture and machine of deterritorialization.)[13]

It is in this role as, we might say, a very broad sort of restrictive practice that the capitalist axiomatic needs and authorizes the state apparatus to modify, discipline and police its proliferating flows. We thus do not see the decline of the state as those in the neoliberal crowd claim; we instead see a shift in the power with which the state may act internally. Saskia Sassen advances the idea that with the globalization of the economy the functioning of the state apparatus in even democratic countries is becoming more centralized, hierarchical and potentially repressive:

> My hypothesis was that state participation in the work of implementing the global economy would redistribute power inside the state, increasing the weight of certain components of the government, notably the Treasury, the Federal Reserve, and finance-related specialized regulatory agencies. The ascendance of these agencies within the government was particularly due to the higher level of strategic importance and complexity of their tasks in a global economy. For the same reasons such shifts took place in a growing number of countries as they globalized their economies ... the increased complexity and technicality of the economy, whether national or global is a key factor in the internal state redistribution of power. Oversight functions increasingly shift out of congress and into specialized government agencies and private sector.
>
> (Sassen 2006: 171)

Notice how this dovetails with the discussion of executive governance in Chapter 1. The acceleration of global capitalism requires an increase in executive authority to police and organize global flows, while the anxiety such acceleration of flows produces on behalf of national populations inflates further the call for stronger executive authority. This resonance (between the requirement of accelerating global flows and reactions to them) will be considered in the last section.

We now have a more complex map of state/economy processes. Rather than assessing activity in terms of an ideal model of state/economy separation, we have a unified space of flows, organized, mediated and disciplined by a supple axiomatic, articulated through state apparatuses.

Regimes of (im)mobility

This account of the global capitalist axiomatic and its interaction with the state-form provides a starting point for our investigation into speed and velocity in the context of globalizing capitalism. It does away with the binary opposition, presented in dominant accounts of speed and globalization, which maps mobile capital flows as in conflict with the static state-form (regardless of whether this stasis of the state is viewed as an obstacle to the efficient functioning of capitalism, as in neoliberal accounts, or as a crucial bulwark against the cruelties and contingencies of capital flows, as in some anti-globalist accounts). We must understand that the global capitalist axiomatic is not premised on a homogenous, uninterrupted, 'flat' space of universally accelerating flows of people, information, capital, resources, etc. Rather, the global capitalist axiomatic only comes into being through a particular process of mediating, moderating, conjoining, disciplining and suppressing flows. The global capitalist axiomatic too must act as both a deterritorializing machine and an apparatus of capture. The state-form (as well as numerous other legal, social, cultural, economic and physical formations) can provide a very useful apparatus with which to form an assemblage, as a way of achieving this coordination of flows.

The goal of this section, then, will be to trace these apparatuses and assemblages; the techniques, structures, agents, formations, objects and subjects which serve to organize and discipline the flows deterritorialized by the global capitalist axiomatic. The concept that I wish to introduce to investigate these assemblages is the regime of (im)mobility. 'Regimes of (im)mobility' refers to the sites and apparatuses throughout the world that regulate, focus, reduce or moderate global flows. In some cases this involves clearing pathways to encourage the acceleration of certain flows (capital, skilled labour, resources); in other cases it means blocking or slowing down other flows (labour markets, migrant flows, black market goods). What's important is that, under this analysis, both mobilization and immobilization belong to the same set of regimes of global production.

The notion of a regime of (im)mobility is suggested by Deleuze in his 'Postscript on Control Societies'. In this essay, Deleuze notes a shift from the 'disciplinary societies' described by Foucault, where power is exerted on a model of interiority, through the disciplining of diverse flows in various static spaces, to a 'control society', which is based on mobile, flexible mediations of flows. In the control society, power is exerted like a '*modulation*, like a self-transmuting molding continually changing from one moment to the next, or like a sieve whose mesh varies from one point to another' (Deleuze 1995: 178–9). That the control society shifts the emphasis from interior disciplinary spaces to exterior modulation of flows does not, however, mean that it is somehow freer:

> We don't have to stray into science fiction to find a control mechanism that can fix the position of any element at any given moment – an animal in a game reserve, a man in a business (electronic tagging). Felix Guattari has imagined a town where anyone can leave their flat, their street, their neighborhood, using their (individual) electronic card that opens this or that barrier; but the card may also be rejected on a particular day, or between certain times of day; it doesn't depend on the barrier but on the computer that is making sure everyone is in a permissible place, and effecting a universal modulation.
>
> (Deleuze 1995: 181–2)

A regime of (im)mobility is this system of variable barriers at the global (and local) level; a complex system of customs and immigration regimes, state economic policies (interest rates, tariffs), political definitions, social movements, physical infrastructures, informational infrastructures, transnational economic collaborations, and cultural and linguistic systems, which mobilize some flows and immobilize others, helping some to accelerate while slowing others to a trickle. Regimes of (im)mobility also serve to delimit the spaces and channels through which flows can travel, using legal technologies, but also economic checks on access, as well as cultural and social pressures which determine spaces of possibility (for example, immigration flows, both legal and illegal, may occur but, through social and cultural processes of delegitimation, are limited in the spaces they can inhabit and the resources they can access). This section aims to map out these regimes of (im)mobility as a way of tracing some of the conjunctions of flows which inscribe global capitalist production. This will not be an exhaustive account of the global economy and its local and national instantiations. Indeed, the very point of the concept of the global capitalist axiomatic is that there are countless actual and potential variations within global capitalism. The goal is simply to draw some broad outlines, while giving concrete examples, that show the way in which global capitalism depends on regimes of (im)mobility.

The typographical encasement of the 'im' in (im)mobility serves two crucial purposes. The first is to indicate that regimes of (im)mobility function reciprocally. This is to say that a regime of (im)mobility functions by creating differential velocities. Every mobility in global capitalism is defined against a relative immobility elsewhere. This returns to my criticism of neoliberalism, that the inequalities of global mobility are not the result of inadequate integration of 'underdeveloped' zones into a universal mobility. Rather, globalizing capitalism is founded on differentials of mobility. The immobilization of agents and flows, the constraint and control of movement, is necessary and is the only way in which velocity comes to make sense. Hence 'regimes of (im)mobility'. They are always multiple.

The second meaning of the 'im' is more complex, and speaks to the way in which the nature and valence of mobility changes with the emergence of a control society and global production. This is because mobility is no longer automatically identified with freedom, if it ever was entirely. In this new world, control and exploitation can be fostered through movement and flow as much as through capture and stasis. Thus '(im)mobility' implies not just a structural reciprocity between mobility and immobility, but also the development of a zone of indiscernibility between the two; the way in which mobility and immobility have begun to resemble one another in key ways.

This indeterminacy travels in two directions. First of all, there is increasingly a form of mobility which does not really move. On the one hand, we will recount tales of forced migrations, refugees, immigrants, legal and illegal, who, though they might be mobile, have little control, freedom or voice in their movement. They are trapped just as surely as those who are immobilized within a national border or even a jail cell. On the other hand, there is a form of elite travel that produces a corporate monoculture, a worldwide infrastructure of similarly configured global cities, hotels, conference centres and restaurants which isolates jet-setters from experiencing anything new or different. Hence Smith notes that '[t]he equalization of geographical differences and the shrinking of world space emerge together; the more accessible foreign parts become, the more similar they seem to home' (1984: 117). Globalizing capital is marked with flows where the movers go nowhere. This is perhaps the great innovation of capitalism. Frantic movement that goes nowhere, effort expended only to end up where you began. (The geographic equivalent of the acceleration of inertia.)

Second, we see how this indeterminacy of the mobility/immobility dyad affects the traditionally assumed stability of immobility. Zygmunt Bauman notes the odd state of affairs in which

> [t]he idea of the 'state of rest', of immobility, makes sense only in a world that stays still or could be taken for such; in a place with solid walls, fixed roads and signposts steady enough to have time to rust. One cannot 'stay put' in moving sands. Neither can one stay put in this late-modern or postmodern world of ours – a world with reference points set on wheels and known for their vexing habit of vanishing from view before the instruction they offer has been read out in full, pondered and acted upon.
>
> (Bauman 1998: 78)

This mobility of immobility again cuts in two directions. On the one hand you have those who are so wealthy, so powerful, so 'networked' they never have to move. The earth travels around them.[14] On the other, you have those who, though they might wish to remain immobile, to retain some sort of static certainty over their lives, cannot do so in late-modernity. New cultural formations are brought forcefully into their world, economic decisions made far away can make their local position in production incredibly profitable or completely obsolete. They simply do not have the option of remaining immobile in this world.

Capital mobility

In tracing the global regimes of (im)mobility which parcel out velocity and access to various agents and flows on the world stage, we begin with the 'fastest' and work our way to the most immobile (remembering, as we do, that the velocity of each actor always exists only in comparison to a reciprocal actor). In the contemporary global economy, we begin with capital itself.

It is one of the great ironies that capitalism, which is said to replace the transcendent attachments of the past with cold material relations, produces something as ethereal and amorphous as capital itself. As we saw in the earlier section, capitalism is defined by freeing a flow of surplus value as capital. It is in the nature of capital to flow, to be mobile, to be 'fast'. In his book *The Magic of the State*, Michael Taussig compares the functioning of money with spirit possession (1997: ch. 13). And in essence, this is the Marxist analysis of capitalism: what is the formula M-C-M' but the symbolic representation of capital's fleeting interaction with production; its momentary possession of materiality before once more being freed, returning to a life that is fundamentally immaterial – capital as 'value-in-process'?

Though diagrammatically this has been true since the early days of capitalism, in practice materiality has always been quite a bit stickier. Historically, production required a dense, rooted infrastructure of land, physically located resources, and variegated and intransigent labour markets. Additionally, capital's movements were hampered by national borders and exclusionary trade regimes, not to mention diseconomies of distance rooted in inefficient transportation and communication technologies. Indeed, even as money, capital was never pure flow, tied as it was to physical currency bound – at least notionally – to precious metal stores.

It is in the era of globalization, with the development of new information and communication technologies, as well as attendant economic, legal and informational structures, that we see the possibility for capital to shift towards a pole of 'pure' flow. The most dramatic example of this immateriality is in currency markets. Saskia Sassen gives us the stunning statistic that 'the average daily turnover in foreign exchange in 2004 [was] $1.8 trillion, equal to almost one-fifth of the total annual value of world trade in 2003' (2006: 250) – $1.8 trillion in transactions and nearly all of it happening virtually, with nothing produced, no service rendered and no good moved, except some electrons in a global infrastructure of fibre-optic cables and computer terminals.

And when this liberated capital does step down from the heights of pure speculation to participate in material production, it now finds a much more fluid and flexible materiality to imbue. With new transportation and communication technologies, the diseconomies of distance are no longer as constraining, and capital is free to travel the globe searching for new opportunities (enhanced by the diminishment of trade barriers). Hence the dramatic rise of foreign direct investment, multinational corporations and the 'New International Division of Labour'.

It is this freedom of capital to participate in global production that leads commentators to declare that 'the world is flat' and that 'the playing field has been leveled' (Friedman 2006: 7). However, we must understand that *this is only from the perspective of capital*. The playing field is levelled *for capital*. The world is flat *for capital*. And this is the starting point of one of the most fundamental regimes of (im)mobility, for, since regimes of (im)mobility are relational, this mobility of capital is necessarily premised on the immobility of something else.

It is said that in globalizing capitalism 'place doesn't matter'. This is close to being true, but misses the point in a crucial way. In the new global economy '*space* doesn't matter' in the sense that new transportation and communication technologies reduce travel costs to the point where distances can increasingly be factored out of cost calculations. However, *place* still matters very much, for if it didn't, this ability to surmount the space between places would be irrelevant. This fact lies at the heart of this regime of (im)mobility. The mobility of capital, its ability to ignore space, is only meaningful in the context of differentiated localities, and differential capacities for producing surplus value. Says Harvey,

> [t]he general diminution in transport costs in no way disrupts the significance of territorial division and specialization of labor. Indeed, it makes for more fine-grained territorial division since small differences in production costs (due to raw materials, labor conditions, intermediate inputs, consumer markets, infrastructural or taxation arrangements) are more easily exploitable by highly mobile capital. Reducing the friction of distance, in short, makes capital *more* rather than *less* sensitive to local geographical variations.
>
> (Harvey 2006b: 101; emphasis added)

The most obvious example of this attentiveness to territoriality is in relation to immobile natural resource deposits. The decrease in transportation costs makes resource extraction more efficient. However, it also amplifies the ability of mobile capital to take advantage of different territorially bound labour markets – to exploit 'human' resource deposits, as it were. And whereas the advantage of different natural resource deposits might be greater yield or higher quality, the advantage of different 'human' resource deposits is specific skills and cheaper labour.

Access to diverse labour pools has been a critical drive in globalizing capital (Amin 1976: ch. 3):

> An outsourcing company coined the term *labor arbitrage* to mean 'the ability to pay one labor pool less than another labor pool for accomplishing the same work, typically by substituting labor in one geography for labor in a different locale. The outsourcing industry is now applying labor arbitrage widely; it is transitioning from a novel approach to a competitive requirement'.
>
> (Ong 2006: 161)

The crucial element in 'labour arbitrage' is that labour markets remain variegated, which is to say that they remain territorially bound and differentiated, in the face of capital mobility and globalized production. If they didn't there would be nothing to exploit through capital mobility. This is where the regime of (im)mobility takes full effect. For capital mobility to be meaningful, labour pools must be immobile. In short, human resources must be as immobile and territorially bound as natural resources. We can thus parse any political, legal, social and cultural apparatuses which seek to fix populations territorially as integrated into this regime of (im)mobility, since they create pockets of human resources to be extracted by capital. Such apparatuses can be externally directed, as in 'first world' immigration regimes which seek to repulse, or at least discipline, incoming 'third world' immigrants, keeping them locked in cheap 'developing' labour pools. (It is only meaningful for GM to be able to move all of its plants to Mexico if Mexicans are unable to come up to America in search of better paying jobs.) These apparatuses can also be directed inwardly, to discipline an internal labour market, inhibiting workers' ability to escape to (or demand) greener pastures (thus the suppression of labour organizing, lobbying for improved labour regulations, etc.). Here we might return to our earlier discussion of the role of the state apparatus within the global capitalist axiomatic. We see how, without the state's borders to police and suppress certain flows, the global capitalist axiomatic would be submerged under a disorderly, discordant tidal wave of deterritorialized flows (similar to how, in Chapter 3, restrictive practices were necessary to suppress the full force of the 'perennial gale of creative destruction').

Zygmunt Bauman lays out this regime of (im)mobility by discussing the equivocation in neoliberal discourse around the apparently laudatory term 'flexibility', depending on whether it refers to capital or labour. Whereas flexibility of capital 'means freedom to move wherever greener pastures beckon' (Bauman 1998: 105), the flexibility of labour means being 'more pliant and compliant, easy to knead and mold, to slice and roll, and putting up no resistance whatever is being done to it' (104). Thus for labour to be 'flexible in the eyes of the investors ... the "suppliers of labour" must be as rigid and *inflexible* as possible – indeed, the very contrary of "flexible": their freedom to choose, to accept or refuse, let alone to impose their own rules on the game, must be cut to the bone' (105). Labour must simply wait, like a subterranean vein of ore, to be mined and used in production.

The dichotomy of capital mobility/labour immobility provides the simplest and most elemental regime of (im)mobility. It might be useful to look at how this dichotomy is concretized in a particular legal and political technology, that of the export processing zone (EPZ).

EPZs (or free trade zones, FTZs) are areas within a country's territory organized around production facilities dedicated to export commodities primarily funded through foreign direct investment. As such, in these areas, checks on foreign capital which might be in effect in the rest of a country (tariffs, limits on capital withdrawal, etc.) are diminished, if not eliminated entirely:

> The EPZ is a combination of old customs areas and export-oriented manufacturing. Thus EPZs combine tax-free holidays with other incentives for foreign investors to set up factories that produce export goods, train low-skill workers, and facilitate technology transfer. The EPZ strategy succeeded export-substitution industrialization in developing countries, driven by the pursuit of foreign exchange earnings.
>
> (Ong 2006: 103)

In short, they are parts of a country's territory that foreign capital can enter, occupy and leave as if they weren't.

There are thousands of EPZs functioning in over a hundred countries worldwide. What is important for our understanding is not how these EPZs make national borders more permeable to foreign capital. If anything, these EPZs can be seen simply as vanguards, small samples of what all economic relations will some day look like. What is important is how the borders of EPZs remain sealed to population movement, limiting the space in which citizens can freely move. Aihwa Ong provides an excellent account of how Chinese EPZs, the 'special economic zones' (SEZs), were set up. Areas such as Shenzen, Zhuhai, Shantou, Xiamen and Hainan Island (105), amongst others, ended up becoming, for the workers and inhabitants, a separate nation, where they were often subject to harsher treatment than they would experience in rest of the country (in addition to the greater isolation and decreased mobility). She notes: 'Not only are migrant workers exposed to the full force of market conditions; they are discriminated against by zone authorities as if they were foreigners. Migrants must obtain a border pass, a work permit, and a temporary resident pass to work in the SEZs' (106). Additionally, zone workers 'are systematically ignored by unionized workers in the rest of china' (106). The Chinese SEZs thus function as legal-territorial modellings of the dominant regime of (im)mobility. They create territorial boundaries which are permeable to capital but impermeable to workers (even when they are citizens of the territory they inscribe). This is exactly the kind of mechanism Deleuze describes as part of the control society. SEZs (and other EPZs) create striated and variegated spaces for the human population, while creating an ever-expanding smooth space of capital. This complex-ification of the previously binary function of borders is part of what Aihwa Ong terms 'graduated sovereignty':

> I thus use the term *graduated sovereignty* to refer to the effects of a flexible management of sovereignty, as governments adjust political space to the dictates of global capital, giving corporations an indirect power over the political conditions of citizens in zones that are differently articulated to global production and financial circuits ... In short, 'graduated sover-eignty' is an effect of states moving from being administrators of a watertight national entity to regulators of diverse spaces and populations that link with global markets.
>
> (Ong 2006: 78)

The shift from sovereignty and a disciplinary society is marked by an increased differentiation of binary and static logics of territoriality. Borders become sub-ject to diverse regimes of (im)mobility, permeable or impermeable depending on the agent or flow. Thus we see how the state apparatus artfully articulates its borders to better produce the necessary axiomatic organization of flows.

Capitalist mobility

The transnational capitalist class

This dichotomy of capital mobility/labour immobility describes the function-ing of regimes of (im)mobility at the most general or abstract level. The example of the Chinese SEZs provides a more specific, and intricately articu-lated, example of this regime. In this section and the next we will look at lower-order regimes of differentiation and articulation.

I will begin with those agents which mediate between mobile capital and immobile labour, the actors and institutions which service, mediate, organize and discipline globalizing capitalism: the transnational capitalist class (TCC) (Sklair 2004: 43). The TCC is of course not a wholly unitary or homogenous group. It constitutes a broad continuum of wealth, power and, most impor-tantly, mobility. On the upper end of the spectrum we have the so-called 'Global Billionaires' (and their slightly less wealthy compatriots), controlling empires spanning multiple countries (45). On the lower end we have what John Friedmann refers to as the 'Technocratic Elite':

> They are found in business, government and international organizations. They are highly educated possessing specialized professional skills, and

some are paid extremely well. Many are economists, accountants, lawyers, engineers, architects and information specialists. Their chief characteristic, however, is a willingness to serve the interest of transnational capital in its global expansion, putting national interests second. They are a highly mobile, polyglot group capable of working under pressure in fluid situations.

(John Friedmann 1982: 318)

The technocratic elite have relatively less control over their mobility than the global executives. All the same, they have access to a mobility unparalleled in history.

The question of mobility at the global level is frequently a question of legitimacy, of who has the legitimate right to transcend certain borders. In principle, the inception of the modern state produced an established regime of legitimate mobility based on citizenship and bounded by territory. One was either a citizen of a territory, and hence legitimately mobile within it, or not (that travellers, tourists, immigrants, 'non-resident' aliens and a host of other non-citizens might be given limited permission to travel within a territory does not change this fact, since their legitimacy was derived from the distinction of citizen/foreigner, bestowed by a sovereign centre). However, with the transition from sovereign, disciplinary society into the global capitalist axiomatic, with its flexible regimes of 'graduated sovereignty', we also see a shift in the regime of legitimacy to a system of 'graduated citizenship' (Ong 2006: 78). Under a system of 'graduated citizenship' the right to legitimate mobility is increasingly determined by one's status in the systems of global production. In many countries, foreign members of the TCC are treated better than foreigners of a lower class.[15] As an example of graduated citizenship, Aiwha Ong describes the system of immigrant classification in Singapore:

> The instrument is the employment pass system, which grades skilled foreigners according to an intricate three-tier system of employment passes. The top criteria are professional qualifications, university degrees, and specialist skills; professionals, administrators, entrepreneurs, and investors are most highly valued. Foreigners are also graded in terms of their basic monthly salaries. The expatriate (a term applied to all white-collar and skilled foreign workers) can obtain permanent residency easily, depending on a point system measured according to skill and income.
>
> (Ong 2006: 186)

At the same time:

> Low-skilled foreigners are also desperately needed, but they are subject to rigorous control. A work permit system is used for low-skilled migrant workers from Southeast Asia, who are brought in on two year contracts. Needed in construction, manufacturing, services, and domestic work,

> migrant workers cannot change jobs and have absolutely no chance to
> become permanent residents.
>
> (Ong 2006: 186)

The status of foreigner is no longer the opposite of the citizen. Rather, it is a continuum of desirability, marking different types of actors with different degrees of legitimacy and mobility. Such a differentiation of the class of 'foreigner' operates in nearly every country engaged in global production.

What is remarkable about this new regime of graduate citizenship is that these striations of legitimate mobility mark not just foreigners, but *citizens as well*:

> Segments of the population are differently disciplined and given differ-
> ential privileges and protections in relation to their varying participation
> in globalized market activities. These gradations of governing ... may
> be in a continuum, but their effects are to fragment citizenship for sub-
> jects who are all nominally speaking citizens of the same country. The
> elites are showered with economic, social, and political benefits, while
> others are abandoned and deprived of basic survival needs.
>
> (Ong 2006: 87–8)

Of course, wealth has always brought with it privilege. What is important here is the new terms, sites and modes of privilege. Legitimate mobility is being ascribed not on the basis of location within territory (i.e. citizen versus foreign) but on the basis of role within global production (i.e. the TCC versus the global proletariat). Thus workers within an EPZ must possess a 'border pass, a work permit, and a temporary resident pass', despite being citizens of that country, while the foreign professional can 'obtain permanent residency easily'.

The citadel and the ghetto

However, the regimes of (im)mobility which govern the mobility of the transnational capitalist class are not just enacted at territorial borders of states (or the administrative borders of EPZs). Nor, for that matter, are they solely articulated through state designations of legitimacy. Regimes of (im) mobility function at multiple different locations and scales and are just as likely to function through social, cultural and infrastructural mechanisms as they are through legal and administrative typologies. An investigation of the 'global city' can provide us with a new perspective on the ways in which regimes of (im)mobility mediate flows at both the global and the local level (and, indeed, complicate the seemingly easy distinction between the two).

Global cities (or world cities) are cities which, in the words of John Friedmann, 'articulate regional, national and international economies into a global economy. They serve as organizing nodes of a global economic system'

(1995: 25).[16] Global cities serve as fixed points in the amorphous infrastructure of global mobility, frequently providing the site of major ports, airport hubs, train lines, etc. This status as a hub of transportation, a point of articulation in a global network of mobility, is important to global actors and organizations. They also serve as centres for business and technological development, and thus the city becomes a point of articulation in a global network of production:

> Spatially fixed and immobile physical infrastructures of transport and communications systems (ports, airports, transport systems) are required in order to liberate other forms of capital and labor for easy spatial movement. Transport investments get drawn towards major centers of production, finance and commerce because that is where they are likely to be most profitable.
>
> (Harvey 2006b: 101)

This dual articulation of global cities as sites of global mobility and global production then results in a tertiary formation, as these cities become home to the transnational capitalist class, who then require places to live, work and be entertained. Global cities become cultural centres, a home for the arts, sites of excitement and Meccas of 'all that money can buy' (Friedmann 1982: 319).

Now, cities have always been centres of wealth and the pleasures that wealth can bring. And they have often been located within a web of global travel.[17] The global city is a novel formation insofar as it is *primarily* a global formation, which is to say that its organization is oriented towards the requirements of global production, even more than the interests or concerns of national, regional or local production. The global city functions as an axiom which harmonizes local production with global production.[18] Warren Magnusson describes the global city as shaped not by the 'Newtonian' space of the sovereign state organized territorially, but rather by a kind of 'political hyperspace', wherein '[w]hat is "here" is not distinct from what is "there," no place can be mapped without locating it temporally, and every domain of activity is relative to the others' (1996: 292):

> Once we take into account the city's relationship to the countryside and other cities, it becomes apparent that urban space is a dynamic presence in the world as a whole. People are within urban space in their airplanes going from airport to airport, and in their cars speeding along motorways. The airport café in Honolulu, which serves passengers on their way from San Francisco to Sydney, is a part of the space of all three cities – and many more.
>
> (Magnusson 1996: 289)

The production of urban space in relation to an infrastructure of global mobility has concrete results for the way in which global cities are organized and constituted. These cities, regardless of their geographic location, provide an environment built to the specifications of the transnational capitalist class. This gives rise to a kind of isomorphism of global practices and cultures. Zygmunt Bauman quotes a story told by Agnes Heller of a member of the technocratic elite, 'a middle-aged woman, an employee of an international trade firm, who spoke five languages and owned three apartments in three different places':

> She constantly migrates, and among many places, and always to and fro ... Let's accompany her on her constant trips from Singapore to Hong Kong, London, Stockholm, New Hampshire, Tokyo, Prague and so on. She stays in the same Hilton Hotel, eats the same tuna for lunch, or, if she wishes, eats Chinese food in Paris and French food in Hong Kong. She uses the same type of fax, and telephones, and computers, watches the same films, and discusses the same kind of problems with the same kind of people.
>
> (Bauman 1998: 90)

One is therefore faced with the irony of the mobility of the transnational capitalist class. By constructing an infrastructure of global mobility, they essentially seek to homogenize their favourite locations, while, as we have already seen, labour markets remain heterogenous. They thus ensure that, in travel, they never have to encounter much new or different. In this sense, travel within the urban hyperspace of global production is the flipside to the modern technology of teleconferencing, or telecommuting (so lovingly described by Thomas Friedman in his account of global capitalism [Friedman 2006: 6]). The latter is travelling without moving, while the former is moving without travelling. Thus we see how the exteriority of the flows of capitalism, which seek to overturn the previous boundaries of geography and politics, are reterritorialized by new logics of interiority and similarity.

However, though this urban hyperspace might be oriented towards global production and mobility, this does not, as much as some thinkers might wish, do away with the fact that they are also bound to immobile and intransigent built environments, rooted in a particular locality.[19] All of the activities of global cities (business, transportation, entertainment) require a substantial underclass of service workers to ensure their proper functioning, in the roles of clerical workers, domestic and janitorial services, entertainment, tourism, food, real estate, etc., workers who must live in the city or the surrounding metropolitan area. The result is the radical partitioning of the global city into what John Friedmann calls the Citadel and the Ghetto (1982: 325). The citadel is the armoured and walled living quarters of the global elite, fortified against the incursion of a threatening and proliferating underclass.[20] This underclass in turn lives in the heavily policed, surveilled and partitioned zones of the global city's 'Ghetto'. A variety of different technological and archi-tectural tactics are brought into play to ensure that, outside work, the underclass is channelled into the ghetto and away from the citadel. Stephen Flusty describes the development of 'interdictory spaces', architectural spaces 'designed to intercept and repel or filter would be users' (Bauman 1998: 20). Mike Davis explores 'slippery spaces' designed to discourage loitering or occupation by undesirables; ironically to enforce mobility on them to more acceptable locations.

The citadel and the ghetto represent the top and the bottom of the global city, with several layers of mobility between, all enforced by an architectural, technological and disciplinary political apparatus, transforming the fabric of the global city into a cluster of regimes of (im)mobility. For some, the global city serves as a launching pad into the circuits of global capitalism. It is a node in a vast hyperspace of global mobility. For others, it serves as an immobilizing force, an architecture of localization and ghettoization. Here we see shades of Guattari's 'sci-fi' key-card city. Only some flows are chosen and released into the wild. They serve the flows of global capitalism by flowing with it. Others serve it by remaining where they are. Which is which is not arbitrary.

Popular (im)mobility

This attention to the differential mobility of different subject groups through intercoded regimes of (im)mobility helps to dispel a common misreading of capitalism: that it is, at root, a homogenizing force. This is a misconception as common among a certain type of Marxist (who still expects the proletarianization of the world) as it is among neoliberal and classical economists (who expect developing nations to develop any day now). This was the crucial fact extracted from our discussion of Deleuze and Guattari; that, far from being a homogenizing force, capitalism is a flexible and supple axiomatic which incorporates, and indeed requires, a heterogeneity of form to reproduce itself. This is why Deleuze and Guattari (following numerous development theorists) state that a global capitalist system can, and must, incorporate numerous non-, extra- and semi-capitalist social formations. Functioning regimes of (im)mobility are crucial to this polymorphy since they ensure that labour pools will stay within these 'pre-capitalist or semi-capitalist' zones and not travel to (hopefully) less oppressive and exploitative ones. This heterogeneity or polymorphy refers not just to broad forms of economic production, but also to general forms of power distribution and organization. Hence, within the control society of (post)industrial capitalism, it is possible for there to exist pockets of industrial, fordist production, disciplinary apparatuses and sovereignty structures. For example, Aiwha Ong describes the existence of 'sweatshop-based systems in North America or neo-Taylorist governmentality in South China' (2006: 136). These zones of pre-(post)industrial production are important, because they are not just *sustained* by regimes of (im)mobility, they *are* regimes of (im)mobility. This is to say that they are apparatuses by which certain agents' mobility is curtailed, while the mobility of others is accelerated and directed.

Let us take the example of migrant domestic labour in Southeast Asia. Southeast Asia is marked by large flows of migrant domestic guest workers; according to Aiwha Ong, 140,000 in Singapore, 200,000 in Malaysia and 240,000 in Hong Kong, primarily from the Philippines and Indonesia. Many of these workers live in conditions that are comparable to slavery, with their space of legitimate mobility sharply circumscribed: 'Foreign maids are sent to be confined in the households that employ them. In Hong Kong, Singapore, and Malaysia, contracted foreign domestic helpers can apply for the renewal of contract but not for citizenship' (202). Furthermore:

> The unregulated nature of domestic employment is based on a logic of incarceration. The employer controls every aspect of the foreign maid's life. It is common practice in Singapore and Malaysia for the employer to hold the maid's passport and work papers, on the pretext of preventing her from running away, but in fact confining her within the household. ... When the maids are allowed days off, Hong Kong and Singapore limit where they can go and when they can go there. Public gatherings of foreign domestic workers are restricted to Sundays and certain urban spaces.
>
> (Ong 2006: 202)

Legalized incarceration leaves domestic workers open to abuse, sexualized violence and, sometimes, murder (195).

The poor treatment of domestic workers is nothing new. What is new is how tied in to the circuits of global production this archaic form of oppression and exploitation has become. On the side of the host country, these workers are necessary for their rise as global cities.[21] From the point of view of the country of origin, the money that these workers send back in the form of remittance payments to support their families is crucial. Indeed, the export of labour has, for some countries, become a critical component of their economy:

> the Philippines actively exports workers overseas because of the inability of its economy to absorb the labor of its citizens. Hence, for each case of successful development through state-sponsored globalization, there seems to be another case of state-driven exportation of labor, as if this interconnection were an outcome dictated by an unseen law of the global economy ... In 1997, the number of overseas contract workers (OCWs) from the Philippines was estimated at 6.1 million. By December 2001, the estimated figure had risen to 7.4 million, representing close to 10 percent of the population and 21 percent of the total labor force. Their contribution to the Philippine economy is indispensable. Remittances by OCWs totaled I.S. $7.4 billion in 2003 and amounted to slightly over 8 percent of the gross national product and 19 percent of the overall export of goods and services.
>
> (Cheah 2006: 186–7)

And yet despite being integrated into the functioning of globalizing capital-ism, these working conditions mimic early capitalist and even pre-capitalist social formations. At work here is a complex regime of (im)mobility which allows workers to be moved without granting them full mobility rights (which would endanger the primary regime of capital mobility/labour immobility). This apparatus supplements the first regime we observed; adding to capital's ability to go where the cheap labour is is the ability to make cheap, pliable labour come to it – labour flexibility as the underside of capital flexibility.

These domestic workers provide one example of how pockets of dis-ciplinary labour, or even neoslavery, can exist within the flows of capitalist globalization. We could provide other examples, such as the case of Yemeni and Pakistani guest workers in Gulf State oil fields or Thai workers in Israel. If we introduce the quasi-legal and illegal practices of human trafficking and people smuggling, we see an even wider band of these practices: Chinese migrants, smuggled into the west coast of Canada and America by 'snake-heads' and then forced to work as slaves in sweatshops; Central and South American illegal immigrants locked in Wal-Mart overnight as cleaning crews; the sale and trafficking of North African migrants in Western Europe; the transnational trade in prostitutes from Eastern Europe and Russia into Western Europe and America. The experience of these migrant workers speaks to the complex hierarchy that regimes of (im)mobility produce within globalizing capitalism. They are simultaneously immensely mobile, travelling distances little seen in history, and profoundly immobile, literally incarcerated in rooms, houses and workshops. They travel the world and cannot escape their immediate surroundings. They see their strange counterpoint in the phenom-enon of those populations who are not swept up in these (forced or unforced) migrant flows, who are, indeed, denied the right to travel (either through legal, economic or infrastructural obstacles) and yet still find their world subject to intense and rapid change and movement. The GM worker in Flint, Michigan, who finds that his plant has suddenly moved to Mexico stays in his town and yet feels the whole earth move out from underneath him. This worker feels the world to be travelling at a bewildering speed, and yet also feels himself to be trapped (whether in his town, his region or his nation).

Always moving and yet confined, confined and yet always moving; this is the contradictory experience of life under globalizing capitalism. This para-dox is solved when we remember that life under the control society and (post) modern capitalism is not marked by a dichotomy between movement and stasis, speed and immobility. Rather, everything is in flow. Everything has velocity, and, as we remember from Chapter 1, velocity is relative and can be attributed to any point in a vector. Hence the world is just as fast for the member of the Chinese sweatshop, or GM worker, who sees the world rushing away from her, as it is for the member of the transnational capitalist class who sees it rushing towards her. The crucial distinction is not to be made on the basis of the quantitative experience of the world as fast or slow. It is the quality of the mobility which is determinative. Do we experience it with a

sense of control and freedom? Do we have choice in the direction and destination of velocity? Do we go where we wish, or do we wish that we could go?
Does the world come to us, or do we come to the world? How far down the
path of a particular flow can we see? In short, do we experience the space of
flows that is life under globalizing capitalism as speed or velocity? To the
members of the transnational capitalist class the space of flows is a space of
velocities, which promises to augment their power and well-being. To the
members of the global underclass, it is a space of speed, of abrupt shift,
swerves, halts and accelerations, all coming with little warning or real promise. Many move between these poles. But the poles themselves are real. And
if uncertainties, escapes and surprising turns sometimes occur within global
flows (which we will discuss in Chapter 5), a very real stratification of flow is
still discernible.

What is important is that this provides a point of commonality, and
potentially solidarity, between members of the global underclass who, though
they are subject to radically different regimes of (im)mobility, share a general
position of insecurity, and exploitation in terms of the global capitalist axiomatic. The migrant worker and the national proletariat both experience the
space of flows as a place of uncontrollable speeds. They exist at the whim of
global capital. They are bound together in their (im)mobility.

Ressentiment *of exteriority*

The problem, of course, is that alliances and solidarities between local and
migrant labour groups rarely develop (the former generally from the developed world, the latter primarily from the developing world). In most places in
the world animosity between the two groups is growing. Despite being subject
to the same system of global capitalist exploitation, first world labour pools
rarely see migrant labourers (or, for that matter, workers in other countries)
as part of the same subject group. The difficulty in making manifest the lines
of connection is the fact that the global workforce 'is now far more geographically dispersed, culturally heterogenous, ethnically and religiously
diverse, racially stratified and linguistically fragmented' (Harvey 2000: 45). In
this case, already held racisms, ethnic nationalisms and xenophobia act to
inhibit a sense of connection between groups. However, it is not enough to
use racist or xenophobic attitudes to explain conflict between local and
migrant labour populations. To do so is to miss the way in which such attitudes are activated, and indeed even produced, through global capitalism and
specific regimes of (im)mobility. This is not to suggest that racialist, nationalist or xenophobic attitudes are purely derivative of economic organizations.
Rather, it is to say that forms of consciousness, whether racial, ethnic,
national or classist, do not exist in isolation, but constantly effect, inform and
meld into one another. For the purposes of our analysis, it is important to see
how the very circumstances of exploitation that are produced by global
capitalism give rise to racialist, nationalist or xenophobic subjectivities that

proscribe alliances and solidarities which could potentially challenge and resist that exploitation.

The most obvious way in which a local underclass is turned against a foreign underclass is through holding the migrants responsible for economic misfortune. This scapegoating can take the form of a narrative about illegal Mexican migrants sneaking into the United States to 'steal' the jobs of Americans, or Chinese and Indian labourers who are 'willing to work for less' in their home countries. Such scapegoating is aided by a failure to differentiate between foreign labour and foreign capital (or, for that matter, multinational or transnational capital). Therefore migrant labour (whether legal or illegal) receives the same status and suspicion as does, say, the influx of Japanese capital in America in the mid-1990s. This is partly the result of the same liberal/ neoliberal ideology of individualism which makes it impossible to view economic disenfranchisement as systematic. When transferred onto foreign workers alone, the movement of migrant labourers is seen as a result of a personal choice, and the willingness of foreign labour pools to work for less is seen as a ploy on behalf of foreign workers to steal jobs from the developed world. If one must conceive of these actions as the result of choices made by free individuals, rather than the coerced decisions of actors in different positions with regards to global capitalism, then one can (1) devalue the moral status of these actors (turning migrants into 'illegals' or 'Queue-jumpers') and (2) see them as opponents competing for work, rather than fellow victims of a general system of economic exploitation.

More specifically, the movement of migrant workers and so-called 'economic refugees' to the developed world is confused by the failure to differentiate between flow as speed and flow as velocity. This is to say that the working class of a developed country is essentially immobile, finding itself without much control, subject to the whim of global capitalism. In this regard, then, it is assumed that since their immobility is tied to a lack of choice, mobility must represent a form of freedom or choice. Hence migrant labourers are attacked for impinging on a labour market that is already economically depressed. Such a perspective fails to conceive of a flow or movement that might be experienced not as velocity, rooted in freedom and intentionality, but as speed, conditioned and forced. In short, they cannot conceive of a mobility that is just as constraining as their own immobility.

It is this last point that speaks to the larger problem of producing developed world/developing world solidarities: the misidentification of those caught up in the flows of globalizing capitalism with the source or cause of those flows. Workers in developed countries feel their own immobility in a world of globalizing flows as impotence and uncertainty. The world moves around them. This sense of impotence and uncertainty is contrasted with a mythologized version of the past, when labour was properly valorized and one's livelihood, as well as one's culture and sense of identity, was secured. This past is mythologized as slow-moving, local and national, where boundaries between inside and outside, foreign and domestic, stasis and movement, were firm.

This sense of uncertainty and impotence is paired with a sense of social and cultural marginalization. This is to say that, with the globalization of capitalism and the rise of the transnational capitalist class, there is a valorization of mobility and the global cosmopolitan culture that it inspires. There has always been a sense of glamour attached to travel. However, in the past travel was something viewed as exceptional, an escape from a static environment, usually as a way to experience a different culture. Now travel, mobility, has become a culture to itself, and those who do not move have a tendency to be viewed, and to view themselves, as 'being relegated to a ... mire of parochialism' (James 2004: 28). Television, movies and magazines bring tales of glamorous people who live in, and travel between, global cities; satellite news constantly describes situations in far-off places; the business news valorizes high-flying executives; and ad campaigns warn people that if they are not jacked into some sort of global information network they will find themselves to be lumbering dinosaurs, left in the dust. The dominant discourse leaves the impression that there is a shame or embarrassment in immobility; that one is *missing out*, left behind in a world that is unfolding elsewhere. Whereas once it was expected that you would live your whole life in the town in which you were born, now it is considered insular and parochial if one does not leave. We may add to this the fact that this cosmopolitan culture tends to inject ideas, cultural objects and mores which are frequently at odds with local culture and customs.

In this sense, the immobile underclass of the first world views globalization as a mechanism not just of economic marginalization, but also of cultural and existential devalorization. It disturbs the cultural context in which they live, marginalizing the values to which they cling. Thomas Frank does an excellent job of describing how a discourse has developed in the American heartland of a cultural elite (located in global cities such as New York and LA and connected to a transnational culture network) that mocks, diminishes and replaces local, authentic, American culture (Frank 2004). The trouble is that, from this position, all flows of globalization are seen as equal in marginalizing and devalorizing local, 'immobile' culture. The arrival of migrant labourers, bringing with them different cultures, styles, mores and languages, are seen not just as coming from another culture, but as a drive to marginalize and displace the true 'authentic' local culture.

We thus have the combination of economic marginalization coupled with a sense of cultural marginalization. This sense of impotence joined to a new cultural essentialism and revaluation crystallizes into a vague, intense sense of resentment against the fluidity of the world and the flows which impinge on the solid ground and strong borders that (supposedly) once underlay economic, social, political and cultural life. This becomes a sort of *ressentiment* against exteriority (the counterpoint to the *ressentiment* against the future we saw in Chapter 1):

> Experiencing considerable anxiety over the dissolution of secure boundaries and familiar borders, groups such as industrial workers and small

farmers are losing their former privileged status in traditional social hierarchies. As people's old identities are subjected to a growing sense of fragmentation and alienation, one possible response to the new challenges of the postmodern world lies in assigning blame to internal and external Others for the desecration of the familiar.

(Steger 2005: 101–2)

This *ressentiment* against the outside is marked by fear and anger at the flows which break up the comfortable stasis of interiority, making lives and livelihoods uncertain. This *ressentiment* then becomes focused on the flows, rather than on the source or instigator of those flows. As William Connolly describes this *ressentiment* against exteriority in the American context:

> Such reactive drives are not too likely to grab hold effectively of the processes of capitalist invention, finance, investment, labor migration, geographic expansion, and intraterritorial colonization, even though these are pre-eminent forces propelling the acceleration of pace ... So now resentment against the acceleration of pace becomes projected upon religious and nationalist drives to identify a series of vulnerable constituencies as paradigmatic enemies of territorial culture, traditional morality, unified politics and Christian civilization. The atheist, the postmodernist, the gay, the prostitute, the Jew, the media, the nomadic Indian, and the Gypsy have all been defined as paradigmatic agents of restlessness, nomadism, superficial fashion, immorality, and danger by defenders of close integration among political territory, religious unity, and moral monism. Such definitions displace upon vulnerable constituencies anxiety about the pace of life and the right in time. The underlying enemy is speed and uncertainty, but it is difficult to grab hold of the capitalist systems in which these processes are set.

(Connolly 2002: 147–8)

Though described here primarily in relation to the American context, this growing sense of *ressentiment* can be seen in numerous countries, through the rise of nationalist, xenophobic and anti-immigration movements, amongst other cultural phenomenon.

Of course, the irony is that, whereas the *ressentiment* against the future discussed in Chapter 1 merely resulted in people being willing to give up their right to political participation in exchange for a sense of security (a bad bargain perhaps, but an exchange nonetheless), the result of this rising *ressentiment* against exteriority is a tendency to reinforce the circumstances and institutions which gave rise to these sentiments in the first place (if occasionally effectively attacking or punishing its most local and vulnerable manifestations). This is to say that political movements rooted in *ressentiment* against exteriority do not in fact challenge the central workings of globalizing capitalism. Rather, they serve to help perpetuate the system. This happens in two ways.

The first is by the exploitation of this *ressentiment* on behalf of right-wing parties who embody a bizarre yet accepted neoliberal/neoconservative consensus; this is to say parties who claim to oppose the perceived cultural attacks on local, immobile cultures, while at the same time enacting neoliberal economic policies, which actually produce and intensify the flows which are seen to threaten the culture of interiority. In America, this has become the norm, with the Republicans as the vanguard of this position and even the Democratic party often using a derivative platform.[22] Says Harvey,

> In the US the moral values that became central to the neo-conservative movement can be understood as a logical outcome of the particular coalition that was built in the 1970s between elite class and business interests intent on restoring their class power and an electoral base among the 'moral majority' of the disaffected white working class.
>
> (Harvey 2006b: 59–60)

However, this rise of political parties embodying culturally conservative yet economically neoliberal policies is by no means constrained to the United States, and is in fact present throughout the developed world (and even in newly industrialized economies and some developing nations):

> The rise of nationalist sentiment in Japan and China, for example, has been marked in recent years, and in both instances this can be seen as an antidote to the dissolution of former bonds of social solidarity under the impact of neo-liberalism. Strong currents of cultural nationalism are stirring within the old nation states (such as France) that now constitute the European Union. Religion and cultural nationalism provided the moral heft behind the Hindu Nationalist Party's success in importing neo-liberal practices into India in recent times.
>
> (Harvey 2006b: 61)

Such political movements become perpetual motion machines. They establish themselves as defenders of a particular community defined in terms of interiority, bolstered by the resentment felt by that community. However, they also enact neoliberal economic policies, which ensure more encroaching economic, cultural and social flows to challenge the interiority of community, ensuring more outrage and resentment, and thus more support for the movement. This is especially ironic because, though nationalist, xenophobic movements and *ressentiment* are not wholly produced or determined by economic flows, it is a sense of economic marginalization and impotence which activates *ressentiment* as a political script, and provides these movements with mass appeal. And yet political parties ensure that no real change to that economic marginalization will take place, by focusing on the cultural aspects, which are themselves derivative of economic flows:

Rather than endorsing fundamental social change in the direction of greater equality, right-wing populists maintain and intensify existing systems of social privilege. As political scientist Chip Berlet points out, populist movements are fueled by people's legitimate grievances against existing forms of domination, but they 'Deflect popular discontent away from positive social change by targeting only small sections of the elite or groups falsely identified with the elite.' Moreover, right-wing populists channel the brunt of people's anger against ethnic minorities, recent immigrants, and welfare recipients. These oppressed and marginalized groups offer easier and more vulnerable targets than political and economic elites.

(Steger 2005: 96)

This targeting of immigrants, and other even more marginalized groups, provides the second way in which the intensification of *ressentiment* serves to reinforce the capitalist regimes of (im)mobility. For the circumscription of the mobility of certain migrant workers, which makes them subject to increased exploitation, is the result not just of legal and political proscriptions, but also of social conflicts and animosities. Thus, for example, the incarceration of domestic workers in South-East Asia discussed on pp. 143–144 requires not just legal circumscription, but also cultural and moral delegitimation. Extreme anti-immigration movements and attitudes in the American southwest stops migrant workers from seeking legal protections. The cultural and linguistic isolation of Chinese diasporic communities in multiple locations makes new immigrants subject to predatory employers and working conditions.[23] In short, a generalized *ressentiment* against exteriority supports a regime of (im)mobility since it limits and circumscribes the spaces (physically, legally and culturally) through which migrants may travel. This leaves them all the more open to exploitation, and thus all the more useful for global production.

The great tragedy of all of this is that these groups – workers in the developed world, workers in the developing world and migrant workers trapped in between – are all in similar subject positions with regard to global capitalism. They all find themselves in a global space of flows, constrained and constricted by an interlocking web of regimes of (im)mobility, experiencing the velocity of production as an uncontrollable, unpredictable speed. The enmity that is experienced between these groups is partly a result of the failure to see these similarities, partly a result of the affective resentment attached to the differences between them. This is not to say that all of these actors are identical, or have the exact same political interest in all situations. I am not here arguing for some form of global proletarian consciousness. What I am arguing is that, by virtue of their shared marginalization through a global set of regimes of (im)mobility, there is perhaps more to be gained from their solidarity and partnership than from their conflict and opposition.

We return, then, to the problem we began with: how to map a world whose territoriality is criss-crossed and deformed by flows of people, goods, information, capital, ideas, diseases, disciplines, organisms, threats and opportunities. If we map the world according to a territorial logic of interiority, then these flows will look like threats to, and attacks on, the static foundation of culture and community. In such a map, the Mexican migrant labourer and the Chinese worker in an EPZ are of the same status as the multinational corporation which transfers away jobs and abandons localities. They are all agents of a globalizing capitalism which seek to dissolve the static social unity of local community. However, if we seek to map not the territorial world, but the political hyperspace of flows, we see that what matters is not always actual mobility or immobility. Rather, it is one's position within a global space of flows, the space within which you can travel, the autonomy with which you move; the question is of an open (im)mobility versus a closed (im) mobility (with numerous layers of ambiguity in between). In such a map we see migrant workers and local workers, peripheral work forces and central work forces trapped in the complementary circuits, close together, and yet prized apart by elaborate regimes of (im)mobility. Such a map could become the blueprint for an attempt to deform and redirect these global flows, to make surprising and unexpected linkages. Such a map might help us to become fellow travellers in the world. This chapter is part of an attempt to draw this map from above. However, we must also engage attempts on the ground to reshape the map, grassroots efforts to forge these linkages, affinities and solidarities across static lines of difference and belonging. It is to these efforts that we will turn in Chapter 5.

5 'A world in which many worlds fit'

On rhizomatic cosmopolitanism

> Many worlds walk in the world. Many worlds are made. Many worlds make us. ... In the world of the powerful there is no space for anyone but themselves and their servants. In the world we want, everyone fits. We want a world in which many worlds fit. The nation that we construct is one where all communities and languages fit, where all steps may walk, where all may have laughter, where all may live the dawn.
>
> (Marcos 2002: 80)

'La puebla, unida, jamas cera vincindo!'

Chapter 4 ended on such a note of despair, as we identified some of the forces and flows which produce separation, antagonism and resentment between the exploited and disenfranchised in different countries. It is worthwhile to take a moment to remind ourselves that this is only one side of the story. I want to begin this final chapter with a story of hope, a story of possibility, a story that reminds us of the things that human beings can do for, and with, one another.

In autumn 2007, the Farm Labor Organizing Committee (FLOC) began a campaign to protect the rights of fieldworkers in North Carolina who pick tobacco for RJ Reynolds. The North Carolina fieldworkers are often subject to inhumane working conditions, with inadequate breaks and water even at the height of the summer heat, frequently without proper safety equipment to protect them from the toxic chemicals in green tobacco. Over the previous two years, at least six workers had died in the fields, usually of heat stroke. FLOC wanted to unionize the workers as a way of ensuring that proper safety regulations were enforced.

FLOC had previously had great success in North Carolina, where a boycott against Mt Olive Pickles led to an agreement with the North Carolina Growers' Association to unionize 6,000 fieldworkers. The RJ Reynolds campaign, however, was a more difficult case, as the pickers were not directly employed by RJ Reynolds, but instead by hundreds of smaller farms to whom RJ Reynolds subcontracted their tobacco growing. Thus, unionizing the workers would involve a long drawn-out, farm-by-farm process. This was further complicated by the fact that the vast majority of these workers were migrant workers from Mexico, in America on guest worker visas. Such workers are notoriously difficult to unionize, since they find themselves uniquely vulnerable to reprisals such as blacklisting and possible deportation (as well as more overt forms of violence and repression without ready recourse). FLOC therefore decided to directly target RJ Reynolds, asking that CEO Susan Ivey meet with them and discuss unionizing the fieldworkers, a request which RJ Reynolds refused. FLOC then began a pressure campaign to try and force RJ Reynolds to meet with them. The kick-off to that campaign was a march, scheduled for late November 2007, in Winston-Salem, North Carolina, home of RJ Reynolds corporate headquarters.

I was part of a group travelling from DC in a bus chartered by the AFL-CIO to take part in the march. FLOC is affiliated with the AFL-CIO, which had sent out messages to all of its member unions, informing them of the protest and urging them to participate if possible. Our bus consisted of a diverse group of unions, including members of the Postal Carriers, Machine Workers, Teamsters and a large contingent from the Seafarers' Union. During the seven-hour bus ride south, a sort of *ad hoc* roundtable discussion on labour issues and immigration was taken up, a discussion which went counter to all of the common expectations of American views on Hispanic migrant labourers. Sentences that began with the phrase 'The trouble with immigrants ... ' went on to say, ' ... is that since they're not born here, they don't know what their rights are, so it's easy for employers to exploit them'. The fear-mongering and xenophobia of a Lou Dobbs were entirely absent. In its place seemed to be a sense of solidarity with fellow workers, and of moral obligation to help those who were being oppressed.

These impressions were only reinforced when we arrived in Winston-Salem. The crowd of protestors, a few hundred strong, was split pretty evenly between the workers themselves (primarily Hispanic, and primarily guest workers) and their supporters, including allied union workers (primarily white or African-American), members of church groups, and anti-capitalist and human rights groups. Before the march, drummers and musicians energized the crowd. Speeches were given in both English and Spanish. Indeed, in defiance of all of the reactionary politics surrounding the question of language in America, throughout the protest everyone seemed to slide easily back and forth between English and Spanish. As seemingly one of the few present with no knowledge of Spanish whatsoever, I felt a bit like an outsider. In what has stuck with me as the most enduring image of that day, I watched as two members of the United Mine Workers, both at least in their sixties, good friends and clearly veterans of more than a few strikes, laughed as they learned to chant 'The people, united, will never be divided!' in Spanish. In the carnival-like atmosphere of the protest, the sense of *ressentiment* against exteriority which I spoke of in Chapter 4 seemed to be entirely absent, replaced with a joyous affect of community and mutual support. These men and women viewed each other as fellow travellers, workers, human beings, and gladly took part in each other's languages, cultures and struggles.

This sort of willingness to extend friendship and connection across lines of culture is just one example of what is termed the increasingly 'cosmopolitan' character of our accelerating world. Indeed, this story, centred as it is on a Canadian academic travelling to the American south to lend support to migrant labourers from Mexico, is a bit parochial compared to some of the other tales of transnational political activism we will encounter. That the acceleration of the world introduces a 'cosmopolitan' character to much of the world's politics and culture is, at this point, a fairly uncontentious claim. However, the meaning of this cosmopolitanism is by no means equally free from debate. Even the meaning of this simple story of hope is ambiguous. How did the different groups I described above conceive of their interactions? Were they thinking in terms of a solidarity of workers? A tactical alliance of political actors? Recognition of a fundamental humanity? What did they think of the differences between them? Did they conceive of them as superficial attributes, or profound differences of culture and identity? And if so, how did they negotiate these differences?

We will return to this story later on, and attempt some answers. In the meantime, in order to continue our analysis of speed and global politics, it is necessary to investigate this term that is frequently allied with it, cosmopolitanism. I will begin by investigating a dominant account of speed and cosmopolitanism, what I eventually term 'arborescent cosmopolitanism', as presented in the works of Immanuel Kant and Martha Nussbaum. I will contest the implicit operation of this cosmopolitanism as a process which seeks to erase difference and produce a homogenizing narrative of global time and space. I will then suggest that 'arborescent cosmopolitanism' is not the only possibility for progressive global politics, and that our investigation into the spatial and temporal dimensions of speed can alert us to an alternative, what I term 'rhizomatic cosmopolitanism' (or perhaps rhizomatic cosmopolitanism*s*). It is my wager that the development of a theory of rhizomatic cosmopolitanism can help to better explain the current landscape of transnational activism and solidarity movements, as well as making us more open and hopeful about the possibility of effective political action at both the global and local levels.

Homogeneity and cosmopolitanism

One of the claims we have encountered time and again is that speed is an inexorably homogenizing or totalizing force. In Chapter 1 we saw Sheldon Wolin argue that the social acceleration of time brings with it the erasure of local difference in favour of large-scale industrial aggregates under the sign of 'inverted totalitarianism'. In Chapter 2, we engaged Paul Virilio's image of speed as the harbinger of a globalitarian society, with the whole world frozen under the synoptic eye of a totalizing war-machine. And in Chapters 3 and 4 we dealt with the idea that accelerative technologies advanced the totalizing grip of capitalist domination, in terms of time (in the foreclosure of the future through capitalist production) and of space (in the complete integration of the world into the global capitalist axiomatic).

We should not, I suppose, find this equation of speed with homogenization surprising, for two reasons. The first is that the most immediate understanding of speed is as velocity, and increased velocity is viewed as a mechanism of increased scope: the drawing together of all things, the dissolution of boundaries and distinctions between times and places. This view suggests that, in an accelerated world, political problems and issues will be of such a vast scope that any politics which wishes to respond to them, even a progressive politics, must also transcend the particularity of locality and produce a united front to act at the level of large-scale aggregates. The second reason is that many of those who valorize speed valorize it precisely *for* its homogenizing effects. We saw one example of this in Chapter 4 with Thomas Friedman's exultation of accelerative communication and transportation technologies, which are said to 'flatten' the world, erasing differences between localities. The neoliberal account of speed glories in the apparent homogenizing power of accelerative technologies to integrate the entire world into the global capitalist system. I challenged this perspective by arguing that the global capitalist axiomatic does not, in fact, produce homogeneity, but functions instead according to a logic of differentiated (im)mobilities. I will also, later, argue that for all of its supposed totalizing power, the capitalist axiomatic also sends out errant and eccentric flows, which produce new escapes, spaces and times (as in Chapter 3, where lines of flight created by technological innovation produced alternative productive spaces).

In this chapter I endeavour to deal with another (potentially) universalizing and homogenizing ideology: cosmopolitanism. Given the fact that we have identified one of the defining characteristics of speed as 'exteriority', it is not surprising that speed should be connected with a perspective that tends to be defined by efforts to 'transcend regional particularism' and achieve a 'universal humanism' (Cheah and Robbins 1998: 22). These days, when someone is described as cosmopolitan it is usually assumed that they are bound up in the network of global flows which we have been charting over the past few chapters.

Any discussion of speed will therefore be incomplete if it does not engage with cosmopolitanism. This does not mean, however, that speed is connected to cosmopolitanism in an unproblematic way. Nor must we accept the idea that cosmopolitanism itself is unproblematic. Indeed, the drive to 'transcend regional particularism' and produce a 'universal humanism' is attached to only one account of cosmopolitanism, which I term 'arborescent cosmopolitanism'. I will argue that arborescent cosmopolitanism's relationship with acceleration is (like that of capitalism, the state or war) a tense and ambivalent one. Accelerative technologies also give rise to another cosmopolitanism, a multiple and less centred cosmopolitanism, which cuts across boundaries while at the same time remaining connected to particularity and locality; a 'rhizomatic' cosmopolitanism. It is to this rhizomatic cosmopolitanism that

I will turn later on in this chapter (pp. 167–178). But first we must investigate arborescent cosmopolitanism and see how speed has traditionally been linked with it.

Arborescent cosmopolitanism

I focus on two major thinkers of cosmopolitanism: Immanuel Kant and Martha Nussbaum. I begin with Kant because it is with Kant that we see a transition from the idea of cosmopolitanism as a moral ideal to the idea of cosmopolitanism as a historical and political state of affairs made possible by material changes. And among these material changes I will argue that it is speed that has pride of place. I then turn to the neo-Kantian Nussbaum as a theorist of arborescent cosmopolitanism to demonstrate its homogenizing tendencies.

Kant's cosmopolitanism was not just a personal moral imperative, requiring the universal application of moral principles regardless of particularities such as citizenship or ethnicity (as it was, for example, amongst the Epicureans or Stoics). Rather, according to Kant, cosmopolitanism must be seen as a potentially existing social and political order, 'a universal civil society administered in accord with the right' (1983: 33). What is more, Kant says, this social and political order should be understood as the very goal of history. In his work 'Idea for a Universal History with a Cosmopolitan Intent', Kant argues that 'nature's supreme objective [is] a universal *cosmopolitan state*' (37–8). Note that what Kant means by 'state' here is '*Zustand*, in the sense of state of things, of the situation, of the real constitution and not of the State with a capital S' (Derrida 2002: 5). Indeed Kant's goal is not a global state, but rather a 'federation of peoples' (although a federation 'administered in accord with right') (Kant 1983: 34). *Idea for a Universal History* describes a collection of changing material forces which provide the conditions of possibility for this federation of peoples. In these material forces, I will argue, speed and acceleration play a crucial role.

The first and perhaps most important force which calls the cosmopolitan state into existence is war. War, says Kant, is an expression of the inherent unsociability of man (32). From the perspective of universal history, however, this unsociability is not purely a negative attribute. For 'the means that nature uses to bring about the development of all of man's capacities is the antagonism among them'. This antagonism also creates the need for, and possibility of, the state and 'law-governed order in society' (31). Were it not for war, 'man would live as an Arcadian shepherd, in perfect concord, contentment, and mutual love, and all talents would lie eternally dormant in their seed' (32).

However, this contradictory beneficence of war can only carry on for so long. At a certain point, the power of war becomes too great, and threatens the very possibility of human existence. This increasing violence of war forces states to come to the realization that steps must be taken to do away with war completely (and hence, to move towards a cosmopolitan international order, administered in accord with right):

> through wars, through excessive and never remitting preparation for war, through the resultant distress that every nation must, even during times of peace, feel within itself, they are driven to make some initial imperfect attempts; finally, after much devastation, upheaval, and even complete exhaustion of their inner powers, they are driven to take the step that reason could have suggested, even without so much sad experience, namely, to leave the lawless state of savagery and enter into a federation of peoples.
>
> (Kant 1983: 34)

Inherent in this increasing savagery of war is the advancement of accelerative technologies which we discussed in Chapter 2.[1] The central point here is that, as the scope of war increases (both in terms of damage and territory), so the scope of the needed political response increases.

The second historical shift which encourages the development of cosmopolitan structures and ideologies is the growth of commerce. In his essay on perpetual peace, Kant discusses how international trade produces an elaborate interdependence between states – an interdependence which, when broken by the new destructiveness of war, damages all involved:

> The spirit of trade cannot coexist with war, and sooner or later this spirit dominates every people. For among all those powers (or means) that belong to a nation, financial power may be the most reliable in forcing nations to pursue the noble cause of peace (though not from moral motives); and wherever in the world war threatens to break out, they will try to head it off through mediation, just as if they were permanently leagued for that purpose.
>
> (Kant 1983: 125)

The globalization of trade, which we discussed in Chapter 4, provides a material incentive to move towards an international system ordered according to a system of right, and away from one based on partial or national interest and determined by force. Indeed, if we assume, as Kant does, the mutually beneficial nature of trade, commercial interdependence produces the growth of a shared global interest.

The third historical shift lies in the improvement of communication and transportation technologies, which leads to increased interaction between the world's peoples and, as such, an increased sense of community which transcends borders. This expanded network of information and belonging means that moral responsibility is felt not just within nations, but across the globe:

> Because a (narrower or wider) community widely prevails among the earth's peoples, a transgression of rights in *one* place in the world is felt

everywhere; consequently, the idea of cosmopolitan right is not fantastic and exaggerated, but rather an amendment to the unwritten code of national and international rights, necessary to the public rights of men in general.

(Kant 1983: 119)

This new communicative interdependence also leads to the dissemination of philosophical, moral, political and social ideas, producing an increasing rapprochement of beliefs between peoples, providing a yet stronger grounding for the federation of peoples and the general cosmopolitan state.

We can see how these different material changes intertwine with one another to produce a historical shift towards a cosmopolitan state in a quotation from Allen Wood, who describes how Kant analyzes a historical moment in which

the positive effects war has had on the development of human faculties are being overtaken by the destructive effects of a system of states whose security is based on military power. If the historical development of our species-capacities is to continue, a system of mutually independent states must gradually grow toward a federal union, naturally grounded on ties of commerce and mutual self-interest, and affected by an increasing unity of principles based on ever-expanding communication and the consequent emergence of a single enlightened world culture.

(Wood 2005: 63)

Wood captures how Kant places an ever-increasing global interdependency at the root of the historical movement towards cosmopolitanism. We can see how this interdependency is a function of acceleration. The growing threat of negative interdependency (war), coupled with the growing benefits of positive interdependencies (trade) and grounded in a growing ideological interdependency (increased communication and travel), provides the foundation for a cosmopolitan state. Kant's narrative is therefore one of the early accounts of how the acceleration and proliferation of global flows lead to a world in which the traditional violence and oppression of the state system is replaced by a global order governed by principles of international law and led by a philosophy of cosmopolitan moral responsibility. It is this narrative that, *mutatis mutandis*, undergirds many contemporary laudatory accounts of globalization. This account of a move towards a more global polity as a result of technological shifts and growing interdependence can be found in thinkers as diverse as Hegel, Marx, H. G. Wells, John Stuart Mill, as well as many neo-Kantian cosmopolitans, such as David Held and Martha Nussbaum.

However, at this point, it is pertinent to discuss the somewhat ambiguous status of the teleology which Kant lays out. For, though Kant provides empirical evidence and conditions for this progressive cosmopolitanization of the world, he does not, in the end, believe that it can be proven empirically. Indeed, according to Kant, the teleology of universal history cannot be proven from *a posteriori* evidence; rather, it must be assumed on the basis of metaphysical and moral commitments which are transcendentally deduced (Kant 2002, 1987):

> I will thus permit myself to assume that since the human race's natural end is to make steady cultural progress, its moral end is to be conceived as progressing toward the better ... It is not necessary for me to prove this assumption; the burden of proof is on its opponents. For I rest my case on my innate duty ... the duty so to affect posterity that it will become continually better (something that must be assumed to be possible).
>
> (Kant 1983: 33)

What this means is that 'cosmopolitanism ... gains a grip in Kant's moral imagination only because it flows from a transcendental imperative to act *as if* the world were filled with a *providential direction* that stretches beyond the reach of human agency. Kant's transcendentalism enables cosmopolitanism to function as a regulative ideal in his time' (Connolly 2002: 180–1). Thus the invocation of a cosmopolitan future rests on a set of metaphysical and ethical assumptions, including the '"apodictic" recognition that morality takes the form of law' as well as a 'base line for the postulates of freedom, god, salvation and ... looser secretions about providence, grace, progress, cosmopolitanism, and an ethical commonwealth' (Connolly 2011). So the narrative of cosmopolitanization that Kant lays out cannot be separated from a particularly situated philosophical (and social and historical) position. We will discuss the implications of this fact shortly. However, at this point, it is useful to shift our focus to another philosopher, one heavily indebted to Kantian philosophy: Martha Nussbaum.

Nussbaum approaches the question of cosmopolitanism not from the perspective of material conditions of historical inevitability, but rather from the perspective of moral imperative, and this dovetails nicely with our discussion of the metaphysical foundations of Kant's cosmopolitan history. Furthermore, since Kant argues that part of the project of universal history is the dissemination of cosmopolitan norms and the development of a universal set of principles of right, Nussbaum's defence of cosmopolitan morality functions as part of his project, since she explicitly couches her discussion of cosmopolitanism in terms of the importance of cosmopolitan education.

The central principle of Martha Nussbaum's cosmopolitanism is the 'moral irrelevance of nationality'. This is to say that, in terms of political and moral decision-making, we should learn to leave behind our particular attachments and instead 'give our first allegiance to what is morally good' (Nussbaum 1996: 5). This sort of cosmopolitanism is a universal moral imperative. However, it takes on a special importance and urgency in an accelerating world where interaction between different national groups becomes increasingly common. Political decisions increasingly cross borders and affect multiple different groups. In such a world, it is necessary that the various actors make decisions on the basis of rational and moral imperatives, rather than an irrational attachment to their locality: 'One of the greatest barriers to rational deliberation in politics is the unexamined feeling that one's own preferences and ways are neutral and natural' (11). Nussbaum advocates a program of cosmopolitan education as way of overcoming this irrational attachment to locality and encouraging 'rational deliberation':

> An education that takes national boundaries as morally salient too often reinforces this kind of irrationality, by lending to what is an accident of history a false air of moral weight and glory. By looking at ourselves through the lens of the other, we come to see what in our practices is local and nonessential, what is more broadly or deeply shared.
>
> (Nussbaum 1996: 11)

For Nussbaum, learning about other cultures is a crucial step towards producing a rational public policy for a newly interdependent world. However, we should be clear about the purposes of this cosmopolitan education. The goal of learning about other cultures is not solely to historicize and localize one's own knowledge. Rather, it is to identify (and discard) that which is local and historically particular, in favour of highlighting what is 'more broadly or deeply shared'. Nussbaum's cosmopolitanism is a process of abstraction. It aims to get underneath the particularities of location and history in order to discern a universal human nature. She recounts the lessons of Diogenes, who taught that

> [t]he accident of where one is born is just that, an accident; any human being might have been born in any nation. Recognizing this, his Stoic successors held we should not allow differences of nationality or class or ethnic membership or even gender to erect barriers between us and our fellow human beings. We should recognize humanity where it occurs, and give its fundamental ingredients, reason and moral capacity, our first allegiance and respect.
>
> (Nussbaum 1996: 7)

Cosmopolitan education, then, is a process of transcendence; transcending our differences and disengaging from local and particular communities (at least in terms of moral and political deliberation) (5).[2] Most importantly, it is a process of transcending passionate affective attachments to particular localities, in favour of the calm and clear-eyed appraisal of universal rational and moral norms. Thus 'the invitation to think as a world citizen [is], in a sense, an invitation to be an exile from the comfort of patriotism and its easy sentiments, to see our own ways of life from the point of view of justice and the good' (7).

This process of abstraction and disengagement does not, of course, require the complete abandonment of all local obligations. But it does require subordinating them to universal rational or moral obligations. Nussbaum maps this hierarchy of obligations using the Stoic imagery of concentric circles:

> They suggest that we think of ourselves not as devoid of local affiliations, but as surrounded by a series of concentric circles. The first one encircles the self, the next takes in the immediate family, then follows the extended family, then, in order, neighbours or local groups, fellow city-dwellers, and fellow countrymen – and we can easily add to this list groupings based on ethnic, linguistic, historical, professional, gender, or sexual identities. Outside all these circles is the largest one, humanity as a whole. Our task as citizens of the world will be to 'draw the circles somehow towards the center' making all human beings more like our fellow city-dwellers, and so on.
>
> (Nussbaum 1996: 9)

Our lives are thus a set of concentric circles describing our moral and social obligations. We are tied to our most immediate circles through affective bonds of familiarity. But, says Nussbaum, if we wish to live rationally and morally (and, for her, the two are the same) we must transcend these smaller circles and disengage from these partial alliances (at least when called upon for moral and political decision-making) and act according to universal rules of rationality dictated to all people equally according to a common humanity. A crucial goal of Nussbaum's political philosophy, then, is to produce an extensive account of this common humanity which can serve as a regulative ideal and ethical grounding for the 'largest circle' of moral concern. This is done through an essentialist Aristotelian analysis which seeks to produce a list of 'thick, vague universals' which describe the fundamental properties without which 'we no longer have a human life at all' (Nussbaum 1992: 215, 207).

If we combine Kantian and Nussbaumian cosmopolitanism, we are faced with a moral and pragmatic duty to learn how to transcend the parochialism of national borders and transfer our allegiance to a global social regime ordered according to universal rules of right. Nussbaum's program of cosmopolitan education helps to loosen the irrational and affective ties of particular loyalty and disseminate the cosmopolitan norms that are necessary to act morally, and also to survive in the accelerating and interdependent world which Kant describes.

Put together, these two narratives produce one of the dominant articulations of cosmopolitanism, which has had considerable influence amongst those engaged in progressive politics. On the one hand, progressives are increasingly unwilling to accept claims to sovereign authority or national self-determination as excuses for human rights violations, and other forms of oppression and exploitation. For these activists, a border should not be allowed to serve as a shield for injustice. On the other hand, in the newly interdependent world there is the sense that many structures of exploitation or oppression now function transnationally and thus any effective resistance must take the form of cosmopolitan transnational organizations. Andrew Herrod describes the common perception that, in terms of labour organization,

> local actions mounted to defend communities against the ravages of, for example, deindustrialization are often seen as hopelessly parochial and destined to be outmaneuvered and defeated by a hypermobile and flexible capital that can always choose to abandon them and relocate to virtually any place on the planet. The only logical response, so it is claimed, is that workers and community activists must develop global campaigns to match the global reach of transnational corporations and global capital more generally.
>
> (Herrod 2001: 51)

Such global campaigns exist to overcome not just exploitative labour practices, but other forms of injustice and oppression as well. Many of these campaigns seek a cosmopolitan ethos as a way of producing more expansive coalitions, as well as a set of settled global norms which can be applied regardless of nationality and borders. By disseminating cosmopolitan values we can establish a regime of universal human rights, and thus identify and bring effective resistance against injustice wherever it may occur. Michal Osterweil describes this as the 'universalizing globalist' perspective:

> According to a 'universalizing globalist' perspective, effective resistance to neo-liberal capitalist globalization must come in the form of a united global movement that has moved *beyond* place-based and local struggles to occupy and constitute *an* alternative global space ... I call this position 'universalizing' because despite some attention to, and acknowledgement of, difference and a certain acceptance of the importance of local practice, this position always works towards establishing a *future universal* political project. It does so on the one hand by stressing the need for disembedded juridical categories such as 'global citizenship' and on the other by its view of place and difference as regressive and provincial, something to be transcended in favour of a common unified movement against capital.
>
> (Osterweil 2005: 25–6)

I will, following Deleuze and Guattari, refer to this brand of cosmopolitanism as 'arborescent cosmopolitanism'. An arborescent structure, say Deleuze and Guattari, is one that is organized around a 'strong principal unity ... that of the pivotal taproot supporting the secondary roots' (1987: 5). Such a structure explains all multiplicity as derivative of a central unity. We can see, then, the Stoics' 'concentric circle' model of moral obligation as an arborescent structure, with each locality or historical particularity splitting off from a more fundamental unity, starting from a foundational, universal truth of humanity. Arborescent systems have the benefit of being able to simplify, or at the very least tame, hugely complex or proliferating systems. A shared human nature, with its attendant universal moral and rational norms, serves as the 'pivotal taproot' from which all local differences are derived.

Arborescent cosmopolitanism is thus an attempt to move our moral allegiances closer and closer to the taproot, attenuating our attachments to particular slender branches. An arborescent cosmopolitanism 'implicitly expects human beings to follow a path of scaling up of their identities until they become abstract bearers of universal rights and duties, who embrace all of humankind yet are "unencumbered" by sub-cosmopolitan attachments. To be cosmopolitan in this way is to become geographically and culturally disembedded, to adopt a view from nowhere that leaves socio-cultural specificities' (Kurasawa 2004: 239).

However, this effort to transcend particularity is a losing proposition because, at the end of the day, there is no 'view from nowhere'. Moral propositions which lay claim to universality have an unfortunate tendency, when investigated closely, to show themselves to be unconsciously particular and partial. As Judith Butler puts it, as enticing as a moral universal is, '[t]he problem emerges ... when the meaning of "the universal" proves to be culturally variable, and the specific cultural articulations of the universal works against its claim to a transcultural status' (1996: 45).

What kinds of violence are done, then, in the attempt to enforce the particular as the universal? What particular assumptions are (re)produced as universal assertions? Which claims and identities, struggles and communities are marginalized, or potentially even erased, when we attempt to enforce this universalistic structure. Again, Judith Butler asks the question:

> What kind of cultural imposition is it to claim that a Kantian may be found in every culture? For whereas there may be something like a world reference in moral thinking or even a recourse to a version of universality, it would sidestep the specific cultural work to be done to claim that we have in Kant everything we might want to know about how moral reasoning works in various cultural contexts.
>
> (Butler 1996: 52)

Indeed, at this point it is useful to return to Kant, for in his work we can very clearly see the rootedness of the supposedly cosmopolitan state that he endeavours to bring about it. For Kant's universal history seems to include only a small portion of the world's population:

> For if one begins with Greek history – the one through which all other more ancient or contemporaneous histories have been preserved or at least authenticated; it one follows the influence of the Greeks on the formation and malformation of the body politic of the *Roman* people, who engulfed the Greek nation, and the influence of the Romans on the

barbarians, who in their turn destroyed the Romans, up to our own time; and if, as episodes, one adds to this the national histories of other peoples, inasmuch as knowledge of them has bit by bit come to us from these enlightened nations; one will discover a course of improvement conforming to rules in the constitutions of the nations on our continent (which will in all likelihood eventually give laws to all others).

(Kant 1983: 38)

This is why Derrida states:

this text, which is cosmopolitical in spirit, according to a law that could be verified well beyond Kant, is the most strongly Eurocentered text that can be, not only in its philosophical axiomatic but also in its retrospective reference to Greco-Roman history and in its prospective reference to the future hegemony of Europe.

(Derrida 2002: 7)

This Eurocentrism of Kant's cosmopolitan project is a result of the fact that the supposedly apodictic and *a priori* metaphysical principles which we noted underlie Kant's universal history are rooted solidly in a particularly European and Christian social milieu.[3]

I would therefore like to argue that the drive of an arborescent cosmopolitanism is not only to draw all the concentric circles of identity and moral obligation towards the centre, but also to expand the inner circle outwards, to turn what was a particular into a universal boundary, encompassing all that is strange and different in familiar codes, understandings and norms. The Other is transformed into the Self by asserting a fundamental unity beneath an epiphenomenal difference, transforming an exteriority into an interiority.

My concern is not with the specific content of the moral and social order which Kant, Nussbaum or any other arborescent cosmopolitan would like to see enacted at the global level. Indeed, I find many aspects of that political order laudable. My concern is with the very idea that an idea can simply transcend the historical location of its formation. This is not to say that cross-cultural points of commonality can't be produced, or negotiations or agreements made. However, rather than having this commonality come about as a result of political engagement, Nussbaum insists that her cosmopolitan project *must begin* by assuming a collection of 'thick, vague universals' which cannot be negotiated or discussed, only accepted. The danger of this assertion of a universal human nature is that it might blind us to different social formations, either newly emergent or as yet unencountered. To identity a set of universal principles will mean privileging one cultural context over others, and will marginalize and potentially erase alternative narratives of morality, politics and rationality. This becomes a real problem when cosmopolitan ideals are put into to play by global governance structures or transnational activist movements. Even the most well-intentioned endeavour, by its reliance on 'universal principles', can overlook local differences and do harm.[4] We can trace a long line of the negative consequences of benevolent universalisms in the modern world, starting with the civilizing missions of the great colonial projects, and working our way up to the International Monetary Fund and World Bank structural adjustment programs, which offer the same remedies to every ailing economy regardless of the particular sources. The point here is to highlight the way in which arborescent cosmopolitanism can lead to *unintended* violence.

To take just one example, we can look at Ethel Brooks' account of the American campaign against child labour in Bangladesh, which resulted in the Harkin Bill and a boycott of Bangladeshi-made garments. Though rooted in the laudable goal of discouraging child labour, 'UBINIG [a Bangladeshi non-governmental organization (NGO) on development issues], along with other NGO and activist groups in Bangladesh, charged the authors of the Harkin Bill and the consumers who boycotted Bangladesh-made goods with protectionism and imperialism' (Brooks 2005: 128). They charged that the American activists acted without a proper understanding of local conditions, such as the way in which a boycott would damage a community dependent on garment work for survival, and ignored the question of what to do with the child workers now put out on the street (128). Perhaps most important of all was the fact that the Bangladeshi workers were themselves excluded from the political process (128). Western activists could have worked with the Bangladeshi workers and learned about local conditions, and sought to empower them politically. Instead, they were treated as mute victims (or, worse, collaborators in the exploitation of children), who could be dealt with abstractly as bearers of universal human rights. The point is not that American activists should not have been concerned about child welfare in Bangladesh, or that they didn't have good intentions, but rather that a cosmopolitanism that seeks to act according to a process of disengagement and abstraction can frequently do harm as a result of its lack of local knowledge and inability to fully acknowledge the differences of others.[5]

By seeking its foundation in a universal humanity, morality and rationality, arborescent cosmopolitanism provides a way of taming or controlling an increasingly complex and interdependent world, where examples of multiplicity and difference seem to proliferate and clash at alarming speed. It provides a fundamental homogeneity at the human level to sweep away the cumbersome and potentially dangerous heterogeneity at the level of territorial particularity. That it does so by elevating one particularity to the level of 'pivotal taproot' and subordinating, potentially violently, all other difference is the price that is paid for this stability and certainty.

The question, then, is this: if acceleration is the condition of possibility of cosmopolitanism, is it also bound to the homogenizing project of arborescent cosmopolitanism? Does the acceleration of modern life provide both the threat which galvanizes the homogenizing project (by constantly producing new and dangerous encounters with difference and multiplicity) and the technological means to produce the totalized and unified world which the Stoics could only advocate as a moral ideal? Does speed, as Virilio, Wolin and Thomas Freidman seem to believe, obliterate difference and create one small concentric world?

Rhizomatic cosmopolitanism

David Held describes how material shifts in the velocity and scope of global politics drive the universalizing project of arborescent cosmopolitanism:

> The locus of effective political power can no longer be assumed to be simply national governments – effective power is shared and bartered by diverse forces and agencies, public and private, at national, regional and international levels. Moreover, the idea of a self-determining people – or of a political community of fate – can no longer be located within the boundaries of a single national-state alone. Some of the most fundamental focuses and processes which determine the nature of life chances are now beyond the reach of individual nation-states.
>
> (Held 2003: 161)

As the problems the world faces expand in scope and the structures of repression, exploitation and violence become global, is it necessary to produce a movement in response equally large in scope? In other words, if we wish to engage effectively and efficiently in global politics, are we doomed by the velocity of the world to recreate the homogenization and transcendence from particularity in our attempt to build an alternative world order? Can we fight global homogenization effectively without becoming it ourselves?

Here it is helpful to return to a critical point in our analysis of speed: the ontological distinction between speed and movement. In doing this we introduced an inherent ambiguity and bivalence into the social acceleration of time. Movement and velocity may be marked by an increase in scope, but speed is marked by an unforeseeable swerve in a teleological projection in space–time. Speed introduces a difference into sameness; a heterogeneity into homogeneity. We saw this in the nomad war-machine that escapes the state-form in Chapter 2 or the creative line of innovation that escapes the capitalist apparatus of capture in Chapter 3. And in this chapter we will see how at the same time as acceleration seems to bind the whole world in one global system it also sets in motion eccentric flows which have the potential to conjugate in odd and unexpected ways.

We have described one tendency of speed as exteriority, the drive to overflow borders and boundaries. However, such an exteriority does not overcome local or national borders only to set up a new border encompassing the whole world. As we saw in Chapter 2, it is the great failure of the worldwide war-machine to think that it can use the speed of the war-machine to enclose the globe. Speed is an anti-boundary phenomenon. The exteriority of speed not only breaks boundaries, but decentres them and undermines their conditions of possibility. In this regard, speed is not a process of transcendence, but a process of deterritorialization (and we would be gravely mistaken in confusing the two). It is true that the act of deterritorialization is nearly always followed by an act of reterritorialization which establishes new borders. But these new borders will not 'transcend' the old ones in a progression towards larger and more 'complete' borders. These new borders will be as contingent as the old ones, ripe for other deterritorializations.

Speed cannot be modelled according to the Stoic's topology of concentric circles, and it certainly does not 'draw the circles somehow towards the center' (Nussbaum 1996: 9). Rather, speed cuts across circles, drawing together what is 'closest as well as farthest away' (Deleuze and Guattari 1987: 3). It is, as we noted in Chapter 1, always a transversal movement. It creates a new map and a new understanding of space. It takes away the unity and the interiority of place (whether local or global).

We saw this in our discussion of (im)mobility in Chapter 4, where places existed neither on their own, unitary and self-sufficient, nor ordered into a hierarchy of size and scope. Rather, they related to one another in a complex and shifting pattern of axiomatic flows. Place became tendentially located in a shifting hyperspace of regimes of (im)mobility (global cities which are 'closer' to one another than to the surrounding territory; lines of travel which are blocked for some agents and free for others; the INA's shifting dynamic map). In this world, locality and globality interplay in surprising and unexpected ways. And none of these relations are abstract or universal. They are particular and rooted. They have territorial and conceptual histories; not essential or unchanging, mind you, but living and effective.

This new space of the world, this interweaving of global and local, decentres and destabilizes old borders, and in doing so does produce a kind of cosmopolitanism. But it is not a universal, singular, arborescent cosmopolitanism; a final, total enclosure to replace all previous partial enclosures. Rather, one of the things this new accelerated world teaches us is:

> Like nations, cosmopolitanisms are now plural and particular. Like nations, they are both European and non-European, and they are weak and underdeveloped as well as strong and privileged. And again like the nation, cosmopolitanism is *there* – not merely as an abstract ideal, like loving one's neighbor as oneself, but habits of thought and feeling that have already shaped and been shaped by particular collectivities, that are socially and geographically situated, hence both limited and empowered.
>
> (Cheah and Robbins 1998: 2)

We therefore see the coming of a new cosmopolitan politics: a politics that goes beyond traditional borders, but without seeking transcendence or abstraction; a politics that finds connection, solidarity and community across borders, but without, for all that, seeking to marginalize or erase difference; that wishes to negotiate agreements and come to decisions, without quashing dissent; that wishes to resist oppression, injustice and inequality, without having to do so under the banner of a timeless and universal rationality and morality; that reflects the new porosity and complexity of space and place in global politics; that rejects the Nussbaumian position that to be effective a cosmopolitanism must assume a 'thick, vague' conception of human nature. As Connolly puts it,

> [Nussbaum] thinks that if [individuals] do not share a thick conception of human flourishing they must appear as strangers to one another. This charge reveals an inability to come to terms with a variety of connections across difference in which people touch each other now in this way and now in that, and through which larger webs of alliance and loyalty are often forged.
>
> (Connolly 2002: 192)

The cosmopolitanism that I seek to flesh out describes such a project of forging alliances and loyalties across difference without asserting an *a priori* commonality of essence.

Many thinkers have advanced different theoretical terms and structures to discuss this new global politics: 'critical cosmopolitanism ' (Mignolo 2000: 724), 'abject cosmopolitanism' (Nyers 2003: 1070), 'cosmopolitanism from below' (Kurasawa 2004), 'creole cosmopolitanism' (Verges 2001: 179), 'rooted cosmopolitanism' (Cohen 1992: 480), 'place based globalism' (Osterweil 2005: 21), and so on. Each of these accounts does important work in mapping the contours of this new global space and politics, and I will try to engage several of them in what follows. However, at the risk of needlessly adding to this collection, I want to introduce a new phrase to investigate the relationship between cosmopolitanism, speed and the new space of global politics: *rhizomatic cosmopolitanism.*

Rhizomatic cosmopolitanism is a practice of global politics that, unlike arborescent cosmopolitanism, is not tree-like. Rather, '[i]n contrast to centered (even polycentric) systems with hierarchical modes of communication and preestablished paths, the rhizome is an acentered, nonhierarchical, nonsignifying system without a General and without an organizing memory or central automaton, defined solely by a circulation of states' (Deleuze and Guattari 1987: 21). The rhizome provides a way of describing the conjunction or connection of multiple and varying flows without subordinating those flows to a higher unity (or, for that matter, freezing those flows into pre-existing unities). Deleuze and Guattari's language of rhizomaticity mirrors the descriptions which many global activists give of their transnational political activities. For example, People's Global Action (PGA, about which more later), a coalition of transnational activist movements, describes itself as embodying '"An organizational philosophy based on decentralization and autonomy." Its defining features include no membership, no resources, and minimal central structures. No one may represent the PGA, nor does the PGA represent any organization or person' (Wood 2005: 100). In describing the coalitions it embodies, the PGA states that '[t]here is no center anywhere that could hope to organize and oversee all this mutual thickening of ties. It would be like trying to instruct a forest how to grow' (99). Subcomandante Insurgente Marcos, head of the Zapatista army, in his address to the First International *Encuentro* for Humanity and against Neoliberalism, a summit of several thousand global activists held in Chiapas, stated:

> This intercontinental network of resistance, recognizing differences and acknowledging similarities, will strive to find itself in other resistances around the world. This intercontinental network of resistance will be the medium in which distinct resistances may support one another. This intercontinental network of resistance is not an organizing structure; it has no central head or decision maker; it has no central command or hierarchies. We are the network, all of us who resist.
>
> (Marcos 2002: 117)

Both these passages speak to the importance of the network form in organizing transnational coalitions. In prior eras, due to problems of communication and transportation over long distances, transnational organizations tended to need to be highly centralized and hierarchical. However, the rise of new accelerative technologies allows transnational organizations to avoid the 'iron law of oligarchy' while at the same time allowing for efficient and effective action. Indeed, these new networked forms of organization allow for greater flexibility and local autonomy, as information and decision-making don't need to pass through a central clearing house.

The advancement of accelerative technologies has been crucial in sustaining the viability of this rhizomatic cosmopolitanism, specifically the development of communications technologies. The internet especially has had a profound impact on the practice of transnational activism, which has allowed for the greater dissemination of information amongst like-minded organizations separated by space:

> prior to the Internet, NGO intelligence tended to be as a consequence more disconnected and sluggish, with the intelligence operations compartmentalized among NGOs spread across the world over multiple state jurisdictions. What intelligence sharing occurred was sporadic and uneven and typically centered on occasional face-to-face meetings supplemented with postal traffic, faxes and intermittent telephone exchanges. The relatively large expenses associated with the last meant that the slower and less interactive modes of the former were more common. NGO intelligence gathering and analysis operated within a similar set of constraints. Prior to the Internet, acquisition of government or international organization documents and reports had to take place through formal postal requisitions,

library searches or trips to departments and ministries, all of which reduced the pace and analytical capacities of individual NGOs most of whom typically operated (and still do) with very modest budgets.

(Deibert 2003b: 178)

However, more than just improving the ability to disseminate information, accelerated communications technologies change (or at least provide the conditions of possibility for changing) the practice of global activism, decreasing the need for hierarchical organization and centralization, and providing new opportunities for networked, decentralized organizations. Rhizomatic cosmopolitanism is 'favoured by the new information technologies and the increasing centrality of information to social life. Whilst those who developed and sell the new electronic media are concerned primarily with control and consumption, the technologies have possibilities that subvert these intentions' (Waterman 1998: 64). The distributed nature of new communication technologies encourages new networked forms of activism. Such networked forms of rhizomatic cosmopolitanism place an essential value on processes of communication and negotiation as a means of mediating difference, rather than arborescent cosmopolitanism's assumption, and potential imposition, of a primal similarity. Thus, '[t]he new global solidarity movements are, in large part, "communication internationalisms". Communication is here increasingly understood not simply as a technical means to be used but as an ethical end to be valued' (215). Macshane looks at changes in the practices of labour union activism which new communications technologies have enabled:

> The traditional pyramid organization of unions with international contacts carefully controlled and monitored at the very peak runs counter to the most useful forms of international contacts, which are horizontal, between workers employed by the same company (or industry) in different countries. Fax, e-mail and cheap travel are also enabling horizontal network-building between workers in different countries, which contrast with traditionally hierarchically-organized trade-union activity. These new developments facilitating international labour contacts pose a challenge to existing trade-union structures and internal communication links. At the same time, they open immense possibilities for labour to regain power and influence. Unions could ride the globalization process by becoming repositories of information about international development as they emerge from, or impact on, the workplace.
>
> (Macshane, quoted in Waterman 1998: 113–14)

This brief discussion of how new communication technologies enable transnational activism gives us some insight into what rhizomatic cosmopolitan political action looks like. At this point it is useful to go more in-depth, looking at the principles of rhizomaticity which Deleuze and Guattari lay out, and how they relate to contemporary global political activism.

Principles of rhizomatic cosmopolitanism

Deleuze and Guattari describe the first principle of the rhizome as the '[p]rinciple of connection' which says 'any point of a rhizome can be connected to any other, and must be. This is very different from the tree or root, which plots a point, fixes an order' (1987: 7). In terms of global politics, this speaks to the way in which new accelerative technologies subvert the traditional hierarchies of scope, creating transversal lines that cut across the concentric circles of the arborescent. The path of connection does not follow a spiralling outwards in scope from local to national to international. Nor do global political initiatives necessarily radiate from the top downwards, enacted by global institutions such as the UN or international NGOs. Such initiatives obviously do exist, and in great numbers. However, what we also see in rhizomatic cosmopolitanisms are allegiances between local groups in different countries which do not travel through larger-scale aggregates. Groups and actors no longer necessarily look to their national government – or international NGOs – to effect change, but make direct connection with other groups engaged in common causes. One excellent example of this is in the context of labour organizing within the globalizing economy. Increasingly, rather than looking to national governments (or international bodies such as the WTO or International Labour Organization), labour unions will reach out to labour unions in other countries with similar interests. Says Michael Hanagan, 'As their hold on the consolidated state has loosened, and as the state's competence in trade policy has declined, trade unions in industrialized countries have begun to consider promoting the unionization of workers in less industrialized countries' (2003: 487). This can lead to lines of support and solidarity across vast distances, connecting deeply disparate localities in common cause. For example, '[i]n 2001 Brazilian Mercedes Benz workers refused to work overtime to compensate for production losses due to a strike of South African autoworkers' (492). Such acts of labour solidarity between international labour movements speak of the increasing ability for transnational connections to occur at all levels.

This is, however, a very simple version of the kinds of interconnection which can take place within rhizomatic cosmopolitanism. There can also be webs of connection which cross borders, jump levels of aggregation and bring together a disparate coalition of actors and forces. Heather Williams describes the struggle for unionization and the enforcement of proper working conditions in the Han Young factory in the *Maquilladora* region of Mexico. At various points this conflict brought together a coalition of labour unions on both sides of the border: elements within the Mexican, American and South Korean governments; the mass media; and multiple human rights groups, labour rights groups and progressive political movements of different scales and locations (Williams 2003). Here we see rhizomatic globalization in action: as a rich web of diverse actors and forces, at multiple different scales of aggregation, linked together and focused on what is, at heart, a local struggle for labour organization. Such complex webs of connection refuse the simple and orderly image of concentric circles of affiliation and community.

Deleuze and Guattari's second principle of the rhizome is the principle of heterogeneity. This is the principle that 'traits are not necessarily linked to traits of the same nature' (Deleuze and Guattari 1987: 21). In the rhizomatic structure, a connection between lines does not necessarily speak to a deeper unity between the two. It is not indicative of the partiality, or contingency of difference, in favour of a more fundamental sameness. Rather, resonances can develop between disparate lines, and a plane of consistency (in the sense of a plane allowing for the functional integration of different machinic assemblages) can be constructed across difference. 'In another sense, consistency concretely ties together heterogeneous, disparate element as such: it assures the consolidation of fuzzy aggregates, in other words, multiplicities of the rhizome type' (507). For the rhizome, connection across difference does not mean resolution or negation of that difference. In terms of a rhizomatic cosmopolitanism, this means that actors and flows which enter into conjunction with one another need not possess some sort of shared primary identity or principles. All that is required is that their immediate goals be able to resonate with one another. For example, we can take the coalition that was formed between the US-based Animal Welfare Institute (AWI) and Samoobrona, a 'militant organization of Polish small farmers', in the attempt to stop Smithfield foods, an American agribusiness corporation, from purchasing 'Polish pork conglomerate Animex and bring[ing] its American-style success story to Poland' (Juska and Edwards 2005: 187), the former because of environmental concerns in Smithfield's production processes, the latter out of fear over how Smithfield would effect the agricultural market in Poland. Juska and Edwards describe how

> difference[s] between AWI and Samoobrona remained, especially in their attitudes toward nature and animals. AWI articulates nature issues as mostly a moral category, having an innate value to be preserved for its own sake. By contrast [Samoobrona] treat nature and animals in a pragmatic way, primarily as a natural resource for human livelihood. However, the compatibility of their ideological critique of corporate capitalism and agreement about preferred strategies and tactics enabled these differences to be negotiated successfully.
>
> (Juska and Edwards 2005: 198)

Campaigns such as these show that 'in a closely knit international economy with easy communication across space and time, actors with different but complementary aims can forge collaborative arrangements' (Tarrow 2005: 162). The point here is that new accelerative technologies provide an environment in which rhizomatic cosmopolitanism can foster transnational coalitions which can effect political change without necessarily requiring, or enforcing, a homogeneity of principles. Heterogeneity can flourish, or at least exist, while allowing for effective resistance against global-level forces (such as transnational corporations).

The third principle of the rhizome is that of 'multiplicity':

> It is only when the multiple is effectively treated as a substantive 'multiplicity,' that it ceases to have any relation to the One as subject or object, natural or spiritual reality, image and world. Multiplicities are rhizomatic, and expose arborescent pseudo-multiplicities for what they are. There is no unity to serve as a pivot in the object, or to divide in the subject. There is not even the unity to abort in the object or 'return in the subject'.
>
> (Deleuze and Guattari 1987: 8)

This is to return to the idea presented above: that rhizomatic cosmopolitanism affirms the multiple. It views the multiplicity of difference present in the world not as arborescent cosmopolitanism does – as particular and contingent deviations from a primary similarity, or as epiphenomenal and illusory – but as real and substantial. What is more, on the other side of things, it refuses to see the rhizomatic assemblage itself as an agglomeration of individual unities (the individuals which add up to the multiple). Each of the points which makes up an assemblage is itself not essentially fixed, but constantly shifting, in time and in space. It is never a being but always a becoming:

> Unlike a structure, which is defined by a set of points and positions, with binary relations between the positions, the rhizome is made only of lines: lines of segmentarity and stratification as its dimensions, and the line of flight or deterritorialization as the maximum dimension after which the multiplicity undergoes metamorphosis, changes in nature.
>
> (Deleuze and Guattari 1987: 21)

It is multiplicity all the way down. This means that acts of rhizomatic connection are themselves processes of becoming which produce change, both in the assemblage and in the lines which are connected. Unlike arborescent cosmopolitanism, which supposedly reveals a latent commonality, rhizomatic cosmopolitan is a never-ending process of constructing an assemblage.[6]

This principle of multiplicity speaks to the way in which the process of transnational activism is not just a process of different agents coming together in recognition of an implicit unity which precedes them (the recognition of the rationally and morally human), or a coded negotiation between pre-existing local unities with established and essential identities and interests. Rather, transnational activism is a process of becoming; becoming at the level of local identities, as well as becoming at the level of an assemblage, a community or a movement, with feedbacks loops linking and affecting the various levels of aggregation. What it will be, what path it will follow, is not predetermined. Transnational activism does not just build new movements, it also builds new actors. This is why, for example, in the realm of transnational labour organizing '[b]oth the IBT and UAW [American Labour Unions] began sending delegations of rank-and-file workers to Mexico in the early 1990s, eroding protectionist sentiments among their workforces and building trust among their Mexican counterparts' (Stillerman 2003: 586). Such interactions do not just discover hidden commonalities and discard inessential or contingent differences. They are intended as a way of producing difference, changing identities and producing new perceptions. Stillerman notes that 'U.S. rank-and-file workers who visit Mexico's assembly plants became radicalized and active spokespeople for transnational solidarity' (591). Campaigns are not necessarily undertaken with a complete understanding of where they will go, or of who the people undertaking them are. This, says, Michal Osterweil, is 'what the Zapatistas mean when they insist on a politics without ideology, without a vanguard, one in which we *caminar preguntando* – walk while questioning' (2005: 23).

The fourth principle of the rhizome is the '[p]rinciple of asignifying rupture: against the oversignifying breaks separating structures or cutting across a single structure. A rhizome may be broken, shattered at a given spot, but it will start up again on one of its old lines, or on new lines' (9). This principle too speaks to the question of hierarchy. Arborescent structures seek to produce ruptures, borders and clear lines of separation between points. Rhizomatic structures, by virtue of the way in which they 'grow from the middle', invariably jump over these ruptures, overgrow blockages, find new passages and unexpected resonances between points. According to our principle of exteriority, lines of acceleration function as movements transversal to a projected line of flight (or potential blockages): 'Transversal communication between different lines scramble the genealogical trees' (11). Rhizomatic structures seek to

> lengthen, prolong and relay the line of flight; make it vary, until you have produced the most abstract and tortuous of lines of *n* dimensions and broken directions. Conjugate deterritorialized flows. Write, form a rhizome, increase your territory by deterritorialization, extend the line of flight to the point where it becomes an abstract machine covering the entire plane of consistency.
>
> (Osterweil 2005: 11)

In terms of a rhizomatic cosmopolitanism, we might see this as the valorization and potential power of apparently isolated and blocked-off points of locality. A traditional critical narrative of globalization states that as localities become integrated into the circuits of global production they become increasingly cut off from centres of power, and hence less capable of autonomous political action and decision-making. The fundamental break between the national level and the global level (at which decisions of economic, social and military importance are made) leaves local actors subject to the whims of global actors. Arborescent cosmopolitanism thus focuses on the need to gain access to these global-level institutions or set up alternative ones as a way of effecting political change.

A rhizomatic cosmopolitan approach does not necessarily eschew the importance of global-level campaigns and institutions. However, it is also aware of how, due to the proliferation of interconnection between global flows, localities can, paradoxically, become more powerful, rather than less. Thus, Andrew Herrod tells the story of the '1998 dispute between the United Auto Workers and the General Motors Corporations':

> In the latter case, the power of workers to take advantage of the vulnerabilities in the production chain presented by GM's corporate and spatial organization and its reliance upon the speedy delivery of components from one plant to another was readily evident. Hence disruptions of work by workers at just two plants in Flint, Michigan, over issues related to local work organization ultimately forced GM to close or to cut back significantly on production at 27 of its 29 North American assembly plants and at 117 component plants located in the United States, Canada, Mexico, and Singapore. In turn, these actions led the corporation to lose production of some 500,000 vehicles, to lay off at the height of the dispute some 193,500 GM workers, and to suffer an after-tax loss of $2.3 Billion for the second and third quarters of 1998. By their local actions, the Flint workers were able to bring to a grinding halt throughout North America the operations of one of the world's most powerful corporations.
>
> (Herrod 2003: 510)

A similar tale can be told of the 1997 strike by UPS workers, in the way in which their local labour activities critically affected the flow of goods within the global economy (510).

Not all localities will be equally capable of effecting change on the global level. But practices of rhizomatic cosmopolitanism make us attentive to the possibility of local action, to the possibility of unexpected resonances and passages developing, jumping over ruptures and blockages. Indeed, it is worth being aware of the way in which even local activities of community building can produce resonance with other localities, and, aided by newly accelerated information and communication technologies, encourage acts of resistance and production, creating webs of mutual support which are locally instantiated but globally resonant.[7] Such an approach revalorizes the local, and presents it as a site of possibility for political action.[8]

The final principle of the rhizome is the '[p]rinciple of cartography and decalcomania: a rhizome is not amenable to any structural or generative model. It is a stranger to any idea of genetic axis or deep structure' (Deleuze and Guattari 1987: 12). This principle speaks to the contingency and openendedness of the process of understanding the contours of the global space, and hence of the pathways of resistance and connection to be found in it.

It may seem confusing to call this principle cartography, but that is only if we think of a map as signifying some sort of fundamental truth about a territory. The fact is, a map is always contingent and partial, always drawn for some purpose, and omitting that which is, at that point, considered irrelevant. It is true that the map frequently gets mistaken for the territory, or, rather, that the truths of the map become reified as the universal truth of the territory. Deleuze and Guattari acknowledge this tendency of the map to get elevated to the level of signifier: 'Does not a multiplicity have a strata upon which unifications and totalizations, massifications, mimetic mechanisms, signifying power takeovers, and subjective attributions take root? Do not even lines of flight, due to their eventual divergence, reproduce the very formations their function it was to dismantle and outflank?' (13). However, such reifications only last so long, and as the totalities of the map begin to rub against the omitted and proliferating contingencies of the territory, its effectiveness begins to falter. And we must return again to the process of mapping: '*the tracing should always be put back on the map*' (13). In spite of the map's contingency, its inadequacy in regards to the territory, the rhizome does not reject it, because the rhizome does not require a universal signifier or a total knowledge of the territory it wishes to inhabit and effect (indeed, it rejects the very possibility of such a signifier). It accepts that, to take action in the world, to effect connections and assemblages, maps are necessary. But a rhizomatic structure is aware of their status as maps, as *mappings*. In terms of rhizomatic cosmopolitanism, this means an awareness of the contingency of one's own map of the world, and a willingness to make changes to the map, as well as to acknowledge the existence of alternative maps. Indeed, it accepts the usefulness of multiple maps (hence the anti-globalization movement taking on of the title 'a movement of movements').

We might then turn to Leslie Wood's account of People's Global Action, a coalition of 'over fifteen hundred organizations, from peasant movements to trade unions', which organizes information exchanges, as well as direct political action, such as the WTO protests in Seattle (2005: 99). Wood describes how the PGA is organized to ensure that all members are able to participate in the continual process of determining its practices and goals:

> From its foundation, the PGA chose to build its collective identity around 'living documents' that would be formally revised at each gathering. Jean Frossholz, who participated in the initial process to write the manifesto, explained how women, native people, farmers, labor activists, and environmentalists worked in small groups to develop their position, gradually drafting an acceptable framework that was brought to the larger body of activists.
>
> (Wood 2005: 110)

At each subsequent meeting, these documents are refined and revised to reflect new understandings and interests. This process of constant redefinition

Table 5.1

Arborescent systems	Rhizomatic stems
Principle of hierarchy: arborescent structures have established hierarchies through which flows must necessarily pass.	Principle of connection: 'any point of a rhizome can be connected to any other, and must be.'
Principle of homogeneity: all differences can be resolved in a more fundamental unity.	Principle of heterogeneity: 'traits are not necessarily linked to traits of the same nature.'
Principle of unity: multiplicities are stable unities, formed through connections between stable lower-order unities.	Principle of multiplicity: 'There is no unity to serve as a pivot in the object, or to divide in the subject. There is not even the unity to abort in the object or "return in the subject".'
Principle of concentricity: spaces are ordered in a nesting hierarchy of importance. Higher-order problems must be challenged at an equal or greater level of scale or power.	Principle of asignifying rupture: 'A rhizome may be broken, shattered at a given spot, but it will start up again on one of its old lines, or on new lines.'
Principle of structure: foundational principles provide a generative order for arborescent organizations.	Principle of cartography: 'A rhizome is not amenable to any structural or generative model. It is a stranger to any idea of genetic axis or deep structure.'

pays careful attention to asymmetries of power between wealthier, typically developed-world organization, and poorer developing-world organizations. As Wood describes, '[i]n reaction to what they perceived as "paternalistic NGOs" the PGA participants worked to build something different. Friederike, a German participant explained; "What matters a lot to me is that it is the only international network where the movements from the South are represented in a way that corresponds to their importance, not like an NGO sponsoring the South or something"' (100). Such an approach ensures the diversity of the maps to which the PGA will have access. The result is a group that, '[c]hallenged by their differences in resources, organizational culture, and coalition experience, and yet pressured to act ... resisted the "iron law of oligarchy" to build a model that would remain both egalitarian and cohesive' (96).

A world in which many worlds fit

At this point it is useful to return to the RJ Reynolds protest with which we began (pp. 153–155). From the perspective of an arborescent cosmopolitanism, this protest marked an example of various actors and groups transcending their particular and local affinities to aid in combating a universal moral indignity. And to some extent this is true. Certainly everyone present thought that the treatment of the tobacco pickers was unacceptable. However, if we look at the event from the perspective of a rhizomatic cosmopolitanism, we can see how much richer and more complex it was. First of all we saw the connection of diverse and heterogenous elements, each with their own particular take on the stakes and interests at play (principles of connection and heterogeneity): the workers themselves, fighting for better working conditions; allied labour unions, connected by ties of affective unity with fellow labourers; church congregations, there out of a sense of moral duty rooted in Christian theology; local and national media outlets, there to cover the story and thus transmit the protestors' voices; transnational academics, there out of a sense of political solidarity (and to acquire some firsthand research); local college kids caught up in the carnival-like atmosphere of the protest. Though many of those present were thinking of the inherent human dignity of the workers, few of them felt the need to transcend their particularity to do so. Instead, the protest was marked by the resonances and interactions of different particular lines, either reinforcing or changing each other (principle of multiplicity): aging mine workers learning to chant in Spanish, young seafarers getting their first taste of social activism and leaving more committed to union activity. The protest itself worked simultaneously at multiple aggregates, trying to resolve a local conflict while at the same time focusing on a national corporation, and to create allegiances between different national labouring bodies (principle of asignifying rupture). And finally, after the protest, all involved were now left to decide where this effort would go next (principle of cartography).

We should not overstate the case. It is not as if arborescent formations were completely absent from this movement. The protest was primarily organized by large, hierarchical labour unions such as FLOC[9] and the AFL-CIO. However, we are not on a crusade to root out all trees. Arborescent formations within the rhizome are inevitable (and desirable to some extent), just as all deterritorializations must inevitably be reterritorialized. The question is: how do the two grow into each other? How do we cross the arborescent with the rhizomatic? How do we grow across enclosures? How do we open up new territories and new planes of consistency?

This image of a rhizomatic cosmopolitanism gives us hope that effective action can be taken against global-level structures of oppression, injustice and inequality, without, for all that, duplicating the homogenizing and totalizing structures which we seek to overturn. We can produce coalitions and communities without therefore erasing or marginalizing difference (or, at the very least, we can seek to minimize the violence that we do). And such efforts are encouraged and aided by the new structure of accelerative technologies. Speed does not mean homogenization and control. It can also mean heterogeneity, resistance and solidarity across difference. A rhizomatic cosmopolitanism makes us attentive to the possibilities these new technologies and structures offer. And a hopeful experimentalism makes us willing to pursue them.

Conclusion

'We have never been territorial'
Fear and hope in an accelerating world

Ressentiment and Left nationalism

At this point it's worth asking why, in the face of so much fruitful activity in the sphere of transnational activism, so many on the Left turn away from these global flows and set their sights resolutely on the national sphere. That conservatives should reject the global in favour of the national is only natural (although, as we saw in Chapter 4, with the development of the neoliberal–neoconservative resonance machine, this becomes somewhat ambiguous). But why is it that, in this time of increased globalization, so many progressives find themselves turning towards what has been termed 'Left nationalism' (Laxer 2001)? By this I do not mean simply the idea that the nation-state is still an important site of political activity in the struggle for justice and equality. As we saw in our survey of transnational activism, the state is often brought into play, either as an agent capable of bringing to bear considerable resources and force or as a site of contestation and pressure. Any rhizomatic cosmopolitan activity will have to take the state very seriously for the conceivable future. Rather, by Left nationalism I mean the belief that the nation, or the nation-state, is the privileged site of political activity and that a bounded territorial model of political community is necessary for the enactment of any effective progressive political movement. We see this in many Left economic analyses, which decry the decline of national labour unions and Keynesianism and fordist production processes. Indeed, this focus on the historically national scope of effective Left economic policy leaves some analysts despairing in the face of a new post-fordist, globalized economy.[1] Others do not go this far, but do believe that the revitalization of the national as the primary political space is necessary to combat the violence and exploitation of globalizing capitalism (as well as a host of other ills). In this chapter, I wish to look to one exemplary Left nationalist text, Richard Rorty's *Achieving Our Country* (1998). The goal here is not just to engage in a critique of Left nationalism, but also to show how this critique once more draws out the dense web of hope, fear and *ressentiment* surrounding the politics of speed, which we have been developing over the course of this book.

Achieving our country

Rorty's text makes the straightforward Left nationalist claim that

> [t]he cultural left often seems convinced that the nation-state is obsolete, and that there is therefore no point in attempting to revive national politics. The trouble with this claim is that the government of our nation-state will be, for the foreseeable future, the only agent capable of making any real difference in the amount of selfishness and sadism inflicted on Americans.
>
> (Rorty 1998: 98)

In response to this he asserts that the 'Left should mobilize what remains of our pride in being Americans' (92).

What is, however, particularly interesting about Rorty, and what makes him so useful for our purpose, is how close his overall theory of political activity comes to the one which we have laid out in Chapter 1, specifically his theory of the temporality of political life. In his account of the philosophy of John Dewey, Rorty advances a political ontology of time that affirms a sense of futurity very similar to that in which speed is rooted. According to Rorty, for Dewey politics is a process of opening up an undetermined future, producing an endless diversity of possibilities:

> Dewey's philosophy is a systematic attempt to temporalize everything, to leave nothing fixed. This means abandoning the attempt to find a theoretical frame of reference within which to evaluate proposals for the human future. Dewey's romantic hope was that future events would make every proposed frame obsolete.
>
> (Rorty 1998: 20)

This temporalization served as a valorization of heterogeneity and contingency: 'What he dreaded was stasis: a time in which everybody would take for granted that the purpose of history had been accomplished, an age of spectators rather than agents, a country in which arguments between Right and Left would no longer be heard' (20). Rorty praises the importance of heterogeneity and difference for a healthy politics:

> Mill and Humboldt's 'richest diversity' and Whitman's 'full play' are ways of saying that no past human achievement, not Plato's or even Christ's, can tell us about the ultimate significance of human life. No such achievement can give us a template on which to model our future. The future will widen endlessly. Experiments with new forms of individual and social life will interact and reinforce one another. Individual life will become unthinkably diverse and social life unthinkably free.
>
> (Rorty 1998: 24)

With such seemingly similar accounts of temporality and the value of heterogeneity in political life, the question then becomes: how is it that his analysis and the one developed in this book arrive at such different points with regard to the question of the nation-state? The answer is that our analysis of speed had a spatial as well as a temporal element. And it is in Rorty's spatial imaginary that he forecloses the possibilities that his temporal ontology opens.

As we saw above, Rorty argues that 'the government of our nation state will be, for the foreseeable future, the only agent capable of making any real difference in the amount of selfishness and sadism inflicted on Americans' (98). In Chapter 5 I challenged this claim, and provided many examples of effective progressive political action which, while not excluding or even diminishing the importance of the nation-state, did not take it as the 'only agent' in the political landscape. Why, according to Rorty, must progressive politics be spatially bounded? Why is the state 'the only agent'?

I would argue that it is because Rorty is not as comfortable with the openness of the future as he would claim. Rorty is aware that an open futurity is not necessarily a safe or happy one, and that '[t]he price of temporalization [is] contingency' (23). In response to the danger of this open temporality, Rorty is moved to affirm a closed spatial dimension to political community. For all of Rorty's valorization of difference early on, such difference can only safely exist for him within the confines of a bounded territorial state and identity: America. He chastises a cultural Left, which, he says, insists on 'asking us to respect one another in our difference rather than asking us to cease noticing those differences' (101). Though Rorty earlier says that 'no past human achievement, not Plato's or even Christ's, can tell us about the ultimate significance of human life' (24), it seems that there is at least one signifier which can be used to parse out (and suppress) identity, difference and possibility. That sign is America. We must learn to 'cease noticing our differences' in the face of our commonality as Americans. Here we see the reappearance of an arborescent cosmopolitan response to difference; its erasure (or, if not erasure, at least implied irrelevancy) in the face of a more fundamental unity. The territory of Rorty's fundamental unity may be smaller than that of arborescent cosmopolitan's, and its future may be more uncertain, but the sense of similarity and homogeneity is the same.

Rorty goes on to criticize those on the 'cultural' and 'academic' Left for their refusal to focus on this national space, allowing their eyes to stray beyond the borders of the bounded American community:

> Union members in the United States have watched factory after factory close, only to reopen in Slovenia, Thailand, or Mexico. It is no wonder that they see the result of international free trade as prosperity for managers and stockholders, a better standard of living for workers in developing countries, and a very much worse standard of living for American workers. It would be no wonder if they saw the American

leftist intelligentsia as on the side of the managers and stockholders – as sharing the same class interests. For we intellectuals, who are mostly academics, are ourselves quite well insulated, at least in the short run, from the effects of globalization. To make things worse, we often seem more interested in the workers of the developing world than in the fate of our fellow citizens.

(Rorty 1998: 89)[2]

In the end, the people (whom Rorty somewhat unreflectively invokes) will find themselves fed up with this 'cosmopolitan' sensibility:

Where, they will ask, was the American Left? Why was it only rightists like Buchanan who spoke to the workers about the consequence of globalization? Why could not the left channel the mounting rage of the newly dispossessed?

(Rorty 1998: 91)

However, as we argued in Chapter 5, this is to ignore the way in which a conservative *ressentiment* against exteriority enters into resonance with neo-liberal globalization, cutting off lines of connection and conjugation between different actors who could fruitfully enter into productive connections across border lines in the struggle against the exploitation of globalizing capitalism. Rorty's Left nationalism potentially reinforces this *ressentiment*, although he does not seem all that concerned (above he seems particularly dismissive of those on the 'academic Left' who have the gall to show concern for Slovenian, Thai or Mexican workers. I wonder what Rorty would have to say to the mine workers I described in Chapter 5?). Indeed, Rorty seems to be underplaying the dangers of nationalism. He is more concerned with the dangerous lack (or perhaps openness is the better word) of political identity which is produced from the cultural Left's perspective of the 'detached cosmopolitan spectator' (105). But, as I have argued, not all cosmopolitans need be detached. Here we see how Rorty's Left nationalism accepts the premise of arborescent cosmopolitanism, i.e. that a movement across borders is necessarily an act of abstraction or transcendence. Both of them privilege the national as the site of an affective attachment to political community, the one positively, the other negatively. And in the case of arborescent cosmopolitanism, this rejection of national borders is only in the service of setting up stronger, more all-encompassing borders at the global level. Both Left nationalism and arborescent cosmopolitanism are then marked by the sense of *ressentiment* against exteriority which we investigated in Chapter 4. Rorty fears how an open spatiality, especially coupled with the open temporality that he supposedly espouses, can do away with the possibility of a unity of identity and action. It is only from within a unitary nation (remember, we must 'forget our differences') that political action is possible. This entire book has argued otherwise.

I do not disagree with Rorty on all points. I specifically agree with Rorty on the importance of pride and optimism in encouraging political possibilities and fostering hope for the future. Rorty begins his book by explaining the stakes of a revalorization of the national:

> National pride is to countries what self-respect is to individuals: a necessary condition for self-improvement. Too much national pride can produce bellicosity and imperialism, just as excessive self-respect can produce arrogance. But just as too little self-respect makes it difficult for a person to display moral courage, so insufficient national pride makes energetic and effective debate about national policy unlikely. Emotional involvement with one's country – feelings of intense shame or of glowing pride aroused by various parts of its history, and by various present-day national policies – is necessary if political deliberation is to be imaginative and productive. Such deliberation will probably not occur unless pride outweighs shame.
>
> (Rorty 1998: 1)

Rorty goes on to argue that, in pursuit of this national pride, we need a program of national education, which could teach Americans the history of their progressive past:

> It would help if students became as familiar with the Pullman Strike, the great Coalfield War, and the passage of the Wagner Act as with the march from Selma, the Berkeley free-speech demonstrations, and Stonewall. Each new generation of students ought to think of American leftism as having a long and glorious history.
>
> (Rorty 1998: 51)

I agree that a sense of pride and of history is important in encouraging political activism. However, I break with Rorty in believing that this pride, and this history, must be national. For Rorty the choice is between a rooted, national history and a rootless, theoretical cosmopolitanism. I argue instead that we can look to a concrete history of transnational activism which can express a sense of pride and activism. I agree that it would be great if students learned about the Pullman Strike and the Coalfield War. But let them also learn about the great transnational labour struggles and solidarities.[3] Peter Waterman tells stories of the amazing acts of sacrifice and solidarity that labour unions in the first half of the twentieth century engaged in. For example, 'during the Swedish General Strike of 1909' Danish trade unions contributed to the Swedish workers' strike fund, contributions which 'amounted to about three days pay per unionized Danish worker':

> projected onto the current American labour force, that rate of voluntary contributions is on the order of four times the current US foreign aid

budget. In both symbolic and concrete terms, international labour solidarity was a force to be reckoned with.

(Waterman 1998: 80–1)

Teach them about these great acts of labour solidarity. Teach them about the Abraham Lincoln brigades who volunteered to give their lives to fight Fascism in the Spanish Civil War. Teach them about the international coalitions which struggled to abolish the slave trade and extend suffrage (Keck and Sikkink 1998: 41–58). About the international movements to ban landmines.

Learning this history would fill us with a sense of pride, and of possibility. More importantly, learning about the wealth of past transnational activity would serve to unveil the dirty little secret of most of this book: *we have never been territorial* – that for all our talk of new internationalisms, the rise of transnational activisms and the aid of new global accelerative technologies, we have never fully resided within the borders which supposedly define us. New accelerative technologies might make the process of global travel and communication more common or make rhizomatic organization easier at larger scales. But in doing so it is only participating in a much longer history of global political activity. An awareness of this history, of the contingency and fragility of borders, might make us more attentive to new political possibilities which accelerative technologies provide us with, and also more hopeful about their potential success.

The politicization of speed

These are difficult times for progressive politics. Wars rage, exploitation and poverty are the norm, and humans the world over continue to be subjected to seemingly endless cruelties and indignities, when they are suffered to live in the first place. Despite the promise of past movements, it often seems that we are worse off now than ever. In response to this, I have attempted to inject a measure of hope into my critique – not an unguarded hope, not even a necessarily optimistic hope (if that's not too oxymoronic a phrase); nor it is a passive or spectatorial hope in a providential future. It is, rather, a hope rooted in one central idea: *that in this world politics is still possible.*

In each chapter I have challenged the position, sometimes on the Right, sometimes on the Left, that, because of the social acceleration of time, meaningful politics is no longer possible. In Chapter 1, it was argued that speed makes democracy untenable and anachronistic, pushing us towards ever-increasing and arbitrary executive authority ('the ticking bomb'). In Chapter 2, it was argued that speed paves the way for a global military state, unresponsive to civilian control or concerns ('There will be no time'). Chapters 3 and 4 examined the claim that speed had allowed economics to trump politics, making democratic governance subject to the necessities of capitalist production ('the acceleration of inertia'). And in this and the previous chapter, I've addressed the argument that the scope of political issues is now so large that only some sort of deracinated, bloodless arborescent global governance structure is possible. In each chapter I encountered some sort of technological determinism, which advanced a particular teleology of history that put speed in the driver's seat, with human civilization dragged along for the ride. In response to this, in every instance I advanced the counter-claim that accelerative technologies did not foreclose the future, but rather opened it. I defended the bivalence of speed phenomena and the ambiguity of these new technologies. I explored the various paths that it, and we, could take. I showed the different assemblages that we could, and do, form with the same speeds and technologies, and suggested how those different assemblages could re-shape the future in different ways (the future of both us and our technology). In short, I argued that speed can still be politicized.

I argued that the tendency to apocalyptic thinking with regards to the question of speed (the tendency to view acceleration as a deterministic line that could be politically engaged with only in futile efforts to turn back the clock) was rooted not in the material facts of acceleration (which showed themselves to be surprisingly malleable) but more often in a sense of *ressentiment* against futurity and exteriority, a calcified resentment against the uncertainties and contingencies which an open future and open borders inevitably bring. This *ressentiment against speed* formed a generalized resentment against a future which seems intransigent to our desire to fully grasp and control it. There is a sort of infantile logic here: if I cannot completely control the future, then I will not control it at all. We see the same sort of response in those conservatives and Left nationalists we have observed. If this world is becoming too complex, too unpredictable, too contingent, then I will shut myself off within the comfortable boundaries with which I am familiar.

None of this is to claim that acceleration does not pose serious challenges to politics, especially a politics which seeks democratic governance, economic equality and pluralistic engagement. I have tried throughout to provide an account of some of the hardships and struggles rooted in the social acceleration of time. But to necessarily take these challenges as insurmountable is to ignore the countless *possibilities* for political action that speed technologies offer. It is to succumb to melancholy, *ressentiment* and apocalyptic thinking.

I do not need the promise of paradise or utopia to think political action worthwhile. I will not demand that the future be laid out before us, devoid of dangerous possibilities or unforeseeable swerves. All I ask is that it be open to us. I look for the possibilities which speed provides, even as I am mindful of its dangers. I have argued that politics is possible today, not just in spite of speed, but because of it. And where there is politics, there is hope.

Notes

Introduction

1 See Harvey (2001, 1990); Mittelman (2000); Sassen (2000).
2 As an example of this, we might look to the passage in Heinrich von Treitschke's *Politics*, published originally in the latter half of the nineteenth century, where he states, 'Speed and cheapness of postage have made our letters so terribly poverty-stricken that the brilliant and witty letters of former times have vanished' (1963: 85–6), suggesting that those who presage the death of the art of correspondence with the development of e-mail have come to the party nearly a century and a half late.

1 The ticking bomb

1 'In the ticking-bomb scenario, the brief period until detonation is a proxy for the premise that there are no alternative courses of action. Torture interrogation is presented as a quick fix. Any alternative would have to promise a quicker fix. Since no one has yet proposed a quicker fix, torture interrogation is considered the winning methodology by default' (Bufacchi and Arrigo 2006: 367).
2 For a more extensive debunking of the ticking bomb scenario, see Bufacchi and Arrigo (2006: 360–1).
3 Scheuerman recounts the passage in John Locke's *Two Treatises on Government*, wherein he argues that 'things of this world are in so constant a flux, that nothing remains in the same state', and goes on to argue that Locke's thesis states that 'Given that the legislature "is usually too numerous, and too slow" only the present-oriented executive is likely to prove able effectively to break with the letter of the law for the sake of rapidly adjusting legislative authority in accordance with immediate or present political needs' (Scheuerman 2004: 38). Scheuerman also notes numerous other liberal theorists who advance similar themes, including Mill, Bentham and de Tocqueville.
4 'In fast-paced crises in which standing rules arguably no longer offer effective political guidance, does it not make sense to turn to the temporally contemporaneous executive, allegedly best equipped to deal with the unexpected and unforeseen? The traditional image of the present-oriented executive as most capable of acting with "dispatch" (or speed) remains a crucial feature of recent liberal democratic thinking as well: President George W. Bush repeatedly appealed to it in the aftermath of September 11, 2001, terrorist attack in order to garner vast emergency authority' (Scheuerman 2004: 94).
5 One of the most extensive and insightful accounts of this broad shift away from democratic deliberation – and even from the organized rule of law – is the work of

Giorgio Agamben, and his discussion of the 'state of exception' (Agamben 2005). For Agamben, the idea of the state of exception – of arbitrary and 'anomic' executive authority in the face of supposed necessity and exigency – becomes the dominant principle around which states are increasingly being organized: 'The state of exception, which used to be essentially a temporary suspension of the order, becomes now a new and stable spatial arrangement' (Agamben 2000: 43). A similar account is developed by Judith Butler in her discussion of indefinite detention in Guantanamo Bay (2006: ch. 3).

6 Though it is important to note that Scheuerman too identifies the liberal narrative of speed as the carrying over of pre-liberal 'reason-of-state' doctrines into liberal thought (Scheuerman 2002: 494).

7 See Bergson (1991).

8 Here Brian Massumi provides a good guide to the way in which Deleuze and Guattari use the concept of essence, saying, '[t]he word "essence" should not be taken in any platonic sense. The essence is always of an encounter; it is an event; it is neither stable nor transcendental nor eternal; it is immanent to the dynamic process it expresses and has only an abyssal present infinitely fractured into past and future' (Massumi 1992: 18).

9 Velocity constitutes a scale of magnitude along which all movement can be situated. It would be useful at this point to note that I am using these terms in a particularly philosophical and colloquial context, and as such I do not feel bound by the technical uses and definitions which the scientific community applies to them. That being said, it should be noted that the ontologies that I am attempting to develop have a sort of rough isomorphism with their scientific definitions, where velocity is a vector measurement which takes consideration of direction (and hence is determined via displacement over time), whereas speed is a scalar, unconcerned with direction and thus less of a relative phenomenon than velocity. However, speed, as it is imagined through the scientific method, will differ from that which I am attempting to develop since, as Bergson pointed out, science can, potentially, only interpolate movement (or at least classical Newtonian movement).

10 See also Deleuze (1988) for a discussion of virtuality.

11 It is interesting to note how this conception of 'the Event' differs from one of its other major articulations, that of Alain Badiou. Whereas, for Deleuze, following Bergson, '[t]he Event' in many ways is the irruption of a kind of newness that is always at play in the flux of duration, for Badiou, the Event is a much rarer phenomenon, taking place against the more homogenous backdrop of what he terms the 'state of the situation'. In his (very critical) account of Deleuze, Badiou states that '[c]ontrary to Deleuze ... I think that the "event dice throws" are all absolutely distinct – not formally (on the contrary, the form of all events is the same) but ontologically. This ontological multiplicity does not compose any series, it is sporadic (events are rare) and cannot be totalized' (Badiou 2000: 75–6).

Though I don't have the time to go into all of the extensive distinctions between Deleuze and Badiou's ontologies, it's worth noting the way in which this different conception of the Event produces a different orientation to speed. For Badiou, the Event exists not as a kind of moment within the durational unfolding of time, but instead as a kind of incursion of the transcendent into the immanent (this, at least, is Deleuze and Guattari's reading of it [1994: 152]). For Badiou this then translates into a philosophy which takes as its primary goal the rejection of speed. '[S]peed exposes us to danger of a very great incoherency. It is because things, images and relations circulate so quickly that we do not even have the time to measure the extent of this incoherency ... Philosophy must propose a retardation process. It must construct a time of thought, which, in the face of the injunction to speed, will constitute a time of its own. I consider this a singularity of philosophy; that its thinking is leisurely, because today revolt requires leisureliness and not speed. This thinking, slow and consequently rebellious, is alone capable of establishing the fixed point, whatever it may be, whatever its name may be, which we need in order to sustain the desire of philosophy' (Badiou 2005: 38).

12 Jean-Luc Nancy provides an excellent account of this relation between event and thought in his *Being Singular Plural*: 'Let us dwell upon this characteristic of surprise. There is, then, something to be thought – the event – the very nature of which – event-ness – can only be a matter of surprise, can only take thinking by surprise. We need to think about how thought can and must be surprised – and how it may be exactly this that makes it think. Or then, we need to think about how there would be no thought without the event of thinking' (Nancy 2000: 165).

13 Though I should note that just as speed is not necessarily fast, so too this 'moment' is not necessarily short, but will rather be determined relationally to the duration of a projection. The 'moment' of speed in evolutionary or geological time will be substantially longer than that of phenomenological or even social time.

14 Again, Nancy's investigation into the nature of the event provides a good account of the complex temporalities and spatialities that it inaugurates: 'The event as such, then, is empty time or the presence of the present as negativity, that is, insofar as it happens and is, as a result, nonpresent – and in such a way that it is not even "not yet present" (which would reinscribe everything in a succession of presents already available "in time"), but is, on the contrary, the sort [of thing] that nothing precedes or succeeds. It is time itself in its appearing, as the appearing that it is' (Nancy 2000: 168).

15 I am borrowing here from Scheuerman's account of this article in his *Liberal Democracy and the Social Acceleration of Time* (2004).

16 I will discuss this issue in far greater depth in Chapter 4.

17 Rosa argues that acceleration is not just separate from economic considerations, but is indeed the driving force behind other formations of modernity, and hence, for him, it can be viewed and analysed in isolation.

18 There are numerous accounts of work within several disciplines which can provide empirical data and examples in support of this thesis. (See Harvey 1990; Bauman 2005, 1998; Simmel 1997; Gleick 2000.)

19 Rosa notes how social acceleration produces an increased 'awareness of contingency', even amongst people who have not experienced any substantial change (2003: 19).

20 In his book *Tabloid Terror*, François Debrix provides an excellent account of how authoritative accounts from government and the media serve to 'restore and impose meaning where none appears to exist anymore (if only for a fleeting moment) and, in the context of this search for rationalizations of the image, to give revenge a "name" ("war on terror," for example)' (Debrix 2008: 4–5).

21 It's useful at this point also to note that, though tending might seem to suggest the same paternalism as intending, since tending seems to imply a hierarchy between the one tending and the thing tended, this is probably either to take the metaphor a little too seriously (whereas flowers might need their best interests interpreted and looked after, humans are capable of simply expressing them) or to mistake its object of reference. This last point is to say that we make a mistake (or perhaps display our own subconscious fears and anxieties, our 'queasiness' about democracy) if we assume that this tending metaphor implies people tending to other people, rather than a group of people tending their own community or sense of identity.

22 As a brief sidebar, it's worth noting that though this chapter and much of this book are concerned with the zone of the future, this should not be interpreted as meaning that I am uninterested in the past, or even that I regard the past as a politically less relevant phenomenon. This point is similar to that which I will repeat frequently, namely that, though clearly I am engaged in an attempt to, in at least

some way, valorize the phenomenon of speed, that does not mean (1) that I don't acknowledge key ambivalences in its functioning and (2) that because of that I am arguing for an equal or attendant devalorization of the use of slowness or immobility. I am simply (well, perhaps not simply) seeking to develop one tool for political activity and insight, amongst numerous others.

23 I am tempted to use the word 'authentic' to describe Wolin's conception of political time, though he himself doesn't use it.

24 It is worth taking a moment to note how the rough contours of this argument correlate to that of another, substantially different thinker, Martin Heidegger. Though I don't have the space for an extensive engagement of the question of Heidegger's relation to speed and technology (for a partial attempt, see Mackenzie 2002), it is perhaps helpful to note how, in Heidegger, there is also a driving suspicion of speed, newness and technology, and a belief that the goal of philosophy is to slow down thought, creating a space for authentic insight.

Now, in principle, Heidegger is not 'anti-technology' (any more than Wolin is). Indeed, he claims 'I am *not against* technology. I have never spoken *against* technology, nor against the so-called demon of technology' (Mackenzie 2002: 125). Additionally, his concept of 'the turning', and the new space for thought that it opens up, carries some similarities to the account of the Event I develop on p. 21 (Heidegger 1977: 48).

And yet, Heidegger's thought is permeated by a certain nostalgia for a time, prior to the age of technological dominance, in which thought and being were more authentically grounded (14–15). Though he doesn't blame technology in essence – nor does he believe that what he terms authentic Dasein can't exist in and among technology and acceleration – he does believe that the pathway to pursuing this goal leads away from technology and acceleration. As Mackenzie puts it, '[f]or Heidegger, technical entities are in a sense ... inauthentic' (Mackenzie 2002: 126–7). The goal of Heidegger's project, then, is to slow down and isolate thought, to allow authentic Dasein to disclose itself: 'The coming to presence of technology threatens revealing, threatens it with the possibility that all revealing will be consumed in ordering and that everything will present itself only in the unconcealedness of standing-reserve' (Heidegger 1977: 33–4). The goal is to clear a space outside and away from technological thinking and away from modern acceleration (40–1). In this, his account of philosophy is similar to that of Badiou's, recounted in note 11, and similar to the politics of Wolin (and of Virilio, whom we will investigate in Chapter 2). And for all of these thinkers (Wolin, Badiou, Virilio, Heidegger) these anti-speed sensibilities have the potential to translate into anti-democratic sensibilities.

25 This is what Henri Bergson means by 'the retrograde movement of the true growth of truth'. It is the idea that newness is never absolute, created *ex nihilo* but must come from, and be rooted in, the past. It is simply a development which could not, in principle, have been predicted before the fact: 'We can always, to be sure, link up the reality once it is accomplished, to the events in which it occurred; but taken from another angle, an entirely different reality (not just *any* reality, it is true) could just as well be linked up to the same circumstances and events' (Bergson 1974: 23).

26 These acts of destruction can be tremendously tragic and deadly, say the 9/11 attacks, which challenged the American narrative of invulnerability and isolation from the rest of the world, or natural disasters brought on by global climate change, which bring into question the sustainability of certain regimes of production and consumption. They can also be glorious and affirmative, such as the destruction of the Berlin Wall, marking the downfall of the oppressive Soviet regime. They can even be both at the same time, such as, for example, John Brown's murder of a group of slave holders, sparking off a grand battle over the soul of a nation.

2 The quick and the dead

1 Though in the last chapter we developed a very particular language of speed, for the time being I will be following Virilio's usage to avoid confusion. This tension will be resolved when we segue into the discussion of Deleuze and Guattari (p. 62).

2 One gets the feeling, however, that, unlike Clastres, Virilio does not see this as an example of the intelligence of the tribe, but rather simply as a mechanical side-effect. Indeed, this is one of the problems with both Virilio's and Clastres' invocation of the pejorative 'primitive'. It suggests a unilinear history of 'progress' from the primitive to the civilized. When we get to Deleuze and Guattari's account, we will see this progressive history, and the insulting designation of 'primitive tribes', challenged.

3 'When there's less than a minute to decide whether or not to push the panic button we will have reached a limit, which is of the automation of war. The decision for war or peace will belong to an answering machine!' (Virilio 1977: 75).

4 See the focus on computer simulation in war planning in Der Derian (2001).

5 'In the 1960's a mutation occurs: *the passage from wartime to the war of peacetime*, to that *total peace* that others still call "peaceful coexistence." The blindness of the speed of the means of communicating destruction is not a liberation from geopolitical servitude, but the extermination of space as the field of freedom of political action' (Virilio 1977: 142).

6 At this point, at least some acknowledgement of the role that the 'military-industrialist complex' plays in this perpetuation and autonomy of the practice of warfare would seem necessary. However, for Virilio, this autonomy of the military seems to be primary, and thus there is very little in the way of an economistic explanation of war.

7 See Marinetti (1909).

8 Although Virilio does call for the need to re-evaluate the ethical status of violence and death. (See Virilio 2002).

9 See Chris Hables Gray's account of the how the *USS Vincennes*, an Aegis class cruiser equipped with automated targeting equipment, shot down an Iranian civilian airliner after mistaking it for a hostile jet (Gray 1997: 67).

10 It is true that Deleuze and Guattari elsewhere develop a theory of the 'primitive' territorial machine; however, for various reasons (the emphasis on speed, violence and unpredictability, starting from Pierre Clastres) it is the nomadic war-machine that more fully relates to Virilio's primitive tribe. We will engage with their account of the 'primitive' territorial machine in Chapter 4 as well as critiquing the language of 'primitiveness'.

11 'We certainly would not say that discipline is what defines a war machine: discipline is the characteristic of armies after the State has appropriated them. The war machine answers to other rules' (Deleuze and Guattari 1987: 358).

12 'Pure' is in scare quotes because it should be understood as an ideal type. As Crogan puts it, 'This means it is as much that the War Machine invents particular historical nomadic societies as it is the reverse – the historical nomads are, like historical States, always an admixture of elements which are becoming-State or becoming-War machine, or between the two, such as transhumance and migration' (1999: 139).

13 'All warfare is based on deception. Therefore, when capable, feign incapacity; when active, inactivity. When near, make it appear that you are far away; when far away, that you are near. Offer the enemy a bait to lure him; feign disorder and strike him' (Sun Tzu 1963: 66).

14 At heart, this is what Clausewitz tries to tell us. His difficulty in describing the make-up of 'military genius' is, in many ways, a result of the difficulty of describing it in terms which the state-form can understand (von Clausewitz 1976: 100–13).

15 Note, however, that this does not require us to leave behind the speed/velocity distinction we made in Chapter 1. Indeed, as we accepted that speed and velocity are two ideal types, constantly in admixture, we might view these two modalities of speed as existing at varying points along the speed/velocity continuum. War-machine-speed closer to the ideal pole of speed, state-speed, existing as it does 'relatively, secondarily', closer to the pole of velocity.

16 Remember here the typology that was developed in Chapter 1, of velocity as a relative movement versus speed as an absolute movement.

17 'This explains the mistrust States have toward their military institutions, in that the military institution inherits an extrinsic war machine. Karl von Clausewitz has a general sense of this situation when he treats the flow of absolute war as an idea that States partially appropriate according to their political needs, and in relation to which they are more or less good "conductors"' (Deleuze and Guattari 1987: 355).

18 See Arquilla and Ronfeldt (1997: 34–5).

19 For a discussion of the militarization of police forces, see Warren (2002); Kraska and Kappeler (1997).

20 'In general, clever and entrepreneurial enemies – even if relatively poor in economic terms – will remain able to thwart many advanced technologies of an adversary, particularly when fighting on their own terrain. Many of the tactics used by North Vietnamese and Viet Cong forces will remain useful in future warfare: using tunnels and bunkers, hugging enemy forces to provide a form of protection from long-range wide-area firepower, storing materials in small amounts through a battlefield, employing large labor forces to transport supplies in modest amounts, and making wide use of pontoons and underwater bridges. Any of these tactics will remain useful even against a foe with foliage- and soil-penetrating radar, other advanced sensors and brilliant anti-armor weapons' (O'Hanlon 2000: 117).

21 For a history of anti-urban tendencies in war, see Shaw (2004).

22 See Friedmann (1982, 1995); Sassen (2000).

23 'Although the element of surprise is not absent in orthodox warfare, there are fewer opportunities to apply it than there are during guerrilla hostilities. In the latter, speed is essential. The movement of guerrilla troops must be secret and of supernatural rapidity; the enemy must be taken unaware, and the action entered speedily. There can be no procrastination in the execution of plans; no assumption of a negative or passive defense; no great dispersion of forces in many local engagements. The basic method is the attack in a violent and deceptive form' (Mao Tse-Tung 2005: 97).

24 Martin Van Creveld does an excellent job of proving this central point through a list of historical failures of states to achieve their military goals against, usually, technologically inferior opponents, including, but not limited to, Soviets in Afghanistan, Cubans in Angola, South Africans in Namibia, Angola and Mozambique, Israelis in Lebanon, Vietnamese in Cambodia, Indians in Sri Lanka. It is for this reason that he says, 'The cold, brutal fact is that much present-day military power is simply irrelevant as an instrument for extending or defending political interests over most of the globe; by this criterion, indeed, it scarcely amounts to "military power" at all' (Van Creveld 1991: 27).

25 'No firm rule of thumb exists but according to one source "a commander is left with the prospect of needing between 9 and 27 attackers per defender in an urban environment" – significantly more than is required in open terrain' (Rosenau 1997: 20).

26 John Mearsheimer makes much the same critique of the RMA in his engagement with Neoconservative doctrine, and its assumptions about being able to globally project overwhelming force (Mearsheimer 2005).

27 See Chomsky (1999); Hardt and Negri (2000: 3–22).

28 See Seymour Hersh's account of the Bush Administration's proposal to use nuclear weapons in dealing with an intransigent Iran (Hersh 2006).

29 'Paul Virilio's analysis strikes as entirely correct in defining fascism ... by the notion of the suicidal State: so-called total war seems less a State undertaking than an undertaking of a war machine that appropriates the State and channels into it a flow of absolute war whose only possible outcome is the suicide of the State itself' (Deleuze and Guattari 1987: 231).

30 Hardt and Negri also advance this critique on a technical level, by noting that the image of terrorist groups as being rhizomatic, or cellular, is frequently mistaken: 'The Colombian drug cartels and al-Qaeda, for example, may look like networks from the perspective of counterinsurgency, but in fact they are highly centralized, with traditional vertical chains of command. Their organization structures are not democratic at all' (Hardt and Negri 2004: 89). We could, undoubtedly, say the same for the local packs of war-machines which the worldwide war-machine unleashes.

31 See Chris Hables Gray's discussion of the different forms of 'Peace warriors' (Gray 1997: 240).

32 See Marcos (2001).

33 '[M]en and women dressed in elaborate forms of padding, ranging from foam armour to innertubes to rubber-ducky flotation devices, helmets and chemical-proof white jumpsuits (their British cousins are well-clad Wombles). As this mock army pushes its way through police barricades, all the while protecting each other against injury or arrest, the ridiculous gear seems to reduce human beings to cartoon characters – misshapen, ungainly, foolish, largely indestructible. The effect is only increased when lines of costumed figures attack police with balloons and water pistols, or, like the "pink bloc" at Prague and elsewhere, dress as fairies and tickle them with feather dusters' (Graeber 2002: 66–7).

34 'Ancient-warfare techniques have been studied to adopt for non-violent but very militant forms of confrontation: there were peltasts and hoplites (the former mainly from Prince Edward Islands, the latter from Montreal) at Quebec City, and research continues into Roman-style shield walls. Blockading has become an art form: if you make a huge web of strands of yarn across an intersection, it's actually impossible to cross; motorcycle cops get trapped like flies' (Graeber 2002: 67).

3 The acceleration of inertia

1 'Any failure to maintain a certain velocity of circulation of capital through the various phases of production and realization will generate a crisis. The time structure of production and realization thus becomes a crucial consideration. Crisis will result if inventories build up, if money lies idle for longer than is strictly necessary, if more sticks are held for a longer period during production, etc.' (Harvey 2006a: 85).

2 'Circulation time thus appears as a barrier to the productivity of labour = an increase in labour time = a decrease in surplus labour time = a decrease in surplus value = an obstruction, a barrier to the self-realization process of capital. Thus, while capital must on one side strive to tear down every spatial barrier to intercourse, i.e. to exchange, and conquer the whole earth for its market, it strives on the other side to annihilate this space with time, i.e. to reduce to a minimum the time spent in motion from one place to another. The more developed the capital, therefore, the more extensive the market over which it circulates, which forms the spatial orbit of its circulation, the more does it strive simultaneously for an even greater extension of the market and for greater annihilation of space by time' (Marx 1973: 539).

3 My thanks to Renee Marlin-Bennett for this point.

4 See, for example, Baudrillard and Virilio. Also look at the discussion of the Frankfurt school's account of technology in Postone (2003).

5 'It has become fashionable, however, to attribute to machinery the powers over humanity which arise in fact from social relations. Society, in this view, is nothing but an extrapolation of science and technology, and the machine itself is the enemy. The machine, the mere product of human labor and ingenuity, designed and constructed by humans and alterable by them at will, is viewed as an independent participant in human social arrangement. It is given life, enters into 'relations' with the workers, relations fixed by its own nature, is endowed with the power to shape the life of mankind, and is sometimes even invested with designs upon the human race' (Braverman 1974: 229).

6 Note that it is here that Marx's and Deleuze's accounts – both of which agree on capitalism's paradoxical relationship with speed – part ways. For Marx, this opposition between acceleration and control is a fundamental contradiction which can only be resolved via dialectical progression. For Deleuze it is a necessary tension which has no predetermined resolution, and can only achieve contingent equilibria determined through specific historical conflicts. This will be discussed in greater detail on p. 104.

7 '[B]oth as a fact and as a threat, the impact of new things – new technologies for instance – on the existing structure of an industry considerably reduces the long-run scope and importance of practices that aim, through restricting output, at conserving established positions and at maximizing the profits accruing from them' (Schumpeter 1950: 87).

8 For discussions of the increasing scope of intellectual property law in terms of patentable knowledge, see Boyle (1996) and Vaidhyanathan (2001). For a discussion of the globalization of intellectual property rights regimes, see Maskus and Reichman (2004).

9 Indeed, some argue that the US patent office frequently acts to give patents on innovations that are considered 'obvious' (one of the criteria for receiving a patent is the non-obviousness of the innovation), and that the patent office encourages applicants to broaden the scope of their patenting claim, encouraging the so-called 'land grab' for intellectual resources. See Stallman (2002: ch.16).

10 'This is why software patents tend to obstruct the progress of software – the work of software development. If it were "one patent, one product," then these patents wouldn't obstruct the development of products because if you develop a new product, it wouldn't be patented by somebody else already. But when one product corresponds to many different ideas combined, it gets very likely your new product (either part or all of your product) is going to be patented by somebody else already' (Stallman 2002: 105–6).

11 '"Restraint of trade" of the cartel type as well as those which merely consist in tacit understandings about price competition may be effective remedies under conditions of depression. As far as they are, they may in the end produce not only steadier but also greater expansion of total output than could be secured by an entirely uncontrolled onward rush that cannot fail to be studded with catastrophes' (Schumpeter 1950: 91).

12 'Today the typical economic unit in the capitalist world is not the small firm producing a negligible fraction of a homogeneous output for an anonymous market but a large-scale enterprise producing a significant share of the output of an industry, or even several industries, and able to control its prices, the volume its production, and the types and amounts of its investments. The typical economic unit, in other words, has the attributes that were once thought to be possessed only by monopolies' (Baran and Sweezy 1966: 6).

13 See Bulow (1986: 746).

14 'RCA at first kept the technology in house, insisting that further tests were needed. When, after two years of testing, Armstrong grew impatient, RCA began to use its power with the government to stall FM radio's deployment generally. In 1936, RCA hired the former head of the FCC and assigned him the task of assuring that the FCC assign spectrum in a way that would castrate FM – principally by moving FM radio to a different band of spectrum ... Soon ... the FCC announced a set of policies that would have one clear effect: FM radio would be crippled' (Lessing 2004: 5).

15 Note that to accept this stance is, implicitly, to decentre labour as the sole source of value in capitalism. This suggests a vital break between Deleuze and Guattari's account of capitalism and Marx's, although Deleuze and Guattari also argue that Marx's account is much richer and potentially rhizomatic than many Marxist accounts give: 'That is why it is unfortunate that Marxist economists too often dwell on considerations concerning the mode of production, and on the theory of money as the general equivalent as founding the first section of *Capital*, without attaching enough importance to banking practice, to financial operations, and to the specific circulation of credit money – which would be the meaning of a return to Marx' (Deleuze and Guattari 1983: 230).

16 J.K. Gibson-Graham (2006) provide just such a minimalist account of capitalism in their text, however with less of a conception of this as merely the kernel of a much larger axiomatic.

17 See Connolly (2008).

18 This question of the multiplicity of capitalism, as well as the ability of the capitalist axiomatic to incorporate non-, pre- and extra-capitalist social formations, will be dealt with more extensively in Chapter 4.

19 'The true axiomatic is that of the social machine itself, which takes the place of the old codings and organizes all the decoded flows, including the flows of scientific and technical code, for the benefit of the capitalist system and in the service of its ends' (Deleuze and Guattari 1983: 233).

20 I introduce the imagery of geography here because of the way that '[g]eography wrests history from the cult of necessity in order to stress the irreducibility of contingency' (Deleuze and Guattari 1994: 96).

21 Though let us understand the term 'decision' here in a social rather than individual form.

22 'The standard notion that incumbent firms saddled with low profitability and high relative costs on their fixed capital stock can be counted on to leave their line once investment in circulating capital ceases to be profitable turns out to be an over-simplification. The corporations that dominated manufacturing across the advanced capitalist world had, through years of experience, built up invaluable proprietary *intangible* assets in their own line but not others – information about markets, relationships with suppliers and customers, and above all technical knowledge. These assets offered them advantages in continuing to produce where they were already located of which they could not avail themselves in any other industry. They could therefore hardly have been expected to close up shop merely because the returns on their existing fixed tangible stock suffered decline' (Brenner 2006: 154).

23 O Riain quotes the manager of an Irish tech firm who states: 'I don't have a budget, it's a customer style relationship within the company and with clients. This has a big impact in that we only provide services that we get paid for. People don't have jobs; they have assignments; these can change every couple of months. There are complaints from some areas, no one is sure who they're working for – I'm saying 'well try and get used to it.' We need to be more able to move people around – we need the flexibility, it's very different from mainframes where you get your production figures at the beginning of the year. Now we have to keep the services very close to demand' (O Riain 2006: 515).

24 Note here the Deleuzo-Guattarian language of 'absolute reterritorialization' should not be taken to indicate some sort of revolutionary overthrow of social relations.

Rather, it is intended to describe the difference between a reterritorialization that returns a line of flight to the same plane of immanence from which it originated, thus reinforcing a particular social order, and a reterritorialization which opens up a new plane of immanence which might challenge the integrity of that social order. I will provide specific examples of this process shortly.

25 'Peer-to-peer (p2p) file sharing is among the most efficient of the efficient technologies the Internet enables. Using distributed intelligence, p2p systems facilitate the easy spread of content in a way unimagined a generation ago' (Lessig 2004: 17).

26 'Indeed, the unique properties of the Internet as a distinct mode of communication center on its dispersed, packet-switching architecture, which breaks up information, sending it along numerous trajectories to be reassembled at its destination. Such a distributed architecture, by its very design, is difficult to control, since there is no central node or gateway through which all information passes. The many peer-to-peer file sharing systems that have been established on the Internet offer a prime example of this particular dimension' (Deibert 2002: 144).

27 See Electronic Frontier Foundation, *RIAA v. The People: Four Years Later*, at http://w2.eff.org/IP/P2P/riaa_at_four.pdf.

28 There are checks and balances on this practice. The party which posted the material can send a counter-notice if they feel that the material doesn't infringe, and the notices are subject to perjury laws if in fact the material isn't infringing or the issuer of the notice doesn't actually own the copyright. The trouble is, however, that fighting a DMCA notice costs time and money, which once again gives the advantage to wealthier corporations versus individuals.

29 'The motivation for this response is obvious. The internet enables the efficient spread of content. That efficiency is a feature of the internet's design. But from the perspective of the content industry, this feature is a "bug"' (Lessig 2004: 193).

30 Electronic Frontier Foundation, *Unintended Consequences: Seven Years under the DMCA*, at http://www.eff.org/files/DMCA_unintended_v4.pdf p.4.

31 'Following the Felten and Sklyarov incidents, a number of prominent computer security experts curtailed their legitimate research activities for fear of potential DMCA liability. For example, when Dutch cryptographer and security systems analyst Niels Ferguson discovered a major security flaw in Intel's HDCP video encryption system, he declined to publish his results on his website on the grounds that he travels frequently to the U.S. and is fearful of "prosecution and/or liability under the U.S. DMCA law." Following the arrest of Dmitry Sklyarov, Fred Cohen, a professor of digital forensics and respected security consultant, removed his 'Forensix' evidence-gathering software from his website, citing fear of potential DMCA liability. Another respected network security protection expert, Dug Song, also removed information from his website for the same reason. Mr. Song is the author of several security papers, including a paper describing a common vulnerability in many firewalls. In mid-2001 an anonymous programmer discovered a vulnerability in Microsoft's proprietary e-book DRM system, but refused to publish the results, citing DMCA liability concerns' (Deibert 2003a: 507–8).

32 'These freedoms are beyond the freedoms promised by fair use. Their precise contours depend upon the choices the creator makes. The creators can choose a license that permits only noncommercial use. She can choose a license that permits any use so long as the same freedoms are given to other uses ("share and share alike"). Or any use so long as no derivative use is made. Or any use at all within the developing nations. Or any sampling use, so long as full copies are not made. Or lastly, any educational use' (Lessig 2004: 283).

33 Indeed, some authors go so far as to note that '[a]n authored-centered regime can actually *slow down* scientific progress, *diminish* the opportunities for creativity, and *curtail* the availability of new products' (Boyle 1996: 119).

34 For a discussion of the importance of experimentation in economic theory and practice, see Gibson-Graham (2006).

35 Indeed, we're increasingly seeing major media companies given up on DRM-based strategies, and moving to other avenues for protecting content.

36 Our investigation of Virilio in Chapter 2 provides an excellent example of these sorts of politics.

37 I think this is somewhat at the heart of what Deleuze means when he says, 'Good people say that we must not flee, that to escape is not good, that it isn't effective, and that one must work for reforms. But the revolutionary knows that escape is revolutionary – withdrawal, breaks – provided one sweeps away the social cover on leaving, or causes a piece of the system to get lost in the shuffle. What matters is to break through the wall ... George Jackson. "I may take flight, but all the while I am fleeing, I will be looking for a weapon!"' (Deleuze and Guattari 1983: 277).

38 The concept of the rhizomatic will be more extensively investigated in Chapter 5.

39 See Deibert (2002) for a discussion of how Chinese hackers subvert the Chinese state's attempts to control and surveille the flow of information.

40 See Deibert (2000).

41 See the work of Citizen Lab, operating out of the Munk Center for International Studies at the University of Toronto, http://www.citizenlab.org/.

4 Regimes of (im)mobility

1 http://www.princeton.edu/~ina/index.html.

2 http://www.princeton.edu/~ina/maps/non_geographic/index.html.

3 'It is generally held that economic development occurs in a succession of capitalist stages and that today's underdeveloped countries are still in a stage, sometimes depicted as an original stage, of history through which the now developed countries passed long ago. Yet even a modest acquaintance with history shows that underdevelopment is not original or traditional and that neither the past nor the present of the underdeveloped countries resembles in any important respect the past of the now developed countries. The now developed countries were never *under*developed, though they may have been *un*developed' (Frank 1969: 4).

4 It's worth noting that Deleuze and Guattari actually refer to the '*savage* territorial machine', in what I've always taken to be an ironic appropriation of Lewis Henry Morgan's typology of human history (the title of the chapter from which this discussion is drawn is 'Savages, Barbarians and Civilized Men'). I will simply refer to the 'territorial machine'. This is for two reasons: (1) to avoid the pejorative connotations of the term, and its unfortunate history within the context of the violence of colonialism; and (2) to avoid the implication of a unilinear evolutionary model of human history (which Deleuze and Guattari reject in multiple instances), or indeed, what is more, to suggest that the territorial mode is completely left behind. Once again, as in our discussion of the conflict between the nomad and the state-form (p. 81), these are not actual historical stages of human evolution, but ideal types, which describe conflicts between organizational forms and social assemblages. Referring to the 'savage' territorial machine suggests a judgement of the sophistication of that mode of organization, as well as the idea that it belongs to an older, more 'primitive' time, neither of which are claims which I believe are present in Deleuze and Guattari's account.

5 See also Polanyi (1944).

6 'Yet exchange is known, well known in the primitive socius – but as that which must exorcised, encasted, severely restricted, so that no corresponding value can develop as an exchange value that would introduce the nightmare of a commodity economy. The primitive market operates through bargaining rather than by fixing

an equivalent that would lead to a decoding of flows and a collapse of the mode of inscription on the socius' (Deleuze and Guattari 1983: 186).

7 'In a word, money – the circulation of money – *is the means for rendering the debt infinite.* And that is what is concealed in the two acts of the State: the residence or territoriality of the State inaugurates the great movement of deterritorialization that subordinates all the primitive filiations to the despotic machine ... the abolition of debts or their accountable transformation initiates the duty of an interminable service to the State that subordinates all the primitive alliances to itself (the problem of debts). The infinite creditor and infinite credit have replaced the blocks of mobile and finite debts' (Deleuze and Guattari 1983: 197).

8 '[P]rivate property presupposes State public property ... and money presupposes taxation' (Deleuze and Guattari 1987: 427).

9 '*The archaic State does not overcode without also freeing a large quantity of decoded flows that escape from it ... the overcoding of the archaic State itself makes possible and gives rise to new flows that escape from it.* The State does not create large-scale works without a flow of independent labor escaping its bureaucracy (notably in the mines and in metallurgy). It does not create the monetary form of the tax without flows of money escaping, and nourishing or bringing into being other powers (notably in commerce and banking). And above all, it does not create a system of public property without a flow of private appropriation growing up beside it, then beginning to pass beyond its grasp; this private property does not itself issue from the archaic system but is constituted on the margins, all the more necessarily and inevitably, slipping through the net of overcoding' (Deleuze and Guattari 1987: 449).

10 'As Braudel says, there were "always two runners, the state and the town" – two forms and two speeds of deterritorialization' (Deleuze and Guattari 1987: 435).

11 See Samir Amin's discussion of how long-distance trade is blocked from developing into capitalism (1976: 30–51).

12 For a discussion of the distinction between social formations and modes of production, and their interaction in capitalist production, see Amin (1976: ch. 1).

13 'The more the capitalist machine deterritorializes, decoding and axiomatizing flows in order to extract surplus value from them, the more its ancillary apparatuses, such as government bureaucracies and the forces of law and order, do their utmost to reterritorialize, absorbing in the process a larger and larger share of surplus value' (Deleuze and Guattari 1983: 35).

14 Hence Paul Virilio's obsession with Howard Hughes, the aviator-turned-shut-in, as the archetypal dromocratic revolutionary – global and yet completely unmoving (Virilio and Lotringer 1983: 77).

15 '[W]e are seeing the formation of specialized cross-border regimes that grant protection to some classes of people (such as the regime for the cross-border movements of professions that is part of the WTO and regional trade agreements) and withdraw protection from other classes of people (undocumented migrants who have lost many protections over the last decade and are now often constituted as semi-criminal subjects)' (Sassen 2006: 36).

16 See also Sassen (2001).

17 For a beautiful description of the deeply cosmopolitan, yet 'pre-globalization' Cairo, see Hobsbawm (1989: 1–2).

18 'For example, much of what we might still experience as the "local" (an office building, a house, or an institution in our neighborhood or downtown) is something I would rather think of as a microenvironment with global span insofar as it is deeply inter-networked. Such a microenvironment is in many senses a localized entity, but it is also part of global digital networks, which give it immediate far-flung span. To continue to think of this as simply local is not useful' (Sassen 2006: 346).

19 'The tendency has been to understand the spatiality of economic globalization in terms of the hypermobility and neutralization of distance made possible by the new technologies. With this comes, inevitably, a notion about the compression of time: instantaneous integration and so-called real-time simultaneity. What such an account tends to leave out of the analysis is the fact that hypermobility and time–space compression need to be produced and that this requires vast concentration of material and not so mobile facilities and infrastructures' (Sassen 2006: 382).

20 'What they also need is the *security of that isolation* – a "non-neighborhood" condition, immunity from local interference, a foolproof, invulnerable isolation, translated as the "safety" of persons, of their homes and their playgrounds. Deterritorialization of power therefore goes hand in hand with the ever stricter structuration of the territory' (Bauman 1998: 20).

21 'Hence, in order to attach educated middle-class women to the profession and high-value service industries, migrant women have to be tethered to the Singaporean home *qua* machine for the reproduction of society and human capital so that the forces of their bodies can be extracted as reproductive labor. The pervasiveness of this double tethering, which is also a dependency, is obvious. Many middle-class working women in Singapore regard foreign maids as a necessity rather than a luxury, so much so that a 1996 academic study suggest that "the maid culture has become a way of life in Singapore"' (Cheah 2006: 202).

22 We can turn to the telling example of CNN pundit and anti-immigrant spokesman Lou Dobbs, who, despite railing against the poor treatment of the middle class and the threat of 'Big Business', as well as the threat of outsourcing and immigration, describes himself as 'a life long Republican' who 'believe[s] deeply in our free-enterprise democracy. I'm a capitalist' (Dobbs 2004: 5).

23 See Ong (1999: chs 2–3).

5 'A world in which many worlds fit'

1 Daniel Deudney provides an explicit account of how the improvement of military technologies, especially transportation and delivery technologies, calls into existence the need for some sort of global governance structure, as a way of mitigating what he terms 'violence interdependence' (Deudney 2007).

2 For a further discussion of cosmopolitanism as 'transcending partiality', see Anderson (1998).

3 'As distance between places becomes abridged and plurality within each becomes enhanced, what appears in Kantian philosophy as an unavoidable moment of universal recognition increasingly becomes a critical site of cultural contestation. Today, the Kantian recognition of the constitutive form of morality is endorsed fervently by some, rejected intensely by others, ignored by many, and strained through a vague sense of uncertainty by yet others. It can be confessed as a contestable act of faith; it might even be imposed through cultural war as the official judgment of an entire country or even civilization. But it cannot be shown without doubt to function, as Kant thought it must, as an apodictic, spontaneous basis of morality achieved prior to moral argument and cultural induction' (Connolly 2002: 183).

4 Says Peter Waterman in his history of cosmopolitanism and internationalism, '"Internationalization," in either the liberal or socialist understanding, implies universalization and is accompanied by a related political/ethical universalism. In both cases the internationalization and internationalism means Westernization. These are, thus, particularlist universalisms in which Western Enlightenment theories, models, aspirations and utopias are offered to, or are imposed on, the rest of the world ("lesser breeds without the law", "peoples without history")' (Waterman 1998: 199).

5 What is ironic is that, in her essay on Aristotelian essentialism, Nussbaum uses a case study of an attempt to encourage literacy amongst women in rural Bangladesh. The process the Nussbaum describes is replete with dialogues between the development agency and the women of the villages, encouraging the shaping of the literacy program to their specific needs and interests (Nussbaum 1992: 236). The trouble is that this case study can be equally well described in terms of a 'rhizomatic cosmopolitanism' which does not require the essentialist commitments that Nussbaum demands. Conversely, she does not do nearly enough to explain how to stop the essentialist position from producing results such as those described in the Bangladeshi child labour case study mentioned on p. 166.

6 'In truth, it is not enough to say, "Long live the multiple," difficult as it is to raise that cry. No typographical, lexical or even syntactical cleverness is enough to make it heard. The multiple *must be made*' (Deleuze and Guattari 1987: 6).

7 See J.K. Gibson-Graham's discussion of community organizing fora (Gibson-Graham 2006).

8 See Osterweil (2005: 26).

9 Although FLOC's organizational philosophy puts considerable importance on decentralization and direct participation.

Conclusion

1 'Thus local actions mounted to defend communities against the ravages of, for example, deindustrialization are often seen as hopelessly parochial and destined to be outmaneuvered and defeated by a hypermobile and flexible capital that can always choose to abandon them and relocate to virtually any place on the planet' (Herrod 2001: 51).

2 Rorty is not the only one to criticize the global leftist 'intelligentsia' as being on the same side as globalizing capitalism. As Gordon Laxer puts it. 'Left globalists ... see the decline of national sovereignty as opening spaces for intense, participatory democracy at local levels. Both tendencies propose essential strategies to multi-faceted efforts to combat corporate globalism. But by accepting corporate globalizers' attacks on all forms of nationalism and attempts to weaken national sovereignty, they inadvertently give up on rooted national solidarities, which can act as mediators between the local and the global' (Laxer 2001: 6).

3 'Yet, international labor organizations and international links among workers have existed in some form since at least the middle of the nineteenth century when, in response to the dramatic economic and political transformations associated with the geographical spread of the industrial revolution across Europe and North America, many socialists, anarchists, trade unionists, and others began to become increasingly concerned that labor protections in one country would be undercut by the lack of equivalent provisions elsewhere' (Herrod 2001: 129).

Bibliography

Adams, W. J. and Encaoua, D. (1994) 'Distorting the Direction of Technological Change', *European Economic Review* 38(3–4): 663–73.

Agamben, G. (2000) *Means without End: Notes on Politics*, trans. Vincenzo Binetti and Cesare Casarino, Minneapolis: University of Minnesota Press.

——(2005) *State of Exception*, trans. K. Attel, Chicago: Chicago University Press.

Agnew, J. (2003) *Geopolitics: Re-visioning World Politics*, London: Routledge.

Amin, S. (1976) *Unequal Development: An Essay on the Social Formations of Peripheral Capitalism*, New York: Monthly Review Press.

Anderson, Amanda (1998) 'Cosmopolitanism, Universalism, and the Divided Legacies of Modernity', *Cosmopolitics*, P. Cheah and B. Robbins (eds), Minneapolis: University of Minnesota Press.

Appadurai, A. (1990) 'Disjuncture and Difference in the Global Cultural Economy', *Public Culture* 2(2): 1–24.

Arquilla, J. and Ronfeldt, D. (1997) 'Cyberwar is Coming!', *In Athena's Camp*, J. Arquilla and D. Ronfeldt (eds), Washington, DC: RAND.

Arrighi, G. (1994) *The Long Twentieth Century: Money, Power and the Origin of Our Times*, London and New York: Verso.

Badiou, A. (2005) *Infinite Thought*, trans. O. Feltham and J. Clemens, London: Continuum Press.

——(2000) *Deleuze: The Clamor of Being*, trans. L. Burchill, Minneapolis: University of Minnesota Press.

Baran, P. A. and Sweezy, P. M. (1966) *Monopoly Capital: An Essay on the American Economic and Social Order*, New York: Monthly Review Press.

Barnett, T. P. M (2003) 'The Pentagon's New Map', *Esquire* (March).

Baudrillard, J. (1994) *Simulacra and Simulation*, trans. S. F. Glaser, Michigan: University of Michigan Press.

Bauman, Z. (2005) *Liquid Life*, Cambridge: Polity Press.

——(1998) *Globalization: The Human Consequences*, New York: Columbia University Press.

Bennett, J. (2005) 'The Agency of Assemblages and the North American Blackout', *Public Culture* 17(3): 445–66.

Bergson, H. (1998) *Creative Evolution*, trans. A. Mitchell, Toronto: Dover.

——(1991) *Matter and Memory*, trans. N. M. Paul and W. S. Palmer, New York: Zone Books.

——(1974) *The Creative Mind*, trans. M. L. Andison, New York: Citadel Press.

Bhagwati, J. (2004) *In Defense of Globalization*, Oxford: Oxford University Press.

Bishop, R. and Clancey, G. (2004) 'The City-as-Target, or Perpetuation and Death', *Cities, War and Terrorism: Towards and Urban Geopolitics*, S. Graham (ed.), Oxford: Blackwell Publishing.

Blank, S. J. (1997) 'Preparing for the Next War: Reflections on the Revolution in Military Affairs', *In Athena's Camp*, J. Arquilla and D. Ronfeldt (eds), Washington, DC: RAND.

Borden, W. L. (1946) *There Will Be No Time: The Revolution in Strategy*, New York: The Macmillan and Company Press.

Boyle, J. (1996) *Shamans, Software and Spleens: Law and the Construction of the Information Society*, Cambridge, MA: Harvard University Press.

Braudel, F. (1992) *The Perspective of the World: Civilization and Capitalism*, vol. III, Berkeley, CA: University of California Press.

Braverman, H. (1974) *Labor and Monopoly Capital: The Degradation of Work in the Twentieth Century*, New York: Monthly Review Press.

Brenner, R. (2006) *The Economics of Global Turbulence*, London: Verso.

Brooks, E. (2005) 'Transnational Campaigns against Child Labor: The Garment Industry in Bangladesh', *Coalitions across Borders*, Joe Bandy and Jackie Smith (eds), Oxford: Rowman and Littlefield Publishers.

Bufacchi, V. and Arrigo, J. M. (2006) 'Torture, Terrorism and the State: A Refutation of the Ticking-Bomb Argument', *Journal of Applied Philosophy* 23(3): 355–73.

Bulow, J. (1986) 'An Economic Theory of Planned Obsolescence', *Quarterly Journal of Economics*, 101(4) (November): 729–49.

Butler, J. (1996) 'Universality in Culture', *For Love of Country*, J. Cohen (ed.), Boston: Beacon Press.

——(2006) *Precarious Life: The Powers of Mourning and Violence*, London: Verso.

Cavell, Stanley (1989) *This New Yet Unapproachable America*, Albuquerque, NM: Living Batch Press.

Cheah, P. (2006) *Inhuman Conditions*, Cambridge, MA: Harvard University Press.

Cheah, P. and Robbins, B. (eds) (1998) *Cosmopolitics*, Minneapolis: University of Minnesota Press.

Chomsky, N. (1999) *The New Military Humanism: Lessons from Kosovo*, Monroe, ME: Common Courage Press.

Cohen, M. (1992) 'Rooted Cosmopolitanism: Thoughts on the Left, Nationalism, and Multiculturalism', *Dissent* (fall).

Connolly, W. E. (2011) 'Shock Therapy, Dramatization and Practical Wisdom', *The Joy of Secularism: 11 Essays for How We Live Now*, George Levine (ed.), Princeton, NJ: Princeton University Press.

——(2008) *Capitalism and Christianity, American Style*, Raleigh, NC: Duke University Press.

——(2005) 'The Evangelical-Capitalist Resonance Machine', *Political Theory* 33(6): 869–85.

——(2002) *Neuropolitics:Thinking, Culture, Speed*, Minneapolis: University of Minnesota Press.

Crogan, P. (1999) 'Theory of State: Deleuze, Guattari and Virilio on the State, Technology and Speed', *Angelaki: Journal of the Theoretical Humanities* 4(2): 137–48.

De Landa, M. (1991) *War in the Age of Intelligent Machines*, New York: Zone Books.

Debrix, F. (2008) *Tabloid Terror: War, Culture and Geopolitics*, London: Routledge.

Deibert, R. J. (2003a) 'Black Code: Censorship, Surveillance and the Militarisation of Cyberspace', *Millennium: Journal of International Studies* 32(3): 501–30.

——(2003b) 'Deep Probe: The Evolution of Network Intelligence', *Intelligence and National Security* 18(4): 175–200.

——(2002) 'Dark Guests and Great Firewalls: The Internet and Chinese Security Policy', *Journal of Social Issues* 58(1): 143–59.

——(2000) 'International Plug 'n' Play: Citizen Activism, the Internet, and Global Public Policy', *International Studies Perspectives* 1: 255–72.

Deleuze, G. (2002) *Nietzsche and Philosophy*, trans. Hugh Tomlinson, New York: Columbia University Press.

——(1995) 'Postscript on Control Societies', *Negotiations*, New York: Columbia University Press.

——(1994) *Difference and Repetition*, trans. P. Patton, New York: Columbia University Press.

——(1992) 'Postscript on the Societies of Control', *October* 59 (winter): 3–7.

——(1990) *The Logic of Sense*, trans. M. Lester, New York: Columbia University Press.

——(1988) *Bergsonism*, trans. H. Tomlinson and B. Habberjam, New York: Zone Books.

——(1984) *Kant's Critical Philosophy*, trans. Hugh Tomlinson and Barbara Habberjam, Minneapolis: University of Minnesota Press.

——(1979) 'Metal, Metallurgy, Music, Husserl, Simondon', trans. T. S. Murphy Gilles, paper delivered in Vincennes, 27 February 1979; available at www.webdeleuze.com.

Deleuze, G. and Guattari, F. (1994) *What Is Philosophy?* trans. H. Tomlinson and G. Burchell, New York: Columbia University Press.

——(1987) *A Thousand Plateaus*, trans. B. Massumi, Minneapolis: University of Minnesota Press.

——(1983) *Anti-Oedipus*, trans. R. Hurley, M. Seem and H. R. Lane, Minneapolis: University of Minnesota Press.

Der Derian, J. (2001) *Virtuous War*, New York: Westview Press.

Derrida, J. (2002) *Ethics, Institutions and the Right to Philosophy*, trans. P. P. Trifonas, Oxford: Rowman and Littlefield.

Dershowitz, A. M. (2006) 'Should We Fight Terror with Torture', *Independent*, 3 July.

——(2004) 'Warming Up to Torture', *Los Angeles Times*, 17 October.

Deudney, D. (2007) *Bounding Power: Republican Security Theory from the Polis to the Global Village*, Princeton, NJ: Princeton University Press.

——(1995) 'Nuclear Weapons and the Waning of the Real-State', *Daedalus* 124(2): 209–31.

——(1980) 'Geopolitics as Theory: Historical Security Materialism', *European Journal of International Relations* 6(1): 77–107.

Dobbs, L. (2004) *Exporting America*, New York: Warner Business Books.

Electronic Frontier Foundation (n.d.a) *RIAA v. The People: Four Years Later*, available at http://w2.eff.org/IP/P2P/riaa_at_four.pdf (accessed 1 January 2011).

——(n.d.b) *Unintended Consequences: Seven Years under the DMCA*; available at http://www.eff.org/files/DMCA_unintended_v4.pdf (accessed 1 January 2011).

Elster, J. (1983) *Explaining Technical Change*, Cambridge: Cambridge University Press.

Foucault, M. (1995) *Discipline and Punish*, trans. Alan Sheridan, New York: Vintage Books.

Frank, A. G. (1969) 'The Development of Underdevelopment', *Latin America: Underdevelopment or Revolution*, New York: Monthly Review Press.

Frank, T. (2004) *What's the Matter with Kansas?* New York: Metropolitan Books.

Friedman, T. L. (2006) *The World Is Flat: A Brief History of the Twenty-First Century*, New York: Farrar, Straus and Giroux.

Friedmann, J. (1995) 'Where We Stand: A Decade of World City Research', *World Cities in a World System*, P. L. Knox and P. J. Taylor (eds), Cambridge: Cambridge University Press.

——(1982) 'World City Formation: An Agenda for Research and Action', *International Journal of Urban and Regional Research* 6(3): 309–44.

Fukuyama, F. (1992) *The End of History and the Last Man*, New York: Perennial.

Gibson-Graham, J. K. (2006) *A Postcapitalist Politics*, Minneapolis: University of Minnesota Press.

Gleick, J. (2000) *Faster: The Acceleration of Just About Everything*, New York: Vintage.

Gonzalez, A. (2002) *Memorandum for the President: Decision Re Application of the Geneva Convention on Prisoners of War to the Conflict with Al Qaeda and the Taliban*; available at http://news.lp.findlaw.com/hdocs/docs/torture/gnzls12502mem2gwb.html (accessed 1 January 2011).

Graeber, D. (2002) 'The New Anarchists', *New Left Review* 13 (January/February): 61–73.

Graham, S. (2004a) 'Introduction: Cities, Warfare and States of Emergency', *Cities, War and Terrorism: Towards and Urban Geopolitics*, S. Graham (ed.), Oxford: Blackwell Publishing.

——(2004b) 'Vertical Geopolitics: Baghdad and After', *Antipode* 36(1): 12–23.

Gray, C. H. (2003) 'Perpetual Revolution in Military Affairs, International Security, and Information', *Bombs and Bandwidth*, R. Latham (ed.), New York: The New Press.

——(1997) *Postmodern War*, New York: Guildford Press.

Guattari, F. (1995) *Chaosmosis: An Ethico-Aesthetic Paradigm*, trans. P. Bains and J. Pefanis, Bloomington, IN: Indiana University Press.

Hanagan, M. (2003) 'Labor Internationalism: An Introduction', *Social Science History* 27(4): 485–99.

Hardt, M. and Negri, A. (2004) *Multitude*, New York: The Penguin Press.

——(2000) *Empire*, Cambridge, MA: Harvard University Press.

Harvey, D. (2006a) *The Limits to Capital*, London: Verso.

——(2006b) *Spaces of Global Capital*, London: Verso.

——(2001) *Spaces of Capital*, New York: Routledge.

——(2000) *Spaces of Hope*, Berkeley, CA: University of California Press.

——(1990) *The Conditions of Postmodernity*, Cambridge: Blackwell Publishing.

Heidegger, M. (1977) *The Question Concerning Technology and Other Essays*, trans. William Lovitt, New York: Harper Torchbooks.

Held, D. (2003) 'From Executive to Cosmopolitan Multilateralism', *Taming Globalization: Frontiers of Governance*, D. Held and M. Koenig-Archibugi (eds), Cambridge: Polity Press.

Herrod, A. (2003) 'Geographies of Labor Internationalism', *Social Science History* 27 (4): 501–23.

——(2001) *Labor Geographies*, New York: Guildford Press.

Hersh, S. (2006) 'The Iran Plans', *New Yorker*, 17 April.

Herz, J. H. (1957) 'Rise and Demise of the Territorial State' *World Politics* 9(4): 473–493.

Hills, A. (2004) 'Continuity and Discontinuity: The Grammar of Urban Military Operations', *Cities, War and Terrorism: Towards an Urban Geopolitics*, S. Graham (ed.), Oxford: Blackwell Publishing.

Hobbes, T. (1994) *Leviathan*, Indianapolis: Hackett Publishing.

Hobsbawm, E. (1989) *The Age of Empire: 1875–1914*, New York: Vintage Books.

Ignatieff, M. (2000) *Virtual War: Kosovo and Beyond*, New York: Picador.

James, P. (2004) 'The Matrix of Global Enchantment', *Rethinking Globalism*, M. B. Steger (ed.), Oxford: Rowman and Littlefield.

Juska, A. and Edwards, B. (2005) 'Refusing the Trojan Pig: The U.S.-Poland Coalition against Corporate Pork Production', *Coalitions across Borders*, Joe Bandy and Jackie Smith (eds.), Oxford: Rowman and Littlefield Publishers.

Kant, I. (2002) *Critique of Practical Reason*, trans. W. S. Pluhar, Indianapolis: Hackett.

——(1987) *Critique of Judgement*, trans. W. S. Pluhar, Indianapolis: Hackett.

——(1983) *Perpetual Peace and Other Essays*, trans. T. Humphrey, Indianapolis: Hackett.

Keck, M. E. and Sikkink, K. (1998) *Activists Beyond Borders*, Ithaca, NY: Cornell University Press.

Kraska, P. B. and Kappeler, V. E. (1997) 'Militarizing American Police: The Rise and Normalization of Paramilitary Units', *Social Problems* 44(1): 1–18.

Kurasawa, F. (2004) 'A Cosmopolitanism from Below: Alternative Globalization and the Creation of a Solidarity without Bounds', *Archive of European Sociology* 45(2): 233–55.

Laxer, G. (2001) 'The Movement that Dare Not Speak Its Name: The Return of Left Nationalism/Internationalism', *Alternatives: Global, Local, Political* 26(1): 1–32.

Lessig, L. (2004) *Free Culture: The Nature and Future of Creativity*, New York: Penguin Books.

Lucretius (1995) *On the Nature of Things*, trans. A. M. Esolen, Baltimore, MD: Johns Hopkins University Press.

Mackenzie, A. (2002) *Transductions: Bodies and Machines at Speed*, New York: Continuum.

Magnusson, W. (1996) *The Search for Political Space*, Toronto: University of Toronto Press.

——(1992) 'Globalization, Movements and the Decentred State', *Organizing Dissent*, W. K. Carroll (ed.), Toronto: Garamond Press.

Mao Tse-Tung (2005) *On Guerrilla Warfare*, trans. S. B. Griffith, Mineola, NY: Dover Publications.

Marcos, Sucommandante Insurgente (2001) *Our Word Is Our Weapon: Selected Writings*, J. P. de Leon (ed.), New York: Seven Stories Press.

Marinetti, F. T. (1909) *The Futurist Manifesto*; available at http://cscs.umich.edu/~crshalizi/T4PM/futurist-manifesto.html (accessed 4 May 2011).

Marx, K. (2000) 'The Communist Manifesto', *Selected Writings*, David McLellan (ed.), Oxford: Oxford University Press.

——(1981) *Capital*, vol. 3, trans. D. Fernbach, London: Penguin Books.

——(1973) *Grundrisse*, trans. M. Nicolaus, London: Penguin Classics.

Maskus, K. E. and Reichman, J. H. (2004) 'The Globalisation of Private Knowledge Goods and the Privatisation of Global Public Goods', *Journal of International Economic Law* 7(2): 279–320.

Massumi, B. (1992) *A User's Guide to Capitalism and Schizophrenia*, Cambridge, MA: MIT Press.

May, C. and Sell, S. K. (2006) *Intellectual Property Rights: A Critical History*, Boulder, CO: Lynne Rienner Publishers.

Mearsheimer, J. J. (2005) 'Hans Morgenthau and the Iraq War: Realism versus Neo-Conservatism', *Open Democracy*; available at http://www.opendemocracy.net/democracy-americanpower/morgenthau_2522.jsp (accessed 1 December 2010).

Meiksins, P. (1996) 'Work, New Technology, and Capitalism', *Monthly Review* 48(3): 99–115.

Mignolo, W. D. (2000) 'The Many Face of Cosmo-polis: Border Thinking and Critical Cosmopolitanism', *Public Culture* 12(3): 721–48.

Mill, J. S. (1998) *On Liberty and Other Essays*, Oxford: Oxford University Press.

Mittelman, J. H. (2000) *The Globalization Syndrome*, Princeton, NJ: Princeton University Press.

Nancy, J.-L. (2000) *Being Singular Plural*, trans. R. D. Richardson and A. E. O'Byrne, Stanford, CA: Stanford University Press.

Naveh, S. (2006) 'Discipline and Punish', *Harper's Magazine* (October).

Negri, A. (2003) 'Kairos, Alma Venus, Multitudo', *Time for Revolution*, trans. M. Mandarini, London: Continuum Press.

——(1991) *Marx Beyond Marx: Lessons on the Grundrisse*, trans. H. Cleaver, M. Ryan and M. Virno, Brooklyn: Autonomedia.

Nussbaum, M. C. (1996) 'Patriotism and Cosmopolitanism', *For Love of Country*, J. Cohen (ed.), Boston: Beacon Press.

——(1992) 'Human Functioning and Social Justice: In Defense of Aristotelian Essentialism', *Political Theory* 20(2) (May).

Nyers, P. (2003) 'Abject Cosmopolitanism: The Politics of Protection in the Anti-Deportation Movement', *Third World Quarterly* 24(6): 202–46.

O Riain, S. (2006) 'Time–Space Intensification: Karl Polanyi, the Double Movement and Global Information Capitalism', *Theory and Society* 3(5–6): 507–28.

O'Hanlon, M. (2000) *Technological Change and the Future of Warfare*, Washington, DC: Brookings Institution Press.

O'Tuathail, G. (1996) *Critical Geopolitics*, Minneapolis: University of Minnesota Press.

Ong, A. (2006) *Neoliberalism as Exception*, Durham, NC: Duke University Press.

——(1999) *Flexible Citizenship*, Durham, NC: Duke University Press.

Osterweil, M. (2005) 'Place-Based Globalism: Theorizing the Global Justice Movement', *Development* 48(2): 23–8.

Patton, P. (2000) *Deleuze and the Political*, London: Routledge.

Perelman, M. (2003) 'The Political Economy of Intellectual Property', *Monthly Review* 54(8): 29–38.

Peters, R. (1996) 'Our Soldiers, Their Cities', *Parameters: The Journal of the US Army War College* (spring): 43–50.

Polanyi, K. (1944) *The Great Transformation*, Boston: Beacon Press.

Postone, M. (2003) *Time, Labor and Social Domination*, Cambridge: Cambridge University Press.

Prigogine, I. (1997) *The End of Certainty*, New York: The Free Press.

Rai, A. K. and Eisenberg, R. S. (2003) 'Bayh–Dole Reform and the Progress of Biomedicine', *Law and Contemporary Problems* 66 (1–2): 289–314.

Reid, J. (2003) 'Deleuze's War Machine: Nomadism Against the State', *Millennium: Journal of International Studies* 32(1): 57–85.

Rorty, R. (1998) *Achieving Our Country*, Cambridge, MA: Harvard University Press.

Rosa, H. (2003) 'Social Acceleration: Ethical and Political Consequences of a Desynchronized High-Speed Society', *Constellations* 10: 3–33.

Rosenau, W. G. (1997) '"Every Room Is a New Battle': The Lessons of Modern Urban Warfare"', *Studies in Conflict and Terrorism* 20(4): 371–94.

Sassen, S. (2006) *Territory, Authority, Rights: From Medieval to Global Assemblages*, Princeton, NJ: Princeton University Press.

——(2001) *The Global City: New York, London, Tokyo*, Princeton, NJ: Princeton University Press.

——(2000) *Cities in a World Economy*, Thousand Oaks, CA: Pine Forge Press.

Scheuerman, W. E. (2004) *Liberal Democracy and the Social Acceleration of Time*, Baltimore, MD: Johns Hopkins University Press.

——(2002) 'Rethinking Crisis Democracy', *Constellations* 9(4): 492–505.

Schumpeter, J. A. (2002) *The Theory of Economic Development*, trans. J. E. Elliot, New Brunswick, NJ: Transaction Publishers.

——(1950) *Capitalism, Socialism and Democracy*, New York: Harper Perennial.

Shaw, M. (2004) 'New Wars of the City: Relationships of "Urbicide" and "Genocide"', *Cities, War and Terrorism: Towards and Urban Geopolitics*, S. Graham (ed.), Oxford: Blackwell Publishing.

Simmel, G. (1997) 'The Metropolis and Mental Life', *Simmel on Culture*, D. Frisby and M. Featherstone (eds), London: Sage Publications.

Sklair, L. (2004) 'The End of Capitalist Globalization', *Rethinking Globalism*, M. B. Steger (ed.), Oxford: Rowman and Littlefield.

Smith, N. (1984) *Uneven Development: Nature, Capital and the Production of Space*, Oxford: Basil Blackwell.

Stallman, R. M. (2002) *Free Software, Free Society: Selected Essays of Richard M. Stallman*, J. Gay (ed.), Boston: Free Software Foundation.

Steger, M. (2005) *Globalism: Market Ideology Meets Terrorism*, Oxford: Rowman and Littlefield.

Stillerman, J. (2003) 'Transnational Activist Networks and the Emergence of Labor Internationalism in the NAFTA Countries', *Social Science History* 27(4): 577–601.

Strange, S. (2000) *The Retreat of the State*, Cambridge: Cambridge University Press.

Sun Tzu (1963) *The Art of War*, trans. S. B. Griffith, Oxford: Oxford University Press.

Suskind, R. (2004) 'Faith, Certainty and the Presidency of George W. Bush', *New York Times Magazine*, October 17.

Tarrow, S. (2005) *The New Transnational Activism*, Cambridge: Cambridge University Press.

Taussig, M. (1997) *The Magic of the State*, New York: Routledge.

Vaidhyanathan, S. (2001) *Copyrights and Copywrongs: The Rise of Intellectual Property and How It Threatens Creativity*, New York: New York University Press.

Van Creveld, M. (1985) *Command in War*, Cambridge, MA: Harvard University Press.

——(1991) *The Transformation of War*, New York: The Free Press.

Verges, F. (2001) 'Vertigo and Emancipation, Creole Cosmopolitanism and Cultural Politics', *Theory, Culture and Society* 18(2–3): 169–83.

Virilio, P. (2002) *Ground Zero*, trans. C. Turner, London: Verso.

——(2000) *Strategy of Deception*, trans. C. Turner, Verso: London.

——(1991) *The Aesthetics of Disappearance*, trans. Philip Beitchman, New York: Semiotext(e).

——(1990) *Popular Defense and Ecological Struggles*, trans. M. Polizzotti, New York: Semiotext(e).

——(1977) *Speed and Politics*, trans. M. Polizzotti, New York: Semiotext(e).

Virilio, P. and Lotringer, S. (1983) *Pure War*, trans. M. Polizzotti, New York: Semiotext(e).

von Clausewitz, C. (1976) *On War*, trans. M. Howard and P. Paret, Princeton, NJ: Princeton University Press.

von Treitschke, H. (1963) *Politics*, trans. Hans Kohn, New York: Harcourt, Brace & World.

Wallerstein, I. (1974) *The Modern World-System*, New York: Academic Press.

Warren, R. (2002) 'Situating the City and September 11th: Military Urban Doctrine, 'Pop-up' Armies and Spatial Chess', *International Journal of Urban and Regional Research* 26(3): 614–19.

Waterman, P. (1998) *Globalization, Social Movements and the New Internationalisms*, London: Mansell Publishing.

Weizman, E. (2007) 'The Art of War: Deleuze, Guattari, Debord and the Israeli Defense Force'; available at http://www.flexmens.org/drupal/?q=the_art_of_war (accessed 1 January 2011).

——(2004) 'Strategic Points, Flexible Lines, Tense Surfaces, and Political Volumes: Ariel Sharon and the Geometry of Occupation', *Cities, War and Terrorism: Towards an Urban Geopolitics*, S. Graham (ed.), Oxford: Blackwell Publishing.

Williams, H. L. (2003) 'Of Labor Tragedy and Legal Farce: The Han Young Factory Struggle in Tijuana, Mexico', *Social Science History* 27(4): 525–50.

Wittgenstein, L. (1958) *Philosophical Investigations*, trans. G. E. M. Anscombe, Upper Saddle River, NJ: Prentice Hall.

Wolin, S. S. (2004) *Politics and Vision*, Princeton, NJ: Princeton University Press.

——(1997) 'What Time Is It?', *Theory and Event* 1(1): 1–10.

——(1989) *The Presence of the Past*, Baltimore, MD: Johns Hopkins University Press.

Yoo, J. (2005) *The Powers of War and Peace*, Chicago: University of Chicago Press.

Wood, L. J. (2005) 'Bridging the Chasms: The Case of People's Global Action', *Coalitions Across Borders*, Joe Bandy and Jackie Smith (eds), Oxford: Rowman and Littlefield Publishers.

Index